DIGITAL RESISTANCE IN THE MIDDLE EAST

Your body is away from me. But there is a window open from my heart to yours. From this window, like the moon, I keep sending news secretly.

Rumi

To those scholar-mentor-friends I have lost recently, Prof. Susanne Hoeber Rudolph, Prof. Lloyd I. Rudolph, Prof. Mary Ann Tétreault and Prof. Allen Greenberger, with gratitude for your love and inspiration.

DIGITAL RESISTANCE IN
THE MIDDLE EAST

New Media Activism in Everyday Life

Deborah L. Wheeler

EDINBURGH
University Press

Edinburgh University Press is one of the leading university presses in the UK. We publish academic books and journals in our selected subject areas across the humanities and social sciences, combining cutting-edge scholarship with high editorial and production values to produce academic works of lasting importance. For more information visit our website: edinburghuniversitypress.com

Edinburgh University Press Ltd
The Tun – Holyrood Road
12 (2f) Jackson's Entry
Edinburgh EH8 8PJ

Typeset in 11/15 Adobe Garamond by
Servis Filmsetting Ltd, Stockport, Cheshire,
and printed and bound in Great Britain by
CPI Group (UK) Ltd, Croydon CR0 4YY

A CIP record for this book is available from the British Library

ISBN 978 1 4744 2255 0 (hardback)
ISBN 978 1 4744 2257 4 (paperback)
ISBN 978 1 4744 2256 7 (webready PDF)
ISBN 978 1 4744 2258 1 (epub)

CONTENTS

FIGURES AND TABLES

Figures

PREFACE AND ACKNOWLEDGEMENTS

In the late 1990s, when initial fieldwork for this book began in Kuwait, the most common response received when asking citizens about their political identity was 'no comment' or 'I'm not that into politics'. Today, citizens in Kuwait and the wider Middle East are increasingly engaged in overt political activity, including widespread labour strikes, frequent protests against corruption, and, as the Arab Springs demonstrate, mass mobilisations to overthrow brutal dictatorships. Why did Arab publics become so agentive and demanding? This book explores the integral role that new media diffusion and use play in empowering Arab citizens, with a focus on the power struggles of everyday life.

A 2013 study by Northwestern University, Qatar, produced evidence of the links between Middle Eastern Internet use and enhanced political engagement. The study included 10,027 respondents from eight Arab nations. A total of 58% of those surveyed felt that they had a better understanding of politics because of their Internet use. Even more surprisingly, 47% felt that their Internet use helped them to have political influence. Likewise, 44% of those questioned felt it was their right to be able to criticise their government online (Northwestern University Qatar 2013). These results are surprising given the authoritarian contexts in which the surveys occurred, including Saudi Arabia, Qatar, the United Arab Emirates and Egypt.

Two years later, a follow-up survey asking the same questions about

Internet use and political engagement, in the same countries, found that 49% of participants felt they had a right to criticise their government online, an increase of 5%; and 50% felt that Internet use made them more politically effective at influencing their government, an increase of 3% (Northwestern University Qatar 2015). From these results, we can conclude that Internet use makes Arab citizens more likely to express themselves politically, and to feel more agentive; and these feelings of civic engagement increase over time.

Using data on Internet diffusion and use in Kuwait, Jordan and Egypt collected between 1996 and 2014, this book similarly argues that Internet use enhances civic engagement and voice in the Arab world. Increasingly, Middle Eastern citizens demand opportunities for meaningful participation in social and political affairs, and expect education, work and lifestyle choices. For example, women in the Arab world have reached the summit at Everest (Saudi), and flown fighter jets in active combat (UAE); citizens in Yemen and Tunisia have won Nobel Prizes. In Egypt, Kuwait, Tunisia, Jordan and Saudi Arabia citizens have organised labour strikes for better pay. In Kuwait, Jordan and Lebanon, angry publics have mobilised against corruption; in Tunisia, Egypt, Yemen and Libya, citizens have overthrown brutal dictatorships through mass mobilisations. This book argues that such restiveness is in part linked with Internet use.

In the process of writing this book manuscript, a number of articles (Wheeler 2006b, 2003a, b and c and 2001a), book chapters (Wheeler 2012 and 2009) and a book (Wheeler 2006a) benefited from peer review and dialogue for which the author is grateful. Only Chapter 5 of this book appears here relatively unaltered from its previously published form (Wheeler 2016). I would like to thank Routledge Press for permission to reprint 'Working around the State: The Micro-Demise of Authoritarianism in a Digitally Empowered Middle East', in Noha Mellor and Khalil Rinnawi (eds), *Political Islam and Global Media* (London: Routledge, 2016). I would especially like to thank Philip Howard, who served as an editor for one of my book chapters (Wheeler 2009) and deserves credit for coming up with the term 'working around the state' to describe the processes of citizen empowerment my research identifies. His valuable influence is still visible in the chapter titles of this book.

A number of institutions supported the evolution of this manuscript.

The Council for International Exchange of Scholars Fulbright Program provided the initial grant (Kuwait 1996–7), which inspired this quest to understand the meaning and implication of new media tools for Islamic societies. A second Fulbright in 2012–13 enabled follow-up research in the Gulf (Saudi Arabia, UAE and Qatar, and a short trip to Morsi's Egypt) where the accumulated impacts of Internet use could be experienced and interpreted in light of questions regarding sustainability and security. The insights collected during this ethnographic study of food, water and energy security inform the pages of this book. Ironically, what seemed like a great diversion in my research interests ultimately presented an overlapping, interpretive sweet spot between decreases in state capacity for meeting citizens' needs and increases in agency among citizens, the disruptive implications of which have yet to fully materialise.

Support from the University of Washington's Center for Internet Studies (2000–1) and the Oxford Internet Institute at Balliol College (2003–4) provided opportunities for developing the comparative case studies upon which this book is based.

Short-term consulting contracts with UNDP Jordan (2004), the Queen Zein al-Sharaf Institute for Development, Jordan (2004), and the Digital Opportunities Trust, Canada (2004–5), provided insights into the links between information technology and socio-economic development, especially as a tool for empowering women.

The University of Bergen, departments of Comparative Politics and Human Informatics, provided a visiting professor fellowship (2005) during which the implications of Internet use in the Middle East were explored with students and colleagues.

The United States Naval Academy Research Center (NARC) grants (2005–11, 2013–15) provided support for summer writing. Likewise, USNA's Center for Middle East and Islamic Studies (now the Center for Regional Studies) provided travel grants to the region, and support for attending conferences to present pieces of this book in the making (2005–12).

Summer teaching opportunities at the American University of Kuwait (2009–11 and 2014) allowed for follow-up ethnographic and survey research and provided important interaction with high-tech youth in a changing socio-political context. I remain grateful to my students at AUK for their

PREFACE AND ACKNOWLEDGEMENTS | xi

help with collecting Internet user data and their keen insights into the ways in which social media use transforms their lives. Were it not for their prodding, I would not have become a smartphone user, and I would be much less aware of what is going on politically at the grass roots of Kuwaiti society.

I wish to offer special thanks to the following people, each of whom left important fingerprints on this project: Laurie Coots, Paula Holmes Eber, Lauren Mintz, Charles Ess, Naomi Sakr, Albrecht Hofheinz, Ildiko Kaposi, David Faris, Mary Ann Tétreault, Leanne Piggott, Gale Mattox, Gary Garrison, Bill Dutton, Hussein Amin, Tim Sullivan, Lloyd and Susanne Rudolph, Abla Amawi and her sister Ayda, Nizar Hamza, Robert Rook, Loubna Hanna Skalli, Ray Bush, Marc Lynch, Noha Mellor and, last but not least, my students. Their generosity in no way contributed to any shortcomings, for which I take full responsibility.

In closing, I want to thank my father, Kenneth Wesley Carter, for his curiosity about the Middle East and the visit to Oxford; my mother, Barbara J. McNair, and my step-father, Bernard B. McNair, for their visits to the field (Cairo, Jordan and UAE), and accounting advice. My spouse, the other Professor Wheeler, has been a constant companion and source of inspiration, throughout life and the writing of this book. Brannon, I hope someday we will write a book together. And finally, to our sons, Jeffry, Zachariah and Franklin Wheeler, thank you for all the sacrifices you made to travel to the Middle East (including hot summers in the Gulf). This book is lovingly dedicated to you, with the hopes that you will all author your own interpretations of the Middle East.

INTRODUCTION

There's really no such thing as the 'voiceless'. There are only the deliberately silenced, or the preferably unheard. (Roy 2004)

The Puzzle

My taxi driver just said he hates Mubarak. What am I supposed to say? Is this guy crazy? Does he want to be imprisoned? Is he trying to get me to say something that will get me arrested or thrown out of the country? The location was Cairo; the year was 2004, yet the conversation seems like yesterday. This was the first time I sensed a loss of fear and discursive inhibition among Egyptians – a new communication pattern?

The taxi driver's forthrightness was not an isolated event. Our grocery delivery man, less than a week later, told me he loved Bin Laden. He thought the Arab world needed more leaders like him, willing to stand up to America. Why was this youth publicly celebrating a known terrorist who had killed nearly 3,000 of my fellow citizens? His words were both an affront to me and risky for his own personal safety, given Egypt's repressive public sphere. What explains these increasingly bold speech acts? Did Internet diffusion and use have anything to do with the changing communication environment in Cairo?

Six years later, an interview with two women for this study in Kuwait directly explains the Internet's potential disruptiveness. A twenty-two-year-old Kuwaiti female, who has 1,314 Facebook friends, sends more than 200 text messages a day, and visits blogs on fashion and photography, observes that the Internet

> allows for a platform for the Arab street to speak their mind while not having to censor their opinions as much, as well as provides a place to organise events etc. . . . This provides Arab society with political freedom and exposure to the rest of the world and vice versa. (Interviewed July 2010, Kuwait City)

Similarly, a twenty-four-year-old Kuwaiti female, who has over 600 Facebook friends, sends over 150 text messages a day, and notes that the Internet 'puts you in touch with any information you need and kills boredom at work', also explains that Internet use

> makes information available more easily and allows for more information to be passed to the general public in a user-friendly way. Blogs open the minds of youths and lessen the gap between men and women and allows [sic] people to make friends through the Internet. (Interviewed June 2010, Kuwait City)

Internet use is linked with at least nine layers of social and political transformation in these two passages. The Internet allows people to speak more freely. It provides citizens with a place to organise. Use of the technology enables exposure to the outside world. The Internet allows users to get information and to share thoughts and opinions more easily. Visits to blogs open the minds of youths. Internet use closes the gender gap, and kills boredom. Last but not least, Internet use allows people to expand their social networks.

These four communication events, two in Egypt and two in Kuwait, represent the types of data used in this book to better understand the role that communication technologies play in change in the Middle East. The ultimate question of this study is why, when the costs for disobedience can be so high, are Middle Eastern citizens in authoritarian contexts oppositional? By interpreting communication events like these four, this book argues that Middle Eastern citizens find the Internet useful in efforts to resist institutionalised power and social norms. Internet use reduces opportunity costs to participation and facilitates the concentration of agency.

The discursive acts analysed throughout this manuscript suggest the need to study politics in authoritarian contexts beneath the surfaces of power, against the grain of norms, beyond organised movements, in everyday forms of digitally enabled micro-empowerments. Doing so illuminates a form of disorganised mass politics transformative of power and civic engagement broadly defined, yet often localised and hidden in the practice of everyday life. James Scott reminds us that 'most of the political life of subordinate groups is to be found neither in overt collective defiance of power-holders nor in complete hegemonic compliance, but in the vast territory between these two polar opposites' (Scott 1990: 136). In this spirit, I argue that new media tools are particularly important for providing spaces for ordinary citizens to resist by having a voice in authoritarian states that seek to deny them this liberty.

Background and Research Methods

In the late 1990s, when research for this book began, there was relatively little data with which to understand new media uses in everyday life. Some initial statistics on diffusion existed, such as those collected by Internet World Stats, the International Telecommunications Union (ITU), and Seymour Goodman's Mosaic Project (<http://mosaic.unomaha.edu/GDI1998/7APGULF.PDF>). Even figures for access, however, were potentially unreliable, because counting IP addresses (Internet World Stats) and collecting data by phone interview (ITU), in a region where public trust is low, can fail to produce reliable numbers (Madar Research 2002; and Najat Rochdi interview, Cairo World Trade Center, July 2004). Moreover, most of the studies of the Internet's use in everyday life focused on Western democratic societies, because these countries were the earliest adopters and had the highest concentration of users of the technology (Chen et al. 2002: 75). Just because the United States was 'the mother ship of the Internet', however, does not mean that new media experiences in the US would replicate globally (Wellman and Haythornthwaite 2002: 10). New media impacts are 'conditioned by social and cultural contexts' (Chen et al. 2002: 110).

More transparent, accountable, democratic, participatory governance in the Middle East was predicted to grow along with Internet diffusion and use. The first article written on emerging new media cultures in the Middle East appeared in 1995 (Anderson 1995). At the time Jon Anderson concluded that 'while the information revolution has not yet reached the Middle East; for the most part it has reached the Middle Eastern Diaspora' (Anderson 1995: 13–14). These knowledge workers and students abroad, Anderson predicted, would 'return and demand or recreate the conditions they have become accustomed to abroad', including new media access. Anderson's findings raised the question of whether or not an acquired taste for information on demand would also include enhanced freedom of expression and civic engagement.

As early as 1999, R. Augustus Norton provided the insight that new media use would increase public voice and abilities to network interests, and in response authoritarian states would 'slowly retreat' (Norton 1999: 20). Marc Lynch predicted new media use would result in the emergence of 'the underpinnings of a more liberal, pluralist politics rooted in a vocal, critical public sphere' (Lynch 2006: 3). Since Middle Eastern governments 'have a heavy hand in controlling print and broadcast media', Internet diffusion and use was expected to create 'digital networked spaces' that were expected to 'offer the possibility of a much richer public sphere than existed before' (Etling et al. 2009: 46). Expectations for new political practices linked with new media diffusion and use were high (Alterman 1998).

Rasha A. Abdulla captures regional enthusiasm for the Internet when she observes,

> The Internet as a mass medium is good news for the Arab people. Arabs should seize the opportunities of what the Internet has to offer. It could be their chance to enhance their lives on many fronts, not the least of which is cultivating a more tolerant and more active civil society. (Abdulla 2007: 155)

In spite of such enthusiasm and great expectations for the Internet's impact, empirical data with which to better understand changes in Middle Eastern information environments were in short supply.

To provide a grass-roots view of emerging Internet cultures in the Middle East, I collected ethnographic data (1996–2014) and structured interviews (2004–11) with Internet users in Kuwait, Jordan and Egypt. The goal was to understand better who had access to the Internet, what users were doing with the tool, and, ultimately, to collect interpretations of social and political changes emerging as a result of new media use. The data were designed to test predictions for sweeping change in the Middle East with empirical evidence derived from testimonies on new media practices in everyday life.

Why ethnography?

In order to extract data on the diffusion, use and impact of the Internet in Middle Eastern contexts, ethnographic research methods were used. Ethnography is defined as 'the study of cultures through close observation, reading and interpretation' (Zemilanski 2008). A number of scholars highlight the utility of ethnographic approaches to political and social change. For example, some argue that ethnography has value because it allows 'the people being studied to "speak," an exercise that gives voice to the powerless, the subaltern and the under studied' (Schatz 2009: 315). Moreover, ethnographic tools 'grant legitimacy to their [the subalterns'] predicaments and concerns' (ibid.). The use of ethnographic tools is said to allow scholars to identify 'UPOs' or 'unidentified political objects' which Cedric Jourde defines as 'political relations and political sites that are generally unseen . . . but are nonetheless meaningful for local political actors' (Jourde 2009: 201).

In Kuwait (1996–7, 2009–11, 2014), Egypt (2000, 2004, 2013) and Jordan (2004 and 2005), ethnographic methods used included hanging out in Internet cafés; visiting community technology centres; interviewing Internet café managers; meeting with Internet service provider employees; consulting with employees at ministries of communication; meeting with international aid organisations and local non-governmental organisations attempting to bridge the digital divide; visiting computer training centres, schools and universities; observing public advertising for the Internet; reading newspapers; visiting with citizens in their homes and places of work and asking them about their Internet access and uses; visiting computer gaming clubs, and mobile phone shops; meeting with local Internet society members; interviewing IT professionals and business leaders. All of these practices were designed to locate evidence of emerging Internet cultures and to isolate 'the voices of the subaltern' and any associated 'unidentified political objects'.

The practice of living in Egypt, Jordan and Kuwait as a family of five – taking the kids to school, getting access to mobile phones, the Internet, satellite television, newspapers and magazines, travelling domestically by air, car, taxi and metro, working (Kuwait as a visiting professor, Jordan as a consultant to the United Nations Development Programme, and Egypt as a visiting researcher at the American University in Cairo), engaging in leisure activities (seeing films, going to cafés, visiting historical sites and places of natural beauty), shopping, getting a haircut, going to the gym, going to social events and parties – all of these everyday activities added insights into norms and norm violations.

In addition to intensive ethnographic research conducted in Kuwait, Egypt and Jordan, comparative ethnographic data on emerging Middle Eastern Internet cultures were collected via short (from one to five months) supplemental research trips to Tunisia (2000), Morocco (1997), UAE (1997, 2010–13), Oman (2004), Qatar (2011–13) and Saudi Arabia (2012–13).

The acts of new media empowerment identified in this book demonstrate what Scott observes about grass-roots resistance in that 'the accumulation of thousands or even millions of such petty acts can have massive effects' on political and social relationships (Scott 2012: xx). Similarly, I argue that micro-changes enabled by new communication practices deserve our attention, because they indicate something meaningful about politics at the margins, among the subaltern. Localised demonstrations of empowerment, although subtle, give us a more complete and sustainable view of the ways in which changing communication patterns are linked with new social practices and power relationships in the persistently authoritarian and patriarchal contexts of the Middle East.

Why structured interviews?

As a supplement to the everyday insights collected through ethnography, observations of emerging Internet cultures in the Middle East were collected via more than 1,000 interviews with Internet users in Kuwait, Jordan and Egypt. With the help of a Jordanian research assistant and students at the American University of Kuwait, structured interviews were collected in 2004 (Amman and Cairo, in Internet cafés throughout the capitals) and 2009–11 (through snowball sampling in Kuwait City, as part of a summer course on Arab Human Development).

The goal of these interviews was to provide another way to understand the Internet's place and effect in users' lives. The interviews aimed to see if the observations collected via ethnographic research methods had merit and meaning in a wider survey of emerging Internet practices. While the interview data are not a representative sample, by locating the subjective responses of individuals (List and Spiekermann 2013), the structured interviews help to identify how the Internet's 'social meanings are bedded down in individual forms of experience' (Bull 2000, quoted in Rippin 2005). Thus, any insights the interview data provide on emerging Internet practices and cultures are of value as a starting point for grasping new media's everyday meanings in the Middle East. The fact that several revolutions emerged, in part because Middle Eastern citizens, 'from the safety of cyberspace, moved towards occupying urban spaces' (Castells 2012: 2), makes the interviews even more important with hindsight because they give a potential window on to the early evidence of engagement and change. All participation in these interviews was voluntary and anonymous.

The interview questions were developed and pilot tested with the assistance of staff at the Oxford Internet Institute where I was a visiting fellow from 2003 to 2004. The same questions were asked in all three countries (see Appendix for the list of questions). The interviews revealed that Internet use was a regular part of everyday life. For example, in 2004, people interviewed in Amman and Cairo spent on average fourteen hours a week online, a surprising finding, given low penetration rates at the time (5% in Egypt, 9% in Jordan). By 2009, the data collected in Kuwait showed that those interviewed spent on average twenty hours a week online, and that nearly 100% of those interviewed had Internet access at home. By 2010, those interviewed in Kuwait were listing '24/7' in response to question twelve, number of hours a day online.

In terms of the impact Internet use has on individual lives, five patterns emerge among those interviewed: social networking, access to uncensored information, civic engagement, pathways out of boredom and ease-of-life factors. Interview results reveal citizens enhancing their agency and voice in the power struggles which define their lives. For example, those interviewed were found to seek entertainment, to pursue engagement with global civil society, to seek jobs, to increase knowledge of English, or to locate a spouse. New forms of risk taking and agency emerged online, with offline implications explored throughout this book.

In part, the findings of my ethnographic observations and wider survey of Internet users are validated by a 2014 survey conducted by the Dubai School of Government, which found that 70% of Middle Eastern citizens surveyed believed that social media use enhances civic engagement (Arab Social Media Report 2014). BBC editor Paul Mason describes these times as 'a new age of discontent' enabled by 'social networks, a newfound self-reliance, and a disjuncture between the young, and an old political order' (Bell 2014). Expressions of discontent and enhanced self-reliance linked with Internet use are explored throughout this book.

Why Kuwait, Jordan and Egypt?

These cases were chosen to provide insights into emerging regional Internet subcultures in comparative perspective. They were also selected because of the differences they possess. Each of the cases comes from a distinct regional subculture: the Gulf (Kuwait), the Fertile Crescent (Jordan) and North Africa (Egypt). Economic diversity is achieved by including oil-rich (Kuwait) and relatively resource-poor countries (Jordan and Egypt). In terms of power structures, one country is a presidency, headed by a former military elite (Egypt), and two are monarchies, where power and legitimacy are awarded based upon family ties (Sabah in Kuwait, and Hashemite in Jordan). Another difference is Internet penetration rates among the cases, which range from 79.9% for Kuwait, to 73.6% for Jordan, and 37% for Egypt (December 2016 Internet World Stats estimates).

In spite of differences of economy, geography, political authority and penetration rates, and in spite of experiencing an Arab Spring or not, these countries share a core of similarities, including new media use patterns. For example, in each of these cases, respective governments provide ease of access to new media tools for their publics, to bridge the digital divide, to spread economic opportunities, and to promote national security. These three countries were among the earliest adopters of Internet technologies for public use (1991–3). In all of these countries, an authoritarian government controls politics. As a result, public information is carefully monitored, and free speech is discouraged. In all of these countries, education levels are relatively high, with youth literacy rates among men and women aged fifteen to twenty-four ranging from a high of 99.2% in Jordan, to 98.6% in Kuwait, followed by 89% in Egypt (92.4% males; 86.1% females) (UNICEF 2013, <http://www.

unicef.org/infobycountry/>; throughout the book, web addresses were last accessed in January 2017 unless stated otherwise). Governments in all three of the cases actively promote education, IT awareness and training/access, to build a knowledge economy to absorb new entrants to the labour force. All three countries suffer from a significant youth bulge, ranging from 56.2% of citizens under the age of twenty-four in Jordan, to 50% in Egypt, and 40.7% in Kuwait (CIA *World Factbook* 2014).

One country selected experienced an Arab Spring revolution (Egypt), while in the other two (Kuwait and Jordan) public mobilisations during the Arab Spring were present, but instead produced relatively small, symbolic changes in formal power relations through reforms. Since the research design and fieldwork for this book took place before the Arab Spring uprisings (although follow-up trips to the field occurred in Kuwait in 2011 and 2014, and Egypt in 2013), the presence or absence of revolution is coincidental to this study.

While the Arab Spring events are spectacular reminders that Arab publics matter, too concentrated a focus on the role of new media in the 2011–12 mobilisations draws attention away from the wider uses of the Internet to improve lives, for, as Manuel Castells observes, 'the fundamental power struggle' in the information age 'is the battle for the construction of meaning in the minds of the people' (Castells 2012: 5). Thus, rather than focus on which new media device mobilised whose public and why, this study focuses on the individual user level of analysis, and asks participants in new media dramas to highlight how access to the Internet has changed their lives, if at all. The results of these narratives are important whether or not they precipitated revolution, because they reflect how real people live in authoritarian contexts where hope gaps are significant, information gaps are purposely maintained by those in power, domination is coerced through intimidation, and the chances of escaping these circumstances are rare.

To see citizens use new media tools to work around the state, to map their way out of hopelessness, to increase their agency and control over their destiny, allows us to understand more fully how change happens in the Middle East. In his study of 'how ordinary people change the Middle East', Asef Bayat argues that change occurs when citizens discover and generate 'new spaces within which they can voice their dissent and assert their presence in pursuit of bettering their lives' (Bayat 2010: ix). I argue that Internet use provides this new space for instigating change.

The following pages support a recent observation made by Thomas Friedman, that 'the role of the Internet was overrated in Egypt and Tunisia' and 'underrated in the Gulf, where in these more closed societies, Facebook, Twitter and YouTube are providing vast uncontrolled spaces for men and women to talk to each other – and back at their leaders' (Friedman 2013). Moreover, this book takes seriously Albrecht Hofheinz's challenge that, 'due to the focus on political change, and the quest for political revolution, the influence of the Internet in the social and cultural realm has been much less in the limelight' (Hofheinz 2011: 1,423). Hofheinz calls on new media scholars to 'acknowledge, but also to take seriously the fact that the Internet and social media are used for much more, and primarily for other things than political activism' (ibid.: 1,424).

Chapter Outline

The chapters that follow examine the implications of the Internet in Middle Eastern contexts with a focus on individual users. Chapter 1, 'A Brief History of Internet Diffusion and Impact in the Middle East', provides an analysis of the relationship between intensified Internet diffusion and evidence of more active citizen engagement in the Middle East. Data on diffusion are provided in charts and tables, while images of Internet-linked change are documented with samples of popular culture including political cartoons, photographs, advertisements, resistance literature and Internet user testimonials. The findings of this chapter are that increased diffusion of the Internet may be linked with more overt impacts of the technology in individual citizens' lives. Thus, states in the region may be increasingly confronted with restive publics demanding more responsive governance.

Chapters 2 to 4 provide case studies of new media use and citizen empowerment in the Middle East. Each one of these cases illustrates the various ways in which Arabs adapt new communications technologies to the practice of everyday life, their hopes and dreams, their struggles and desires for change. By considering information technology diffusion rates, corruption indicators, freedom measurements, and narratives of Internet users in context, patterns in both causes and outcomes of IT-inspired change are investigated.

Chapter 2, 'IT 4 Regime Change: Networking around the State in Egypt', takes as a starting point Gene Sharp's observation that 'the exercise of power depends on the consent of the ruled who, by withdrawing that consent, can control and even destroy the power of their opponent' (Sharp 1973: 4). While this observation applies across the cases, in the Egyptian case in particular Internet use allowed citizens to experiment with withdrawing their consent, in ways that were destructive to the status quo over time. This experimentation in having a voice, both online and off, subverted state control of public discourse, resulting in 'the exchange of ideas, information and models' which 'created an active citizenry' (Bayat 2010: 247). Throughout the Egyptian case study, explanations for an empowered citizenry linked in part with new media use are considered. While the rise of the Sisi presidency reinstated a politics of repression and rule by fear, because the problems and capabilities that produced the Arab Spring have not changed, we can expect ongoing examples of public withdrawal of consent.

Chapter 3, 'No More Red Lines: Networking around the State in Jordan', seeks explanations to Jillian Schwedler's observation that in Jordan 'There are no more red lines' (Schwedler 2012). The chapter explores answers to the question of why King Abdullah and Queen Rania became sources of public critique and opposition by members of Jordanian society in 2012. It examines how enhanced civic engagement and political activism emerged, and isolates the role of Internet use in promoting new levels of social and political awareness, and collective demands for change. Evidence for this chapter comes from ethnographic insights and Internet user testimonials, which reveal subtle forms of empowerment and enhanced voice among citizens.

In Chapter 4, 'Hurry Up and Wait: Oppositional Compliance and Networking around the State in Kuwait', ethnographic research and structured interviews gathered between 1996 and 2014 in Kuwait are interpreted in light of recent examples of public mobilisation in the emirate. The chapter argues that use of new media tools profoundly altered social and political practices and expectations. In Kuwait, according to participants interviewed for this study, Internet use removes inhibitions, gives the public a voice, encourages people to demand access to current, transparent news and information, and enables Internet users to become more engaged and active in the world. For example, in the words of one fifty-five-year-old female Kuwaiti participant, the Internet 'opens the eyes of the younger generation and because of this, they find more freedom to exercise and they can compare freedom in their countries to that in other countries' (interviewed July 2009, Kuwait City). Explanations for the increasingly volatile political and social environment in Kuwait are explored throughout the chapter in light of ethnographic data and interviews with Internet users.

Chapter 5, 'The Micro-demise of Authoritarianism in the Middle East: Working around the State in Comparative Perspective', illustrates the core argument of this book: that ordinary people can create change through small acts of digital resistance. In the service of this argument, the chapter highlights three forms of digital resistance in the Middle East: digital disclosure to confront bad governance; people-to-people diplomacy; and social media for social change. These three examples of 'digital resistance' are based upon public media campaigns against the Egyptian, Turkish, Kuwaiti, Israeli, Iranian and Saudi states. As documented in this chapter and throughout the book, enhanced citizen capacity to network and voice opposition to bad governance and unmet needs is a force for change in the Middle East.

Chapter 6, 'Fear the State: Repression and the Risks of Resistance in the Middle East', provides an overview of the ways in which the Arab state is using repression to discourage resistance post-Arab Spring. This chapter balances the cyber-optimism of the manuscript with a bow to the cyber-pessimists. The ways in which the Egyptian, Jordanian and Kuwaiti states have used new media tools to enhance surveillance capacity are studied throughout the chapter. Moreover, analysis of each state's cyber- and counter-terrorism legislation is used as evidence of the state's discouragement of cyber-activism through coercion. The ultimate conclusion of the chapter, however, is that coercion does not lead to stability, but rather encourages subtler forms of opposition, which accumulate energy, feeding on each act of rights violation, hastening the next explosion of revolutionary change.

A conclusion provides the final summation of this book's message – that in spite of all the challenges Middle Eastern citizens face (or perhaps because of them), everyday activists continue to leverage new media tools to carve out spaces for agency and voice. Substantiating this claim is the goal of the pages that follow.

1

A BRIEF HISTORY OF INTERNET
DIFFUSION AND IMPACT IN THE
MIDDLE EAST

For governments wishing to control the flow of information, insurmountable problems emerge. Many governments, for example, have announced their intentions to control what their citizens can receive over the Internet. These announcements merely indicate these governments' ignorance. (Thurow 1998: 17)

Technology and globalisation has put power once reserved for states in the hands of individuals . . . Technology is empowering civil society in ways that no iron fist can control . . . The upheaval of the Arab world reflects the rejection of an authoritarian order that was anything but stable, and now offers the long-term prospect of more responsive and effective governance. (Excerpts from President Barack Obama's West Point Commencement Address, 28 May 2014)

M y Introduction uses four communication events from the summers of 2004 (Cairo) and 2010 (Kuwait) to signify the emergence of a new (more contentious) Arab public (Lynch 2006, Murphy 2009). To contextualise these events in the wider discourses and meanings of emerging Arab Internet cultures, this chapter provides the back-story with which to understand why these communication events were such transformational moments.

With Internet use becoming a more ubiquitous part of everyday life in the Middle East, a wide community of interdisciplinary scholars seeks explanations for the technology's longer-term implications (Lynch 2012, Seib 2012, Howard and Hussain 2013, Lacroix 2011, Faris 2013, Fekete and Warf 2013). Few if any of the existing studies, however, provide an ethnographically grounded history of Internet diffusion at the grass roots, among non-activists. Throughout this chapter we will consider representations of new media disruptions in everyday contexts as a way to decipher the history, meaning and implication of emerging Arab new media practices. Four overlapping tropes of communication and change frame this history: fear, need, resistance and revolution.

The main argument of this chapter is that the wider the diffusion and the more concentrated uses of the Internet become, the more overt the impacts are on citizen agency and power relations broadly defined. The implications of new communication practices are often subtle alterations of everyday norms, but nonetheless are potentially transformative of power relations where they matter most, in citizens' daily lives. For example, as early as 1995, a nineteen-year-old student from Jeddah, Saudi Arabia, observes that, with the Internet, 'a lot of my friends and I communicate with students all over the world to see how they live . . . We've made friends with male and female students in the States and we correspond sometimes daily' (Wavell 1995: 1). The process of 'seeing how others live', making friends beyond kin networks, and engaging in conversations that transcend national and gender boundaries are transformational practices within Saudi society because they breach norms for social engagement, with potentially significant consequences as youths experience freedoms online they are denied in real life.

Similarly, in Libya, an Internet café user observes that 'people here really avoid talking about politics', but just being online and chatting, having wider access to information, 'has had a profound political effect already' (Saunders 2004: 3). These two passages, and others examined in this chapter, suggest that new media use is agentive. The technology is empowering, because its use shapes how people think and act, and, as Castells observes, 'The way people think determines the fate of norms and values on which societies are constructed' (Castells 2007: 238).

Engaging online beyond norms can enhance civic engagement by spreading 'fellow feeling' among those who might not otherwise interact. As John Stuart Mill foreshadowed, more than two centuries ago,

It is hardly possible to overstate the value, in the present state of human improvement, of placing human beings in contact with other persons dissimilar to themselves, and with modes of thought and action unlike those with which they are familiar ... Such communication has always been, and is peculiarly in the present age, one of the primary sources of progress. (Quoted in Sunstein 2001: 191)

People in the Middle East dissimilar to one another interact daily online and off, and have been more civically engaged than ever before. Raymond Williams calls processes such as these 'a long revolution'. A long revolution occurs when 'processes of communication and economic development feed processes of democratic behavior' (Williams 1961: xii). To see the long revolution in action, Williams encourages us to look for processes of 'deep social and personal changes', which 'appear as scattered symptoms of restlessness and uncertainty' (ibid.).

Images of restlessness and uncertainty linked with changing communication patterns and social practices are interpreted in this chapter as evidence of a long revolution. Data were collected during fieldwork journeys to the Middle East between 1996 and 2014, and include key artifacts, statistics, new media participant narratives and ethnographic observations. Collectively, these narratives and representations illustrate processes of disruptiveness linked with new media diffusion and use. Throughout this analysis we see why Internet use can be 'a weapon of destabilisation' one user at a time (Wavell 1995: 1). As detailed in the pages below, with each new journey to the field I observed shifting narratives and communication practices, as Arab societies moved from fear, to need, to resistance, to revolution, by using new media in norm-breaching ways, to enhance freedom and political efficacy.

Fear: New Media Threat Narratives

In mid-July 1995 ministers of information from around the Arab world met in Cairo to discuss two threats to the region: terrorism and satellite TV. Egyptian Minister of Information Safwat El-Sharif (1983–2004) summarised regional concerns about new media when he observed, 'it is an extremely sensitive period because the Arab mind is subjected to infiltration by a satellite culture falling from an open sky and bringing traditions and values foreign to our society. This is threatening our identity and our culture with the worst dangers' (El-Sharif 1995, quoted in Wheeler 1995). Ironically, El-Sharif was the founder of Egypt's Nilesat.

In part, fear of new media is associated with Western technological and cultural invasion. For example, in 2003, Robert Mugabe called the Internet 'a tool of British imperialism' (Fleck and La Guardia 2003: 14). More specifically, Mugabe cited the UK, the US and Australia as 'using their information superiority to challenge our sovereignty through hostile and malicious broadcasts calculated to foment instability and destroy the state through divisions' (ibid.). That same year, Islamic conservatives in Iran observed that 'the Web' is 'the West's latest high tech weapon in its assault on Islamic values' (Theodoulou 2003: 7).

A decade later, concerns about new media use having a negative impact on states and societies persist. For example, in May 2014, a Saudi cleric 'issued an edict against online chatting between the sexes, equating such activities to the prohibitions on the physical mingling of unrelated men and women' (Gladstone 2014). In the words of Sheikh Abdullah al-Mutlaq, 'the devil would be present when women talk to men on social media network sites' (quoted in Gladstone 2014: A11). In spite of these concerns, Saudi Arabia remains one of the most active social media environments, with an estimated 51% of the population using Twitter (Mari 2013) and 30% of all tweets from the Middle East originating in the kingdom (Arab Social Media Report 2014).

Similarly, Turkey's head of state Recep Tayyip Erdogan observes, 'We will not allow this nation to be victims of YouTube or Facebook. We will take whatever steps are necessary, including shutting them down. These people or these organizations encourage all kinds of immorality and espionage', and in this sense, 'Facebook and YouTube have started taking on a characteristic that threatens national security' (quoted in Idiz 2014). In spite of the prime minister's attempts to shut down social media sites when discourse becomes too oppositional, Turkey remains one of the most wired locations in the Middle East, with an estimated 60% penetration rate (Internet World Stats 2015, <http://www.internetworldstats.com>).

During my initial fieldwork in Kuwait (1996–7), the 'new media as threat' narrative was common, as represented in the cartoon in Figure 1.1, published in Kuwait's most widely read newspaper *Al Rai Al Am* ('Public

Figure 1.1 'New Media Wars', *Al Rai Al Am*, 25 July 1997, p. 13.

Opinion'). While the image can be interpreted on many levels, the main message for the purpose of this analysis is that new media like satellite TV are a threat, and Arabs are ill equipped to resist. In this image, satellite TV is an impenetrable fortress, while Arabs try to joust at it from horseback. Both the horse and the rider are sweating bullets at the enormity of the challenge. The satellite fortress is unmoved by such fear, and remains dominant in this fight.

Furthermore, a sheikh in the al-Jahra region of Kuwait, known for its Islamic conservatism and tribal values, contributed to the 'new media as threat' narrative by issuing a fatwa in 1997 declaring that new media devices are *haram* (forbidden) in Islam. In response to this edict, residents were encouraged to bring their VCRs, satellite dishes, videotapes and other new media devices to the city centre for a public burning. The event made front-page news in *Al-Watan* ('The Homeland'), Kuwait's second most widely read news source (29 January 1997: 1).

During a discussion at the Ministry of Education in Kuwait (1997), I learned that some households would not allow marriages for their sons to brides who have satellite TV at home. The reason was fear that these young women would be influenced by Western cultural norms and thus not good Muslim companions and mothers. In today's world, with satellite TV in nearly every home (an estimated 98% of people in the Middle East watch

TV daily), requirements for a 'suitable' marriage have to be redefined, as few marriages would occur if 'no satellite' standards are maintained, given the ubiquity of the technology (Northwestern University Qatar 2015).

A different kind of fear factor took shape in 1997, when a Bahraini opposition member became the first Arab citizen arrested for his or her online activity (Freedom House 2013). This case provided the earliest evidence that states were using the Internet to police Arab citizens' oppositional imaginations. The main message of this highly public act was: don't assume you have freedom online.

Another facet of Internet fears emerged during a lecture I delivered at the American Cultural Center (1997) in Damascus. The presentation was about Internet use and change in the Middle East. Several people in the audience expressed fears about the unverifiable nature of information available online. More technocratic audience members feared that a US trade embargo against Syria, which prohibited the import of Netscape browsing software, and other web tools, would delay Syria's entrance into the information age. Syria was listed as a state sponsor of terrorism, and as a result could not import Netscape or any strong encryption software, necessary for developing e-commerce. Syrians were thus forced to use text-based protocols like Gopher – assuming they could find an Internet connection through dial-up services available via Lebanon. The desire to connect was palpable among young Syrian students and businessmen in the audience, but such techno-enthusiasm was doused by a state fearful of empowering the public, and a global community concerned about enabling terrorists.

Diffusion rates

When the Internet first became available in the Middle East in the 1990s, fear factors and high costs for service made Internet access rates lower than in any world region. As revealed by the chart below, nine years after the first Internet connection in the region was established in Tunisia (1991), regional penetration of the Internet for most countries did not exceed 10%. During this first phase of diffusion, no one expected Internet use to have a noticeable impact, because too few people had access (Alterman 1998).

In the 1990s, both the largest number and the highest concentration of users per capita were in the United Arab Emirates. Rather than operating in a

Table 1.1 Internet users in the Middle East 2000

Country	Population	Internet users	% population with Internet access
Morocco	28,827,000	100,000	.35%
Algeria	30,506,000	50,000	.16%
Libya	5,346,000	10,000	.19%
Tunisia	9,452,000	100,000	1.0%
Egypt	69,359,979	450,000	.65%
Jordan	4,853,000	127,300	2.6%
Syria	16,511,000	30,000	.18%
Lebanon	3,772,000	300,000	8.0%
Yemen	18,182,000	15,000	.08%
UAE	3,238,000	735,000	23.0%
Saudi Arabia	20,808,000	200,000	1.0%
Qatar	617,000	30,000	5.0%
Kuwait	2,228,000	150,000	7.0%
Oman	2,402,000	90,000	4.0%
Iraq	24,652,000	12,500	.05%
Iran	65,620,000	250,000	4.0%
Bahrain	650,000	40,000	6.0%

Sources: Internet World Stats, UNDP Arab Human Development Report 2011, and CIA *World Factbook*.

culture of fear, leadership in UAE distinguished itself by promoting access to IT for economic and social development. As part of this mission, the Emirates Center for Strategic Studies and Research in Abu Dhabi hosted a conference and subsequently published a book entitled *The Information Revolution and the Arab World: Its Impact on State and Society* (ECSSR 1998). The centre director, Dr Jamal S. Al-Suwaidi, in his introduction to the volume, notes, 'to say that this fast and rapid influx of technology has radically altered the way everyday affairs are conducted is clearly both an understatement and a cliché' (Al-Suwaidi 1998: 1).

During the conference Muhammad I. Al-Ayish argued, 'Access to telecommunications services is increasingly becoming one of the minimum necessary conditions for successful national development and for active participation in the global economy of the twenty-first century' (Al-Ayish 1998: 141). The high level of Internet penetration in the United Arab Emirates comes from the government's belief that strong information infrastructure 'is the backbone of social change and economic progress' (ibid.: 142). While

Emiratis were proactive in using new media tools for social and economic re-engineering, many countries in the region continued to see the information age as a new wave of 'electronic colonialism' (interview with US Embassy employee Rabat Morocco, 1997).

Need: IT4D and the Quest for Universal Access

No matter how well articulated by conservatives, the 'fear-based' approach to the Internet was eventually subverted by a more pronounced 'need-based' approach. We see the need for IT expressed by Syrian technocrats, and in the United Arab Emirates' belief that a society cannot develop and fully participate in world trade without an ability to communicate globally. Characteristic of the need phase was Dubai's building of Media City to bridge the digital divide and grow the knowledge economy. Other countries in the region, like Egypt, Jordan and Tunisia, that lacked oil wealth relied on foreign aid to build the information revolution infrastructures throughout their country. With higher youth unemployment rates (26%) than anywhere else in the world, leaders in the Middle East saw the information revolution as a vehicle for job creation (Coy 2011).

My ethnographic work in Egypt and Jordan (2000–5) revealed that information technology was imagined to be a silver bullet with which to connect people to jobs, to give people new skills in order to be absorbed into the global economy; to stimulate new private-sector growth opportunities with which to empower women, and to solve the problems associated with the youth bulge via job creation. Promises of building a knowledge economy, empowering women, and youths, characterise public discourse during this phase, as Arab publics came to see Internet access as a right, rather than a luxury. Strong growth in Internet diffusion is symptomatic of the perceived need for the Internet becoming more widespread.

Public access to the Internet was expanded during this phase by a coalition of partners and development projects that put governments, international aid organisations and global capital together in attempts to bridge the digital divide in the Middle East. Examples of these partnerships include Intel Computer Clubhouses in Jordan (<http://www.nakhweh.org/en/organizations/1--Intel-Computer-Clubhouse>) and the United Nations Development Programme government of Egypt-funded Technology Access Community Centers pro-

Table 1.2 Internet users in the Middle East 2000–2005

Middle East and North Africa	Population (2005 est.)	Internet users December 2000	Internet users March 2005	Percentage growth (2000–2005)
Algeria	32,557,738	50,000	500,000	900.0%
Bahrain	707,357	40,000	195,700	389.3%
Egypt	69,954,717	450,000	3,000,000	566.7%
Iran	68,458,680	250,000	4,800,000	1,820.0%
Iraq	26,095,283	12,500	25,000	100.0%
Jordan	5,788,340	127,300	457,000	259.0%
Kuwait	2,530,012	150,000	567,000	278.0%
Lebanon	4,461,995	300,000	500,000	66.07%
Libya	5,980,693	10,000	160,000	1,166.7%
Morocco	31,003,311	100,000	1,000,000	900.0%
Oman	2,398,545	90,000	180,000	100.0%
Qatar	768,464	30,000	140,800	369.3%
Saudi Arabia	21,771,609	200,000	1,500,000	650.0%
Syria	18,586,743	30,000	610,000	1,933.3%
Tunisia	10,116,314	100,000	630,000	530.0%
UAE	3,750,054	735,000	1,110,200	51.0%

Source: Internet World Stats.

ject (<https://www.isoc.org/inet99/proceedings/3c/3c_1.htm>). IT4D projects like these aimed to help states to help their publics find new forms of hope and employment through IT diffusion and use. Assumptions were that effective management (including censorship and punishment for misuse) of new media capabilities would empower the state to control oppositional imaginations and public consciousness, at the same time helping to solve the job and education gaps stimulated by the youth bulge (Morozov 2011b, Kalathil and Boas 2003).

An increase in arrests of Internet users who crossed red lines in their oppositional voices occurred during this phase of information society construction. In Tunisia, for example, President Ben Ali imprisoned Zouhair Yahyaoui, one of the first online journalists to be incarcerated for testing the boundaries of Internet freedom. He was arrested for his online magazine, *TuneZine*, in which he published regular satire of Ben Ali's government. He was found guilty and spent eighteen months in prison, where he was tortured. He was eventually released in 2003. In 2005, he died of a heart attack at age thirty-six, in part because of his poor treatment in prison (Global Voices 2005). In 2005, five Middle Eastern countries – Iran, Libya, Saudi Arabia, Syria and

Tunisia – made the 'Internet Enemies list' constructed by Reporters without Borders (Reporters without Borders 2005). Internet monitoring by the state made oppositional behaviour in the Internet age potentially more dangerous for individuals and movements than before, because of the increased abilities of states to spy on publics.

In April 2000, First Lady of Egypt Mrs Suzanne Mubarak provided opening remarks for the Third Mediterranean Development Forum meeting in Cairo. The theme of the conference was 'Voices for Change, Partners for Prosperity'. She noted, 'To the voices of change, I have joined my own voice.' Adding a prescient prediction, Mrs Mubarak warned, 'We must promote growth with equity, the alternative is not only unjust but a prescription for civil strife' (Widdershoven 2000: 50). Evgeny Morozov provides a more cynical view of this process of IT4D when he observes, 'Authoritarian regimes . . . have been actively promoting a host of e-government initiatives . . . not because they want to shorten the distance between the citizen and the bureaucrat, but because they see it as a way to attract funds from foreign donors such as the IMF and the World Bank while also removing the unnecessary red-tape barriers to economic growth' (Morozov 2011b: 87).

For states, the main goal during this period was increasing access to capital and jobs for the ever-increasing entrants to the labour market. New media tools, however, empowered citizens for missions beyond state intentions. The Internet became a location to train for the new economy, as demonstrated by the advertisement in Figure 1.2, from a Knowledge Station in Jordan. The perceived need to bring Internet access to the region also resulted in new business opportunities, like Internet cafés (see Figure 1.3). Within public access points, however, Arab citizens would acquire new tools with which to enhance their everyday lives. For example, an Internet café manager in Cairo observes,

> The Internet is good in the sense that it helps people see how others are living out of Egypt, to exchange ideas and improve their English. They become more open minded, less uptight. They practise freedom of opinion and thought and they learn things from the Net, even in chat. It's also a way to have access to jobs abroad. (Interviewed May 2004, Cairo)

Through processes of increased agency, Internet users experienced processes of transformation in their everyday lives, even if relatively benign, such as

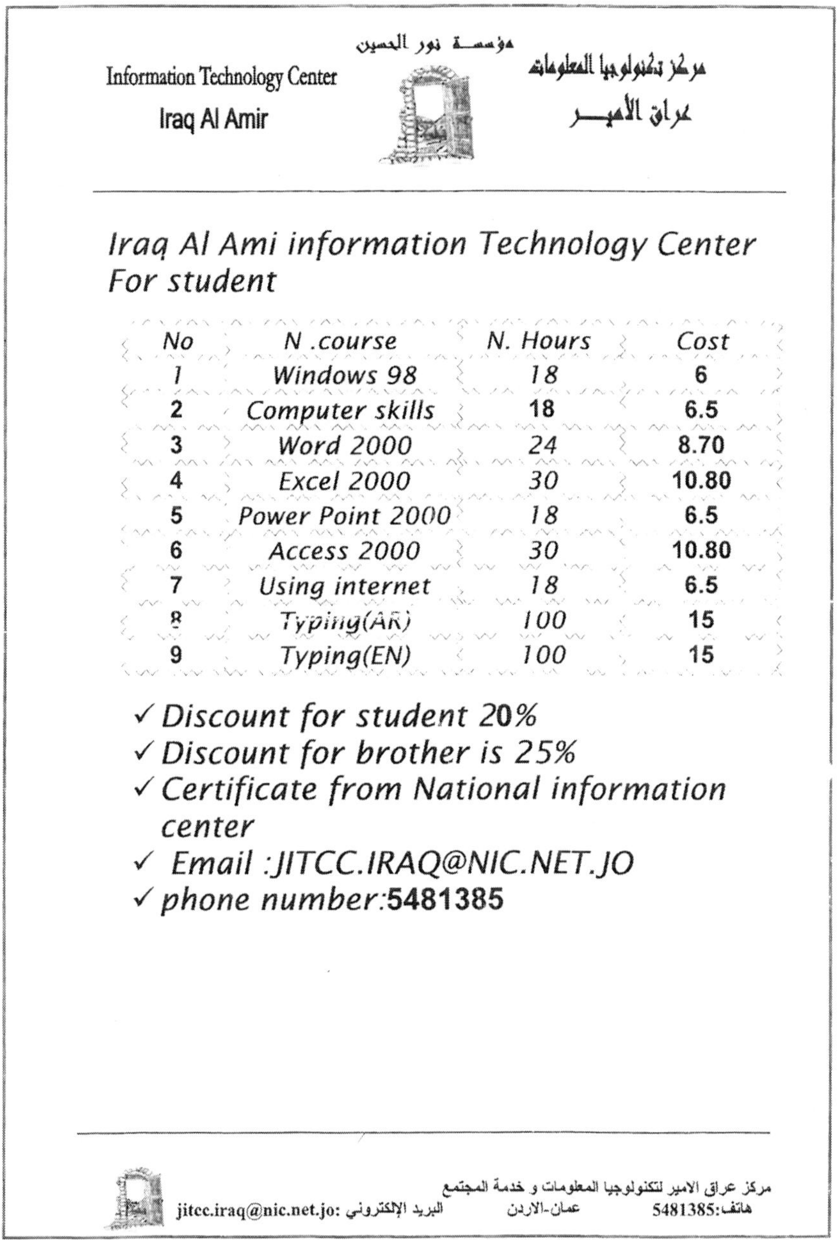

Information Technology Center
Iraq Al Amir

مؤسسة نور الحسين

مركز تكنولوجيا المعلومات
عراق الأميـــر

Iraq Al Ami information Technology Center For student

No	N .course	N. Hours	Cost
1	Windows 98	18	6
2	Computer skills	18	6.5
3	Word 2000	24	8.70
4	Excel 2000	30	10.80
5	Power Point 2000	18	6.5
6	Access 2000	30	10.80
7	Using internet	18	6.5
8	Typing(AR)	100	15
9	Typing(EN)	100	15

✓ Discount for student 20%
✓ Discount for brother is 25%
✓ Certificate from National information center
✓ Email :JITCC.IRAQ@NIC.NET.JO
✓ phone number:5481385

jitcc.iraq@nic.net.jo :البريد الإلكتروني   عمان-الاردن   هاتف:5481385   مركز عراق الامير لتكنولوجيا المعلومات و خدمة المجتمع

Figure 1.2   Advertisement for courses offered at a community IT access centre, Iraq al-Imir, Jordan.

Figure 1.3   Internet and satellite business, Wadi Musa, Jordan.
Photo: Deborah L. Wheeler, 2004.

seeking a new job online, trying to get married to a foreigner or to get a visa out of the Middle East, practising English online, or learning about the outside world and how they 'seemed to have more freedom' (interviewed May 2004, Cairo). All of these experiences, however, require risk taking and problem solving, and result in enhancements of individual power and autonomy in everyday life. In these small acts we see reflections of activism, even if individual mobilisations are directed at improving one's quality of life.

Governments, too self-assured of their abilities to police online behaviour, potentially underestimated the residual effects of new communication tools at work in empowering their publics. At times it may have seemed to the untrained eye that 'the Internet has provided so many cheap and easily available entertainment fixes to those living under authoritarianism that it has become considerably harder to get people to care about politics' (Morozov 2011b: 81).

On the ground, however, citizens are clear about why the Internet matters in their lives, and their explanations go well beyond entertainment factors. For example, a forty-eight-year-old Muslim man from Cairo observes,

> I find the Internet a great device to improve oneself, and to add to my knowledge and education, to keep up with the changes around us in business and all aspects of life. I use it to know what's going on in the Arab world and all over the world with better coverage than TV and newspapers that don't provide enough detailed information. (Interviewed May 2004, Cairo)

Along with attempts to widen access to information, Arab citizens use the Internet to look for pathways out of hopelessness. For example, a Jordanian university student observes,

> The Internet solves the problem of boredom. I meet friends here on the Net and we chat, joke, exchange ideas, argue in debates – it's interesting and better than hanging out all the time in cafés smoking water pipes. (Interviewed April 2004, Amman)

The residual effects of finding entertainment, news and civic engagement opportunities online allow participants to develop opinions, to meet and date new people, and to encounter new cultural terrain and ideas, potentially inaccessible in real life. These digital practices have the power to change identities, attitudes and action, beyond authoritarian state control.

Resistance: Rapid Diffusion, Small (Political) Rewards

Over time, as more users experience micro-forms of empowerment through their Internet use, the potential political importance of the Internet becomes more overt in user testimonials and popular culture. For example, a Kuwaiti college student observes, 'The Internet made Arabs more active in reaching out to others to find ways to express freedom . . . It taught the Arabs a lot regarding the values of democracy and freedom' (interviewed July 2009, Kuwait City). As public awareness of the Internet grows, demands for access also increase. Given state incentives for building IT infrastructures to promote economic development, a hand-in-glove relationship between state and

Table 1.3 Internet users in the Middle East 2000–2009

Country	Population (2009 est.)	Internet usage 2000	Internet usage 2009	% population (penetration)	% growth (2000–2009)
Bahrain	728,290	40,000	155,000	21%	287.5%
Iraq	28,945,569	12,500	300,000	1%	2,300.0%
Jordan	6,269,285	127,300	1,500,500	23.9%	1,078.7%
Kuwait	2,692,526	150,000	1,000,000	37.1%	566.7%
Iran	66,429,284	250,000	32,200,000	48.5%	12,780.0%
Lebanon	4,556,561	300,000	700,000	15.4%	133.3%
Oman	2,452,234	90,000	285,000	11.6%	216.7%
Qatar	824,355	30,000	219,000	26.6%	630%
Saudi Arabia	24,069,943	200,000	2,540,000	10.6%	1,170%
Syria	19,514,386	30,000	1,100,000	5.6%	3,566.7%
UAE	3,981,978	735,000	1,397,200	35.1%	90.1%
Yemen	21,306,342	15,000	220,000	1.0%	1,366.7%
Algeria	33,506,567	50,000	1,920,000	5.7%	3,740%
Egypt	72,478,498	450,000	5,000,000	6.9%	1,011.1%
Libya	6,293,910	10,000	205,000	3.3%	1,950%
Morocco	30,534,870	100,000	4,600,000	15.1%	4,500%
Tunisia	10,342,253	100,000	953,000	9.2%	853.8%

Source: Internet World Stats.

society's shared interests emerges, potentially explaining a surge in Internet use during this period (see Table 1.3).

Under the noses of states, experimental risk taking made relatively easy by new media tools helped to precipitate demands for change in the region. Arab citizens practised oppositional behaviour online for more than a decade prior to the Arab Spring revolutions. New electronic public spheres emerge through online chat forums, blogs, in Internet cafés, among friends and strangers far and wide, via tweets, YouTube videos and Facebook groups. In these contexts, Arab publics eroded their fears and experimented with new media tools to work around the state. Publics ultimately changed the norms of authoritarian rule by refusing to consent to bad governance (Bayat 2010).

Clay Shirky, professor at New York University, explains processes of communication and change applicable to the Middle East when he observes,

> As the communications landscape gets denser, more complex and more participatory, the networked population is gaining greater access to infor-

mation, more opportunities to engage in public speech, and an enhanced ability to undertake collective action. (Shirky 2011: 29)

In the Middle East, we saw this 'enhanced ability to undertake collective action' in Egypt's 2004 Kefaya movement (Oweidat et al. 2008), in Lebanon's 2005 Cedar Revolution (Knudsen and Kerr 2012), in Kuwait's 2006 Orange Revolution (Nordenson 2010), and in Iran's 2009 Green Movement (Mottahedeh 2015). Each of these events represents an example in which small cracks in authoritarian systems emerge, due to micro-changes in the collective action problem whereby citizens lose their fear and inhibition, realise shared misery, and act to create change, in part because they have found ways to effectively leverage new media networks. For example, in the case of Kefaya, a RAND study observes,

> It used electronic messages, including text messages between cell phone users, to publicize its rallies among members and the general public. It pursued a multifaceted Internet strategy to disseminate its message. It published advertisements online, finding these to be more effective than print advertisements in publications the authorities could confiscate. It propagated banners and political cartoons using its own Web page and those of sympathetic bloggers. It documented abuses by state security officers using digital photography and distributed the images online. (Oweidat et al. 2008: ix)

Through digital resistance and street protests, the Kefaya movement in Egypt ended 'the population's aversion to direct confrontation with the regime' (ibid).

A textual example to illustrate this process of losing fear and gaining agency was published in *The Star* newspaper (Lebanese, English language daily) on 25 November 2004 (Figure 1.4). Even the mundane experience of leveraging social media to find a better job can be understood in the Middle East as a subversive act, according to this ad. For example, if you can have a new boss at work, using IT tools, why should the head of state be any different? Both bosses and heads of state can be 'managing dictators'. If you don't like those in power over you, use IT tools to get free. It's time to revolt: on the job and against the state. The message of

Figure 1.4   A call to revolt, *The Star* (Lebanon), 25 November 2004.

this advertisement for Bayt.com, an online job recruiting service similar to Monster.com, is that there is a link between shifts in discourse, expectations and possibilities for change. Changes in one's personal life are not that different from demands for better governance, as implied in this ad. Both levels of change require significant power shifts, yet are enabled by digital communication. Changes in the way people communicate and live subsequently alter expectations for good governance and more freedom on the job.

When looking for clues with which to understand the precipitating factors behind waves of disruption in the Middle East, this chapter suggests we focus on small changes in Internet users' lives, shifts in public discourse, like this ad, and in dress rehearsals for mass-based collective action, in popular culture, social media sites, and in Internet user testimonials. For within these realms we see signs of change, which represent transformative politics emerging, as evidence of a 'long revolution' (Williams 1961).

Revolution: The Arab Spring and Beyond

Historians will remember the years between 2010 and 2015 as a time of significant political change in the Middle East and North Africa. Ordinary people, armed with new media tools, shared demands for change and collectively swept away dictatorial regimes in four countries (Tunisia, Egypt, Libya and Yemen), attempted to do so in an additional two (Bahrain and Syria), while in other regions, citizens pushed for significant reforms (Oman, Jordan, Morocco), and in others, an insurgent Islamist movement would leverage social media and extreme violence to re-establish a transnational Islamic Empire (IS in Syria and Iraq). When trying to isolate the causes of such unrest, one variable is constant among the cases: an increasingly wide diffusion and use of the Internet and social media devices. Whereas in the first phase of Internet diffusion and impact in the Middle East and North Africa, only one country, the United Arab Emirates, had greater than 10% Internet

Table 1.4 Internet users in the Middle East 2015

Country	Population (2015 est.)	Internet users (November 2015 est.)	Penetration rate
Bahrain	1,346,613	1,297,500	96.4%
Iran	81,824,270	46,800,000	57.2%
Iraq	33,309,836	11,000,000	33.0%
Jordan	6,623,279	5,700,000	86.1%
Kuwait	3,996,899	3,145,559	78.7%
Lebanon	4,151,234	3,336,517	80.4%
Oman	3,286,936	2,584,316	78.6%
Qatar	2,194,817	2,016,400	91.9%
Saudi Arabia	27,752,316	18,300,000	65.9%
Syria	22,878,524	6,426,577	28.1%
UAE	9,445,624	8,807,226	93.2%
Yemen	26,737,317	6,029,265	22.6%
Egypt	88,487,396	48,300,000	54.6%
Libya	6,411,776	2,400,000	34.4%
Tunisia	11,037,225	5,408,240	49.0%
Algeria	39,542,166	11,000,000	27.8%
Morocco	33,322,699	20,207,154	60.6%

Source: Internet World Stats.

penetration, by 2015 estimates, no country in the Middle East remained below the 10% penetration threshold. While no country in the region has yet to achieve universal access, three have come close: Bahrain with 96.4%, UAE with 93.2%, and Qatar with 91.9%. David Faris defines 'high connectivity' as a country having 'a penetration rate above 25%' (Faris 2013: 180). Using this definition, by 2015 only Yemen remained a low-connectivity country.

This chapter argues that the more ubiquitous access to the Internet becomes within a society, the more likely perceived social and political impacts of the technology's use become. While statistics can easily illustrate the first part of the equation, that there is increasingly universal access to IT in the Middle East, the second part of the equation, which attempts to link such access with significant social and political change, is more difficult to prove. Icons like the one in Figure 1.5, however, help to illustrate the process, beyond nodes and noses, so to speak (Alterman 2000a). This text was found in my mailbox when I returned home from work while teaching at the American University of Kuwait in June 2011. At the time, the Egyptian and Tunisian revolutions had ended, while the Libyan, Yemeni and Syrian uprisings were ongoing. This text is an information sheet about the Syrian revolution. It details the massacre of Syrian civilians and provides Quranic references to condemn the Syrian regime for the killings. How amazing that a piece of resistance literature from Syria would make it all the way to my home postbox in Kuwait, I thought. The prominent placement of the Twitter, Facebook and web connections on the front cover reveals the degree to which new media are being used to network and share information. By going to the organisation's website and clicking on the 'about' page, which is only available in Arabic, one learns that *Wathakkir* is an Islamist publishing house and organisation located in Kuwait. It was established in 2006, and distributes texts and advice for spreading Islamic awareness. The site has articles, streamed audio of sermons, speeches, political commentary on the Syrian massacre and more.

While the Syrian revolution is still ongoing, the presence of activists in Kuwait, spreading information about the perilous circumstances of Syrian civilians, reveals why controlling the spread of information is no longer possible for governments in the region. Assad can murder his citizens, but he can't keep the whole world from watching. The more brutally he behaves, the more

Figure 1.5   The Syrian revolution: *Wathakkir* movement's resistance literature. (For more on this movement, visit <http://wathakker.info/?lang=eng>.)

illegitimate his regime becomes. Activists throughout the region and the world can work around his state to mobilise public opinion and to attempt to shape policy decisions in their calls for action. The photographs of children being shot in their homes at point-blank range reveal extreme state brutalities and call on global citizens to act. The dissolving of borders, the broadening of activist pools, the ease with which video, audio and photos are distributed over global networks, the collecting of grass-roots civilian voices, and money to support the cause, all of these revolutionary acts are enabled by new media technologies. Together people, new media and well-articulated causes challenge the old rules of the game – including what Arab publics do, what they want, what tools they have available with which to work for change, and what impact they can have on social and political processes.

At the same time, as revealed by the persistence of the Syrian regime, and the recent military coup in Egypt that brought former general Sisi to the presidency, the new Arab public does not necessarily get to control the endgame. States and militaries remain powerful actors, the most powerful in some cases. Tunisia, with its significant transition to democratic, civilian rule, the first to fall and the nation to lead, remains a beacon of light for those still living in precarious positions as a result of the Arab Spring uprisings. Recent terrorist attacks against tourists visiting the pretty Mediterranean country reveal that security concerns besiege even the most promising states and societies in the region.

Conclusion

Citizens in the Middle East regularly use new media technologies to work around the state. These processes threaten the status quo, because Middle Eastern governments and religious leaders 'depended so heavily on their ability to dominate, and control the public sphere' (Lynch 2012: 11). A loss of control over what the public knows, says and does is a force for change in the Middle East, and new media tools are implicated in this process, from the first satellite waves to the growing ubiquity of Facebook, which is the Middle East's most commonly used social networking tool (Dubai School of Government 2014). New media practices embolden some Middle Eastern citizens to openly confront state power, while at the same time offer quiet, nearly invisible opportunities for enhanced civic engagement and agency to anyone with a connection. The growing presence of new media access and use multiplies the potential effects of new communication patterns on power relations broadly defined. If there is even an ounce of truth to President Obama's West Point speech, which opened this chapter, we should focus our gaze on the ways in which average citizens use the Internet to work around power constraints in their everyday lives, as demonstrated in the next four chapters.

2

IT 4 REGIME CHANGE: NETWORKING AROUND THE STATE IN EGYPT

The exercise of power depends on the consent of the ruled who, by withdrawing that consent, can control and even destroy the power of their opponent. (Sharp 1973: 4)

Always it is interesting, is it not? To look rearward from the present moment to those earlier present moments from which it has arisen. If one perspicaciously from effects to causes traces the development of anything, one sees with clarity how infallibly one thing leads to another. And yet, sometimes it is easier from the present to look forward and predict an outcome than it is to look backward and determine a cause. (Hoban 2002: 63)

In 1998, S. A. Slama, a well-known columnist in Egypt, stated that 'any country, institution or individual who wants to catch up with the advanced world should use the Internet' (Slama 1998: 10). Yet in the year 2000, when research for this chapter began, only 450,000 Egyptians had Internet access (July 2000 estimates, <http://www.internetworldstats.com>). A study by Madar Research, however, suggested that Internet penetration rates in the Middle East were notoriously unreliable, because they failed to take into account Internet use at a public access point (Madar Research 2002). Perhaps the Internet was more important to Egyptian citizens than counting IP addresses indicated?

With this question in mind, I travelled to Egypt (initially in 2000, with two follow-up research trips in 2004 and 2013) to learn about public awareness and use of the Internet. I also wanted to see if the government was attempting to bridge the digital divide, and to see if Internet cafés and community access points were providing more connectivity than aggregate statistics suggested. I also wanted to interview government officials, business professionals and international aid workers to understand the motivations of those building an IT infrastructure in Egypt. Moreover, participant observation and interviews with Internet café users aimed to explore Egypt's emerging Internet culture.

What I found is that although the technocratic elite saw the Internet as a vehicle for job creation and capital accumulation, citizens viewed the Internet as a tool with which to achieve a better, more informed life. The main argument of this chapter is that the government of Egypt and its IT advisors, under the direction of Ahmed Nazif, former Minister of Communications and Information Technology (1999–2004) and Prime Minister (2004–11), underestimated the importance of everyday forms of new media empowerment in the lives of aggrieved citizens. These findings result from data collected on three research trips to Cairo in 2000, 2004 and 2013. In addition, my research assistant conducted interviews with Internet café users in Cairo in May and June 2004, when efforts to bridge the digital divide in Egypt peaked.

The ultimate goal of these fieldwork experiences and interviews was to investigate emerging Internet cultures in Cairo, and to determine if participants linked any detectable changes in the practice of everyday life with their new media use. This is why the conversation with the taxi driver in which he directly insulted Mubarak, and the words of the grocery delivery boy who celebrated Bin Laden and indirectly insulted me, were so significant. They indicated an important initial change in public culture and communication openness in the practice of everyday life, in sharp contrast to the repressed nature of public discourse observed in my field research in 2000.

While it is not the goal of this chapter to explain the Egyptian Arab Spring revolution that began on 25 January 2011 in Tahrir Square, one cannot ignore history. History sometimes happens when we are planning for other things. In the spirit of Adelbert Delarue, Russell Hoban's lead character in *The Bat Tattoo*, this analysis looks rearward from the present moment and uses fifty Internet café interviews to see if we can derive any insights into mundane forms of communication and change which may indicate something consequential about the initial effects of public empowerment in a digitised Egypt. Evidence of citizens leveraging the Internet to remove consent and to seek empowerment emerge from the interviews (Scott 1990, Sharp 1973), even if such changes, in 2004, are localised in the power struggles that constrain their everyday life.

As Delarue observes, it is sometimes easier to 'look forward and predict an outcome'. The brutal military dictatorship under the quasi-civilian leadership of 'retired' General Sisi reveals the degree to which people make history, but not 'as they please'. Marx observes that 'the tradition of all dead generations weighs like a nightmare on the brains of the living' and with these words appropriately describes the dialectic of military strongman rule in Egypt (Marx 1885: 5).

As Gene Sharp cautions, however, the removal of consent can be brutal on authoritarian regimes. Applied to Egypt, Sharp's insight means that General Sisi can arrest and torture the opposition, attempt to muzzle students, kill people at football matches, and coerce compliance through arbitrary arrests, torture and executions, but he cannot take away the agency of a public empowered by new media. The genie is out of the bottle, so to speak (Clarke and Kanke 2010: xiii). Egyptian citizens used their voices and organising skills to topple the previous regime. Thus everyday people mired in even more hopeless circumstances than those which gave impetus to the last revolution collect steam for the next phase of explosive change. The words of President Erdogan should be kept in mind. He astutely observes, 'If we look at history, we will see that regimes which persecute [their people] do not remain standing' (Weymouth 2012: B1). The ultimate conclusion of this chapter is that as Egyptians continue to find digital micro-paths to consent removal, future eruptions of mass civic engagement are likely.

Constructing Egypt's Information Society

An insulated core of government technocrats closely associated with the Mubarak presidency transitioned Egypt to the information age. Members of this inner circle include Hisham el Sharif, director of the Information Decision and Support Center and founder of the Regional Information

Technology Institute; Tarek Kamel (interviewed June 2004, Cairo), builder of Egypt's first connection to the Internet, director of the Smart Villages programme, founder of the Egyptian Internet Society, and former Minister of Communications and Information Technology; and Ahmed Nazif, former Prime Minister.

My field research in 2000 and 2004 revealed that building an information society in Egypt was a public-private partnership, including government officials, leading businessmen, representatives of multilateral aid organisations and multinational corporations. Collectively these individuals and organisations worked to fund, build and promote public awareness and use of emerging Internet infrastructures through push-pull strategies. During these two fieldwork visits to Cairo I interviewed more than forty officials from these three sectors – the government, the business community and the aid community – and through these meetings engaged with the future of Egypt as they imagined it.

For example, in an interview with Heba Ramsey, an employee at the Regional Information Technology and Software Engineering Center, she summarised the government's IT vision as far as youths and the general public are concerned by observing,

> We want to make sure young people in Egypt are encouraged not just to be users of the technologies, but to go beyond what is there/available – to become creators of our collective global future; not just the rich, but all sectors of Egypt . . . We are serious about using IT to better our country. (Interviewed June 2000, Cairo)

The government's effort to diffuse IT capabilities throughout Egyptian society resulted in a wide range of public-private partnerships to wire Egypt. Internet cafés mushroomed. More than fifty newly licensed Internet Service Providers (ISPs) competed to provide connectivity to the emerging information society. E-commerce struggled to take root in Egypt, due to a lack of credit card availability among average citizens. Communication technology issues emerged in newspapers and television (in English and Arabic), fostering public demand for IT. New e-government projects aimed to close the service gap between citizen and state by providing online portals through which to buy train tickets, reserve flights or pay bills.

Multinational corporations such as IBM, Microsoft and Nokia assisted Egypt with PC, software and mobile service provisions. IT training centres emerged throughout Egypt, even in the poorest neighbourhoods and villages. Likewise, computer/Internet training was integrated into public and private education, public libraries and community centres (Wheeler 2003b: 139).

Egypt's budding information society illustrated that new media were an important part of daily life for some citizens. But how would new media and communication opportunities affect the average or disenfranchised citizen's life? One optimistic analyst in a report prepared for USAID Egypt predicted that the country's transition to the information age would result in 'efficiency, transparency, and productivity' in both daily life and the economy (Mintz 1998). In 2000, however, most of the people building the IT revolution in Egypt focused on the business implications of constructing an IT revolution – the so-called efficiency and productivity pay-off. Efforts at this stage were concentrated on middle-level management training, as well as the training of elite youths who would someday fill those middle- and upper-level management positions. The poor and marginalised, like the child below, can't even afford proper shoes, or school, and are unlikely to benefit from increased Internet access.

The barriers to participation in the emerging information society in Egypt were significant. The words of a manager at IBM Egypt provide a glimpse of the emerging digital divide, in spite of state efforts to bridge it. He observes:

> The information revolution will make the barriers between rich kids and poor ones more exaggerated than ever before in Egypt. It's inevitable. All of these tele-centres in Upper Egypt to provide Internet access to poor kids are a joke, and a complete waste of resources. How many of them know English, or even how to read? (Interviewed August 2000, Cairo)

Because IT access was considered a luxury, it was assumed by the architects of the information society that IT could target economic development and private-sector growth, while keeping those with significant grievances from participating. The poor, the illiterate and the remote would not have time, money, access or skills with which to use the tool. The IT

Figure 2.1   Poor boy selling bread, Cairo. Photo: Deborah L. Wheeler, March 2013.

revolution would be a surgical strike to make part of Egypt look like India or Singapore. IT would build a Bangalore in Cairo, while keeping the rest of Egypt looking much like India's underclass: poor, underdeveloped and disenfranchised.

Would this be a communications revolution for all Egyptians, rich and poor, or would it exaggerate the overt gaps between haves and have-nots by adding information poverty to Egypt's already significant social problems? With such low connectivity figures for the country at this time (less than 1% of the population having access), the populist message rings hollow. Eventually, however, Internet cafés, TACCs (Technology Access Community Centers) and reduced costs for access would spread the information revolution beyond its initial target audience, laying the foundations for the marginalised to have a voice.

Table 2.1 Internet access in Egypt 2000–2015

Year	Internet users	% of population with access
2000	450,000	.65%
2001	600,000	.85%
2005	3,000,000	4.3%
2008	10,532,400	12.9%
2009	12,568,900	15.9%
2011	21,691,776	26.4%
2015	86,895,099	53.2%

Source: Internet World Stats.

Do the People Want IT?

If 2000 was the year to understand the state's vision for expanding the knowledge economy by building an information society for development, fieldwork in 2004 produced a clearer picture of Internet use in everyday citizens' lives. Through structured interviews with fifty Internet café users in Cairo, we see that over time 'the Internet is creating better informed citizens with more social capital and expectations for more responsive government' (Wheeler 2007a: 332).

Access to the Internet surged in Egypt between 2000 and 2015, as revealed in Table 2.1. Part of the explanation behind this surge is that the government and the private sector in January 2002 introduced a free dial-up service (General Dynamics 2004: 3). Anyone with a home phone line could dial up to the Internet for the price of a local call (a fraction of a cent). Another factor contributing to increased Internet penetration was the establishment of community technology centres built by a partnership between the United Nations Development Programme and the government to close the digital divide. These state-owned community access points were especially important in providing connectivity in rural and poor areas where market forces were too weak to sustain private-sector cafés. Complementing this process of widening communal access to the Internet were a series of private-sector Internet café businesses, which in 2002 numbered more than 400 but were concentrated mostly in Cairo, Alexandria and tourist locations like Luxor and Sharm el-Sheikh (Madar Research 2002).

In addition, the Microsoft Corporation/Government of Egypt's 'A

Table 2.2 Sample of free internet dial-up numbers in Egypt

T. E. Data	0777 7777
Link.Net	0777 0777
Masrawy	0707 0101
Balooshy	0707 0707
Yalla	0707 4444
Misr Net 2	0777 0888
Access	0777 0999
Internet Egypt	0707 7777

Source: American Chamber of Commerce in Egypt, <http://www.amcham.org.eg/Egypt%20 section/FreeInternet.asp>.

Computer for Every Home' project, launched in November 2002, provided low-cost loans for PC acquisition. The programme was designed to enable poorer Egyptians to buy a computer in an effort to bridge the digital divide. An estimated 300,000 Egyptians acquired PCs in the first few years of this project, through interest-free loans, at a cost of $15 a month for up to forty months (Microsoft 2002). This programme more than doubled the number of Egyptians who owned computers (Namatalla 2006). Programmes designed to diffuse information technology, training and use resulted in a rapid increase in Internet access and carried the effects of the information age beyond the wealthy and well-connected in Egypt.

Public Access Points and Voices of the IT Revolution in Egypt

Najat Rochidi, former director of the ICT Dar project at the United Nations Development Programme regional headquarters in Cairo, explained in an interview that more than 85% of all Internet access in the region takes place in a community access point (café or technology centre). In order to better understand Internet use among those who were not able to afford a PC or to have Internet access in their homes, a research assistant and I interviewed Internet café users in various neighbourhoods in Cairo. The resulting patterns among participants' voices allow us to see transitions in social consciousness and civic engagement emerging even in this small n study. While the findings are not intended to represent all Egyptians, or even all residents of Cairo, the interview data reveal potentially hidden forms of empowerment. And since a revolution occurred six years later, in part because citizens leveraged new media tools, any small indications of Internet use to violate norms and enhance citizen voice are data worth considering.

These testaments to new communications tools and their transformational effects tell us how a small handful of Egyptians exercise their rights to know, to express, to meet and to participate in events shaping their society and world. Who are these fifty individuals? They are Internet café users residing in one of five Cairo neighbourhoods: Dokki, Mohandessen, Garden City, Downtown and Agouza. They range in age from seventeen to forty-eight. In terms of education, they range from a high school dropout to Egyptians with a Bachelor's degree. No one interviewed had higher than a Bachelor's degree. Twenty-one of the fifty are still students. In terms of marital status, thirty-six are single, three are engaged, five are married, two are separated, three are divorced and one is a widow. Gender-wise, twenty-five are female and twenty-five are male. In terms of religion, four are Christian and forty-six are Muslim. Four of those interviewed are not students and are unemployed. One of those interviewed owns her own business and one is a housewife; forty-four are either a student and/or employed. Twenty-six of those interviewed only have access to the Internet at a public access point. Of the remaining twenty-four, only two have access to the Internet at home. The rest only have access at work or university, but explain that they come to an Internet café because they cannot use the computer at school or work freely. Only six out of the fifty were formally taught to use the Internet via a course or on-the-job training. The remaining forty-four were taught informally by friends and family members, suggesting that the spread of Internet knowledge is a social (media) phenomenon. Thirty of those interviewed have taught someone within their social network (mostly friends and family members) how to use the Internet, so knowledge of the Internet and its use builds social capital. The average number of hours per week spent online is 13.5. In terms of online activity, the most popular pursuit is email (98%), followed by chatting (88%), study (56%), work/business (40%), music (38%), news (28%), seeking advice (28%), sport (26%), health (26%), religious purposes (18%), gaming (18%) and shopping (8%). What these statistics suggest is that Internet use is primarily for communication or engaging others in chat. It is also used for business- or school-related purposes, and for entertainment.

The fact that 96% of those interviewed for this study only have access to the Internet away from home means that connectivity estimates of 5% may underestimate the scope of Egypt's emerging information society in 2004–5. How do we count those with access at school or work, at a community access point, or on their mobile phones (88% of those interviewed own a mobile phone)? In countries where most people go online at a public access point or on their phones, counting IP addresses could grossly underestimate the number of new media users.

The most accurate way to study access to the Internet – and, more importantly, how such access affects individual lives – is to ask actual users of the technology in context about their new media practices. Moreover, interviewing people about their Internet use at a public access point like a café gives us access to a broader cross section of Egyptian society – not the elites, but rather the everyday Egyptians, people without access to enough capital to afford Internet connectivity at home, which requires a computer and a home phone line.

Small n ethnographic research, like this case study, which includes interviews with open-ended questions, supplemented by participant observation, gives the researcher 'causal process tracing' which 'allows us to specify the nature of the linkages between initial conditions and outcomes with greater precision than is possible in large n quantitative studies' (Wickham 2002: 20). Studies that employ ethnographic research 'are able to explore the micro-dynamics' of 'mobilization in settings on the periphery of the formal political system and hence to clarify the mechanisms through which individual grievances are converted into collective action' (ibid.).

Moreover, focusing on micro-political transformations at the grass roots in everyday Egyptians' lives, in the words of another small n ethnographer, Asef Bayat, allows the researcher to trace 'the quiet encroachment', in other words 'the silent, protracted, but pervasive advancement of the ordinary people on the propertied, powerful or the public, in order to survive and improve their lives' (Bayat 2010: 56). Inspired by the work of Wickham and Bayat, this study uses a relative handful of interviews with Internet café users in Cairo in an attempt to identify micro-political transformations in the practice of everyday life.

Internet Impacts

An Internet café manager interviewed for this study summarises uses and impacts of the Internet in Egypt when he observes,

> The Net helps people see how others live out of Egypt and to exchange ideas and improve their English. They become even more open minded, less uptight and closed minded through such exchanges. They practise freedom of opinion and thought; they learn things from the Net. It's also a way to have access to jobs abroad. (Interviewed May 2004, Cairo)

This narrative contains many layers of meaning for our topic at hand – Internet and empowerment in Egypt. The manager argues that Egyptians are using the tool to learn how others live, which implies that such glimpses could lead Egyptians to press for improvements in their own country. People are teaching themselves new things, which is a form of empowerment, especially when improving their English, and practising freedom of opinion and thought. They are expanding their potential agency in trying to get new jobs. The end result is that Egyptians are becoming more open minded, less uptight, more free and open in their interactions with others. All of these experiences stem from new media use. Collectively, digital communication opportunities enhance individuals' lives by giving them access to things reserved for the powerful in Egypt – command of English, job opportunities, a chance to know life and living beyond Egypt's borders, a chance to become better educated and more open with opinions. In all, this Internet café manager states that Egyptians who use the Internet are more powerful, more knowledgeable and freer as a result, for reasons explored more systematically in the sections that follow.

Getting a job

Several Internet café users interviewed for this project state that they use the Internet to look for jobs. One young man who is unemployed notes,

> The Internet keeps me busy and fills up the loads of free time that I have now recently being without a job. It's a great way to meet new people, express oneself without drawbacks. One can express thoughts and opinions

freely. It helps me look for jobs everywhere. It is a gate to an unlimited world of socialising, job opportunities, [and] fun. I discovered and learned many things from the Net. It educates people. (Interviewed June 2004, Cairo)

Another Internet café user, who is thirty-five, Muslim, male and single, notes:

With the Internet I made many new friendships in Arab and foreign countries and a foreign female friend came and visited me. It was great to meet her in person. We are close friends now and she is trying to help me find a job abroad and have the chance to travel out of Egypt. You know the economy here is getting worse; salaries are so low. What chance does a person have for a good life? The Net is a door to opportunities and hopes. (Interviewed May 2004, Cairo)

'The Net is a door to opportunities and hopes'; cyberspace is a place to express dissatisfaction with poor salaries and to try to find a way out of hopelessness. It's a place for constructing new friendships and interactions with others outside of Egypt, for experiences out of reach for the average Egyptian who can't afford travel abroad, or English lessons. Online, even unemployed Egyptians can have a voice. They find some space for fun, to meet new people, to try to find a job, or a path to a better life. All of these experiences can be empowering by providing perceived pathways out of hopelessness, or at least increased expectations for finding a way out.

Learning new things

Several of those interviewed for this study state that they use the Internet to learn new things and to practise their English. 'It's better than a language school,' observed one Internet café user (interviewed June 2004, Cairo). An Internet café manager in Cairo summarises the educational benefits of IT access by observing,

It's a great invention and source for information and education. We are in a changing world and we need to follow up with the move of countries around the world. It educates people, and broadens their mental horizons. Though chat is a waste of time, it is improving people's English language. (Interviewed June 2004, Cairo)

Affordability and ease also expand people's online access to information and knowledge. For example, a nineteen-year-old male, Muslim student from Mohandessen neighbourhood in Cairo observes,

> Internet is really useful when I need info for school tasks and reports. It saved me time and money to get books or info from other sources. I enjoy my time surfing and chatting, and sending jokes and cards and emails to friends I made on the Net. It's very entertaining, especially [as] we don't have much of a chance to travel to other countries like the people who come here – tourists. (Interviewed June 2004, Cairo)

Knowledge for school, saving money on information acquisition, expanding social networks, and being a virtual tourist all add up to a good time with consequential effects – such as seeing how others live, enjoying one's free time, enhancing human and social capital, and increasing civic engagement and self-sufficiency.

Enhanced freedom

A recurring theme within the interview results is the experience of perceived freedom online. In the testimony above, the young man notes that online 'one can express thoughts and opinions freely'. Similarly, the Internet café manager quoted at the beginning of this section states that Internet users 'practise freedom of opinion and thought' and that such practices make Internet users 'more open minded'. As another example of enhanced freedoms online, one young woman interviewed for this project observes,

> It's interesting to chat and make new friends. I like talking to foreigners; I'm not that keen on the closed Arab mentality. I like people who are themselves in chat, no masks. In person they put on masks. (Interviewed May 2004, Cairo)

Similarly, another young woman observes,

> I enjoy my time surfing and chatting. I made many friends in the Gulf, Syria, Spain and Greece. I enjoy discussing cultural things and our differences. I realise there is a lot more to people and life than what I used to know. They have more freedom and choices than we do in Egypt. (Interviewed May 2004, Cairo)

Collectively, these narratives attest to the ways in which Internet access and use breaks the fear barriers which inhibit expression in Egypt. With Internet access, Egyptians are experimenting with new kinds of self-expression on taboo topics, like divorce, engaging more actively in political debates, and discussing similarities and differences across national boundaries. In the words of a thirty-year-old Muslim Internet user from Agouza, 'using the Internet and chat is a great way to socialise and meet people that one gets along with easily' (interviewed May 2004, Cairo).

Enhanced global understanding and civic engagement

The end result of widening access to new virtual publics is, in the words of one Internet user who is ninteeen, Muslim, female and single, an expanded sense of global understanding. She notes,

> I love chatting with people of different ages and cultures. I believe the Internet is bringing people closer all around the world. It lets them enjoy their humanity without prejudice or segregation. (Interviewed May 2004, Cairo)

Similarly, an Internet café manager in Cairo notes, 'the Internet is a way better way of getting info about anything and it is also good for having friends from different countries' (interviewed May 2004, Cairo).

In terms of what is being discussed across borders, one twenty-seven-year-old single Christian female from Cairo notes that because of the Internet 'I know people from all over the world and we have discussions from politics to social issues to religious debates' (interviewed May 2004, Cairo). A twenty-one-year-old single Muslim female notes that the Internet is good for 'knowing in details about news of events in the Arab world and we discuss them in chat forums. The Net is a great invention to get to know new people and exchange opinions' (interviewed May 2004, Cairo). Another view of enhanced civic engagement is provided by a seventeen-year-old female Muslim, who notes, 'Internet use is fun. I got to know many people and make new friendships. I have friends here, but through the Net I got to know people out of Egypt and to know how they live and think. We discuss many issues' (interviewed May 2004, Cairo). All this engagement across cultures and boundaries, according to one Internet café manager, is 'educating people and broadening their mental horizons' (interviewed May 2004, Cairo).

Breaching norms

Adding a personal and political touch to these observations, a thirty-one-year-old Muslim woman who is separated and considering a divorce notes,

> The Internet has helped me greatly with information concerning my marital status and problems. Also I get information related to my work but mainly chat helped me a lot in taking things easy. I get support and advice from women in other countries who went through separation and divorce. This means a lot to me, especially as this issue is sensitive in the Arab world and here in particular. I can't discuss my private problems with family, and even with friends who know me and my husband. Some things are very private but talking about it with women on the Net helped me a lot, and some of these women became my best friends and I hope that one day we can meet. (Interviewed June 2004, Cairo)

Online communication allows Egyptians to subvert conservative norms and constraints on public engagement. Enhancing one's social networks and knowledge capital results from being able to discuss one's personal problems with a wider audience while avoiding social costs. Coming to voice is a form of resistance for marginalised groups who have 'previously never had a public voice' (hooks 1989: 12).

Similarly, a seventeen-year-old female who is Muslim attests to the ways in which the Internet gives people access to subjects that are personal and potentially embarrassing when she notes, 'on the Internet, I find all the information I need. It is especially useful when I need information about health issues. I have a health problem and I feel comfortable to know and read about it from the Net in privacy' (interviewed May 2004, Cairo). This process of learning to deal with one's personal problems beyond the confines of face-to-face family-and-friend networks is empowering for Egyptians, because wider access to information without social consequences teaches people to problem solve through individual ingenuity. It also shows people that norms and sanctions on what can be discussed privately and publicly are easily breached online. This is a form of empowerment through risk taking, which at relatively low cost allows Egyptians to find their voice, and to speak more openly than is the norm.

Expanding agency

All of these agency-enhancing experiences – whether widening one's social circle, trying to find a job, getting advice on taboo subjects, engaging in cross-cultural debates, learning new things or practising one's English – draw users to the technology, changing their consciousness and civic engagement one click at a time. We likewise see agency-enhancing experiences in the testimony of a twenty-year-old Muslim male from Agouza neighbourhood in Cairo:

> Online I like to educate myself, to gain knowledge and be cultured, to feed my brain with useful material. I enjoy surfing websites and chatting and talking to people. The Net made me less reserved and less serious with people. It helped me greatly with my study. (Interviewed June 2004, Cairo)

Another Internet café user who is seventeen, male and a student observes of the Internet, 'I am an addict to it; it nourishes my interests and ambitions' (interviewed May 2004, Cairo). Another Internet café user who is female, twenty-three years old and Muslim summarises the main points of this argument when she observes, 'the Net is an open gate for personal freedom and self-expression' (interviewed June 2004, Cairo). Demonstrating the clear link between online and offline behaviour, one twenty-three-year-old Muslim male Internet café user observes, 'I used to be so serious and dull. Now I am more social, since chat encouraged me to express myself and be less worried and have less anxiety about expressing my crazy open-minded trains of thought' (interviewed June 2004, Cairo). Another Internet café user puts the Internet's impact in more concrete terms when he observes, 'the Internet is providing a way for modernising people and it helps us to become a more open society' (interviewed June 2004, Cairo).

Taken collectively, all of these testimonies represent a process of increasing 'people power' in Egypt. At the grass roots, one click at a time, an Egyptian public learns to expect more from their lives. Internet café users find new tools with which to expand connections, knowledge and opportunities. Risk taking in breaching norms, in offering opinions and in civically engaging heightens political awareness, and transcends regimes of fear.

What happens when access to the Internet grows; when more norm-breaching behaviour and increasingly free expression accumulate? John Pollock provides an answer when he observes, 'social media has created bridges, has created channels between individuals, between activists, between even ordinary men, to speak out, to know that there are other men who think like me. We can work together, we can make something together' (Pollock 2011: 78).

Did collective consciousness for change have its roots in relatively mundane acts of self-expression and agentive behaviour online? This chapter argues that such communication acts have clear spillover effects in the practice of everyday life – visible as early as 2004, in the oppositional discourse of my taxi driver who insulted Mubarak; in the verbal resistance of the grocery delivery boy who publicly celebrated Bin Laden; and in the various forms of agency and change expressed in Internet café interviews.

Something to Get Angry About: Unemployment, Repression, Corruption and Using the Internet as a Tool for Mobilisation

While the section above argues that new media access plays a role in increasing risk-taking behaviour both online and off, civic engagement and demands for change are also evident in overt collective-action events in Egypt. For example, 'in 2004, there were 266 acts of protest; and by 2008, they reached 630' (Bakr 2012: 67). By 2010, 'daily protests averaged 5 a day' (ibid.). Mobilisation targeted Mubarak's leadership failures in three main areas: unemployment/underemployment among youths, repression and corruption. Tufekci and Wilson found, in their interviews with Tahrir protesters, that 'social media in general, and Facebook in particular, provided new sources of information the regime could not easily control and were crucial in shaping how citizens made individual decisions about participating in protests' (Tufekci and Wilson 2012: 363). Exploring the conditions in Egypt, which make citizens angry enough to risk mobilisation, will add to our understanding of Internet culture in Egypt.

Unemployment and the youth bulge

Youth unemployment and poverty are symptoms of corruption and nepotism in Egypt. Although the economy flourished under Mubarak, new wealth generation and opportunity were not spread evenly. Unlike the Nile, trickle-down economics did not flow very far. The bulk of Egypt's wealth and opportunity remained concentrated in the hands of a small circle of National Democratic Party loyalists, high-ranking military officers, and crony capitalists in Mubarak's network. The rich and powerful got richer, while the masses suffered. In the two years preceding the Arab Spring revolution in Egypt, '90 percent of the unemployed in Egypt were between the ages of 14 and 40' (Baroi 2012: 113). Moreover, of the unemployed youths, 88% are educated (ibid.). What results is that 'they come into the street against unemployment and state owners who failed to provide them jobs' (ibid.).

For example, while Muhammad Abul Enein, multi-millionaire founder of Cleopatra Ceramic Group, also known as 'The Tile King', considers adding a few more private jets to his corporate fleet, striking workers in his factory make around $233 a month. Corporate greed and abuse of workers were among the reasons for the Egyptian revolution, with frequent labour strikes preceding the Tahrir uprising. Slogans include 'Revolution, revolution until victory; revolution against the thieves of Egypt' (Charbel 2012).

In the words of businessman Abul Enein, political stability is required for economic development, and economic development helps all Egyptians (Jarjoura et al. 2011). While Abul Enein saw himself as 'the noblest businessman on earth' (Abo Alabass 2012), angry workers chanted 'There is no God but Allah, and Abul Enein is Allah's enemy' (Charbel 2012). This disconnect between rich and poor, powerful and relatively powerless, was at the heart of the Tahrir uprisings. Standing at the top of the pyramid, so to speak, gazing out over vast economic development opportunities including industrialised agricultural projects, electricity and steel industries, communications companies, textile and tile factories, gold mines and so on, Egypt's rich businessmen saw a land of opportunity in which political freedoms were easily traded for vast access to capital. The masses could not tolerate stability balanced on their own suffering indefinitely, especially when new communication technologies provided them pathways to enhanced voice and agency.

Repression

In order to keep people from openly criticising the government, most of the state's public spending supported the Ministry of Interior. The burned-out carcass of the Mogamma building, where the Ministry of Interior was located prior to the revolution, still stands on the edge of Tahrir Square and is a poignant reminder of networking around the state. While the Internet was unfiltered and free, this belied the fact that an entire branch of the Interior Ministry was dedicated to cyber policing. Open networks meant a bird's-eye view of 'illicit' activity for the regime, which led to arrests of homosexuals (Wheeler 2001c, 2002), the beating to death of Khalid Said (Londono 2011), and arrests of workers, such as the October 6th Movement activists (Faris 2013), and Islamists (Wickham 2013). Cyber-policing strategies regularly earned Egypt 'Enemy of the Internet' status (Reporters without Borders 2010a). According to Reporters without Borders, an Enemy of the Internet is a state that participates in 'active intrusive surveillance of news providers, resulting in grave violations of freedom of information and human rights' (Reporters without Borders 2012a).

In Egypt, a puzzling opening for public dissent emerged in 2005,

Figure 2.2   Ministry of Interior building, Cairo. Photo: Deborah L. Wheeler, March 2013.

Table 2.3 Freedom in Egypt 2002–2015

Year	Freedom	Civil rights	Political rights
2002	6.0	6.0	6.0
2003	6.0	6.0	6.0
2004	6.0	6.0	6.0
2005	5.5	5.0	6.0
2006	5.5	5.0	6.0
2007	5.5	5.0	6.0
2008–11	5.5	5.0	6.0
2012	5.5	5.0	6.0
2013	5.0	5.0	5.0
2014	5.5	5.0	6.0
2015	5.5	5.0	6.0

Source: Freedom House (<www.freedomhouse.org>).

resulting in a slight improvement in Egypt's freedom ranking. In explaining the improvements in freedom and civil rights, one observer points out,

> In a perverse way it was this absolute certainty that Mubarak and those who were a part of his power system had nothing to worry about from any internal source, which included a total disdain of the people that allowed a certain amount of political freedom to exist. (Bassiouni 2012)

The Tahrir uprising which overthrew Mubarak reveals the degree to which the state miscalculated the ingenuity of a digitally enabled, disenfranchised public.

Egyptian corruption

In 2007–9 Egypt experienced a sharp increase in corruption perceptions. Among the key demands of the uprising was an end to corruption and kick-backs that favoured officials and businessmen close to the Mubarak regime (Sorensen 2012). A Chatham House report notes, 'Corruption is a serious problem in Egypt, contributing to high levels of poverty and unemployment' (Chatham House 2012: 2).

Corruption, in the words of former US Ambassador to Egypt Frank Ricciardone, 'remains a significant impediment to growth' and development in Egypt (Grimaldi and O'Harrow 2011: 1A). Crony capitalism and the concentration of wealth and power in Egypt gave rise to a people's power revolu-

Table 2.4 Corruption in Egypt 2001–2015

Year	Rank	Score	Countries with same score
2001	54th	3.6	El Salvador, Turkey
2002	62nd	3.4	El Salvador
2003	70th	3.3	Bosnia, Morocco
2004	77th	3.2	Benin, Mali
2005	70th	3.4	Croatia, Saudi Arabia
2006	70th	3.3	Brazil, China
2007	105th	2.9	Argentina, Albania
2008	115th	2.8	Maldives, Mauritania
2009	111th	2.8	Algeria, Indonesia
2010	98th	3.1	Mexico, Burkina Faso
2011	112th	2.9	Kosovo, Senegal
2012	118th	32	Gabon, Columbia
2013	114th	32	Indonesia
2014	94th	37	Armenia, Liberia
2015	88th	36	Peru, Morocco

Source: Transparency International. Note that the raw score system changed for the 2012–2015 data. Prior to 2012, the ranking was based upon a score between 1 and 10, with 10 being super clean and 1 being highly corrupt; beginning in 2012, the scale was 1–100, with 100 being the cleanest.

tion designed to more evenly distribute a chance for a good life. Whether or not the ideals that brought people collectively into Tahrir Square will be realised remains one of the country's biggest challenges. The military coup to depose Morsi, the popularly elected president of Egypt, the declaration of the Muslim Brotherhood (MB) as an illegal terrorist organisation, and the imprisonment of MB leaders and democracy activists resulted in a surge of repression which breeds public wilfulness to resist. The questionable circumstances surrounding the election of the former general Sisi (Kirkpatrick 2014), and the fact that the Egyptian economy has become markedly worse, with double-digit inflation (Taborda 2015), a depressed tourist market and capital flight, make the dreams of Tahrir for bread, freedom and dignity (Mellor 2016) unlikely to materialise. The decrease in perceived corruption in Egypt is promising, but the decline in freedom, civil liberties and economic opportunity are causes for concern, as such processes have stimulated unrest in the past.

The dreams of Tahrir remain dreams deferred. Sometimes a dream deferred festers and explodes. As Faris observes of Egyptians engaged in movements for change, 'they remain defiant, and they still express that defiance through social media' (Faris 2013: 204). Faris advises, 'don't be surprised if in a decade or two, they do indeed belatedly inherit the beautiful revolution they authored' (ibid.).

Conclusion

Pollock closes his essay on the role of social media in the Arab uprisings with a quote from George Washington: 'Liberty, when it begins to take root, is a plant of rapid growth' (Pollock 2011: 82). This chapter has illustrated how new media use prepared the ground for liberty to take root in Egypt, both in everyday forms of empowerment and in Tahrir-sized mobilisations. Online experimentation, risk taking, enhanced freedom of expression, networking, learning, debating, civic engagement, problem solving and public mobilisation allow liberty to take root. Collectively, such acts 'restored the meaning of politics . . . It revalued the people, revealing them in all their complexity – neither heroes nor saints, but citizens' (Ghobashy 2012).

With several years' hindsight, the growth of liberty in Egypt seems as endangered as the cherry tree George Washington allegedly chopped down. The roots of liberty, however, remain in the everyday lives of citizens and their potentially empowering new media practices. A coup and economic decline cannot make the people forget what they accomplished in ending the Mubarak regime; in captivating global attentions; in gaining self-sufficiency to problem solve. The fatigue of living in an unstable post-revolutionary society, in a state where institutions, currency and food reserves are failing, means that the fight is only beginning. Years of misuse of public funds, corruption, poverty and widening hope gaps limit opportunities for optimism. The Egyptian people, however, are resilient, resourceful and highly capable, so one must put one's faith in their creative use of scarce resources, because they have surprised the world before, throughout history, both ancient and near, and are likely to do so again. The expectation for disruptiveness and a renewed faith in people power remain the legacy of Tahrir. Citizens of Egypt, like the burnt carcass of the Mogamma building, await renewal and reform.

3

NO MORE RED LINES: NETWORKING AROUND THE STATE IN JORDAN

The Jordanian Spring will culminate into the elections, which will usher in the Jordanian Summer – our season of hard work and delivery. The Jordanian Summer will start with the upcoming new Parliament and will proceed from under its dome as the harvest season to build on the historic reforms achieved so far. (AFP 2012)

What is going on around us, in terms of the Arab Spring, is not far from you. So beware from a patient person's anger, for we have run out of patience, and we have made up our mind. We do not believe in the existence of a true will to reform. You have closed all outlets that lead to reform. By doing so, you have sanctioned for us all the doors of peaceful escalation that will transform the Jordanian street that is already prepared. (Fox 2012)

Jordan has been deeply touched by the Arab uprisings – not because the regime has had to confront a mobilised citizenry demanding its fall, but because of the gradual accumulation of too many crossed red lines to ignore, cutting across many segments of society (Schwedler 2012).

In 2011–12, Jordan experienced its version of the Arab uprisings as the country was rocked by a series of street protests, organised via social media. The passages above illustrate facets of new media armed citizen engagement, broadly defined as *hirak* movements, versus a monarchy trying to preserve the status quo. The Jordanian opposition includes a weak coalition of contentious forces united in their shared interest in change. On the streets were East Bank Jordanians, youths and Islamists, all of whom have supported the monarchy in the past. The street protests were surprising, because of the broad coalition of activists, and the direct confrontation with the king.

Social media supported resistance in Jordan reflects a public increasingly disappointed by the stagnating economy, unemployment, hyper-inflation and increases in perceived corruption. The immediate triggers to the street protests were economic, including a lifting of fuel subsidies in 2012 (Haddad 2012) necessitated by the country's crippling debt, which had climbed to more than 70% of GDP (IMF 2012). The Jordanian government was so fiscally challenged in 2012 it could not pay public-sector salaries, and the enforced lifting of fuel subsidies resulted in an immediate 50% increase in fuel prices (Al-Khalidi 2012). A $2.0 billion IMF Stand-By Arrangement provided a quick injection of cash with which to stabilise the country's economic haemorrhage, but it came with strings attached, including tax reform, a reduction in government jobs, and general subsidies cuts, in order to generate revenue that could balance budgets and target social-welfare spending on the poor (Kostial 2012).

Demands issued to the king by the National Front for Reform, and by tribal organisers, however, were more than economic in motivation. In the words of one opposition organiser, 'before stability and food, the Jordanian people seek liberty, dignity, democracy, justice, equality, human rights, and an end to corruption' (Berger 2015: 245). Reinstating fuel subsidies to quieten protests and borrowing money with which to pay salaries were relatively easy for the state. The more serious demands for democratic change and an end to corruption, however, would require a fundamental reordering of power relations.

A significant disconnection between the monarchy's commitment to slow reform and the protesters' demands for significant change, both economically and politically, is explored in this chapter. Schwedler highlights the degree to which politics in Jordan are changing by stating, 'There are no more red lines' (Schwedler 2012). The king and his family are no longer off limits, and demands for change are increasingly public, and bold in their overt challenge to the regime. Why did Jordanians become so oppositional, in an authoritarian context where the risks of confronting the monarchy are so high?

This chapter examines the role that new media diffusion and use play in promoting social and political awareness, and collective demands for change in Jordan. The starting point for this analysis is 200 Internet café interviews conducted by a Jordanian research assistant and me in 2004, in neighbourhoods throughout Amman and neighbouring Zarqa. These data are used to trace micro-changes in communication practices and various forms of risk taking by everyday Jordanians, which may in part explain a more explosive public sphere in the kingdom. In the pages that follow I will argue that the government's desire to build an information society in Jordan for economic and social development enabled new levels of citizen awareness and agency, and an unruly public sphere in 2012. By 2015, however, the public sphere puzzlingly shifts its support in favour of the monarchy, in what has become a typical pattern in Jordan, characterised by a cycle of unrest – protest – protect the monarchy. This dialectic is explored more completely below.

Understanding Jordan

As Karla Cunningham notes, 'economic crisis has often translated into political instability in Jordan' (Cunningham 2002: 256). What is relatively new, however, is that in 2012, the explosiveness of public unrest, and the direct affront to the monarchy, limited 'the range of the regime's responses' (ibid.). The stakes are high because if the king cannot deliver on the promises of reform, then the street protesters in 2012 had a message for His Majesty:

> Once upon a time there was Husni Mubarak and his wife Susanne and Bin Ali and Leila, and Qadaffi and his rats, and Ali Saleh the coward, and Bashar, your time has come to an end. Get ready Abdallah; Bashar your time is coming to an end; pack your clothes Abdallah. (Street chants, Haya al Tafila, East Amman, 8 September 2012. (<http://ireport.cnn.com/docs/DOC-841095>)

This unprecedented confrontation with the king by opposition forces was compounded by the Syrian refugee crisis, which at that time had brought 656,400 registered refugees to Jordan (UNHCR 16 September 2012 estimate, <http://data.unhcr.org/syrianrefugees/country.php?id=107>), all of whom added stress to the country's weak economy and fragile natural resource infrastructure. An impending disaster brews in Jordan, yet, surprisingly, the state survives. What explains the monarchy's viability in the face of severe threat?

Jordan is the 'little country that could'. It has survived in spite of steep odds throughout its history. As the king reiterated in an appearance on *The Daily Show* with Jon Stewart in 2012, when asked how his country was doing, he offered, 'We've seen better times' (<http://www.cc.com/video-clips/ar2432/the-daily-show-with-jon-stewart-king-abdullah-ii-of-jordan-pt--1>). Part of Jordan's problem is that the country is overrun by refugees once every decade or so. Previous waves from conflict in Palestine and Iraq merge with the most recent waves of Arabs fleeing civil war in Syria (*Jordan Times* 2012b, Martinez 2015). The country has few natural resources, except for cheap phosphate for fertiliser exports (Terrill 2009) and tourism. The number of tourists visiting Jordan declined 50% in 2015 (AP 2015). The country is energy-dependent on neighbours, and fluctuations in oil import prices strain the country's budget. Jordan is one of the most water-scarce places on the planet. The country has a higher debt per capita than any other country (ESCWA 2005: 2, Karimeh 2014). Jordan has experienced several foiled (2004, 2012) and successful (2005) terrorist attacks. The November 2005 triple suicide bombing on three hotel lobbies in Amman killed sixty people including Mustapha Akkad, the Hollywood producer of the *Halloween* movies and the film *The Message*, about the birth of Islam. Al Qaeda of Iraq claimed responsibility for the bombings (Gazal 2015). Jordan is a fractured society, ethnically, religiously, tribally, class-wise, gender-wise. Jordan has serious social problems, with poverty, unemployment and a massive youth bulge among the greatest domestic challenges. Politically, Jordan is divided by a well-organised Islamist opposition, both moderate, parliamentary Muslim Brotherhood forces, and extreme, extra-parliamentary *Salafist* forces. Moreover, Jordan is divided by political forces which are pressing for change and those supporting the status quo. Forces for change include a volatile mix of women's rights and human rights activists, democratic reform forces, Islamists who want more Shari'ah observances in everyday life, and youth movements seeking to close what Queen Rania calls the 'hope gap' (Reese 2015). On the other side of the political spectrum, those forces that want to maintain the status quo include a motley crew of traditional East Bank tribal elders, private-sector business elites, Christians, and some conservative Islamists loyal to the king.

To manage economic and social challenges, King Abdullah II has attempted several intersecting programmes designed to make Jordan 'the Singapore of the Middle East' (Al-Bawaba 2000); in other words, to develop a high-tech economy to compensate for a lack of natural resources and keeping political change in check with gradual reforms. The king's plan is to build an oasis of prosperity in a desert of hardships – starting with limited resources, and integrating Jordan into the global economy. In the service of this goal, the king has liberalised the economy, opened up to foreign direct investment, signed free trade deals, and built Qualified Industrial Zones, to add new jobs and boost GDP (Rad 2011). He has revolutionised the educational system. For example, in order to graduate students who are fluent in English (an estimated 45% of Jordanians speak English fluently), computer literate (the Ministry of Education in Jordan requires computer literacy for each graduate) and trained for the knowledge economy, King Abdullah created the Jordan Education Initiative (<http://jei.org.jo/en-us/>) and the Intel Computer Clubhouse programme (<http://www.queenrania.jo/en/media/articles/intel-computer-clubhouse>), and he added English and IT training to the primary and secondary public school curriculum.

The king has built 'Knowledge Stations' (<http://www.ks.jo/default_EN.htm>) in every town and remote village throughout the kingdom (see Figure 1.2). Knowledge Stations are staffed with local youths who have been trained in community and communication development strategies to leverage the digital economy in the service of lifting Jordanians out of poverty. The king has also launched several phases of political reform, including establishing a Ministry of Political Development (Baylouny 2005) and a government-sponsored human rights agency (<http://www.nchr.org.jo/english/home.aspx>). Moreover, the king has tried to stamp out corruption, sometimes appearing incognito and visiting government agencies to rate his treatment. For example, was he asked for a bribe for services? If so, this agency would be fined, and the offending agent fired. A special award for good governance was developed to encourage a cleaner, more transparent business environment in the public sector.

Key to building all of these changes was establishing an IT infrastructure and making sure Jordanians were computer literate. Even the Ministry of Interior General Directorate of Intelligence has a website (<http://www.gid.

gov.jo/en/help.html>) where citizens can submit tips on out-of-the-ordinary events to protect Jordan's security. Knowledge Stations, Internet cafés (see Figure 1.3), computer clubhouses in poor neighbourhoods, computers and Internet access in schools, low-cost dial-up services for homes – these were all part of the plan to make Jordan the Singapore of the Middle East.

Given all the challenges that this nation faces, including a citizenry by design wired for change, how does the king maintain stability and manage incremental reforms? In the face of bad neighbours, crippling debt, austerity measures, sectarianism, unemployment, poverty, inflation, resource strain and another wave of Syrian refugees, how does the state survive? In a poignant turn of events, whereas 2012 was the year of Jordan's (mild) Arab Spring, by 2015, the only street protests taking place were against the Islamic State for murdering a Jordanian pilot. Opposition was replaced by mobilisation in support of the king and the nation.

While some point to foreign aid as the reason the state survives (Haddad 2012), the charisma of the head of state is also a contributing factor. Jordan is a kingdom of cool. The head of state was on *Star Trek* (<https://www.you tube.com/watch?v=Kmut6FJ1d4M>) and is building a billion-dollar amusement park in Aqaba (to bring jobs to the south) with a *Star Trek* theme (<http://www.emirates247.com/news/region/aqaba-to-have-star-trek-park-2011-05-22-1.395806>). He is former head of the Jordanian special forces (<http://www.businessinsider.com/king-abduallh-of-jordan-is-a-total-badass-2015-2>), an elite Cobra helicopter pilot and a rally car racer, at work on a Jordanian-built race car (<https://www.youtube.com/watch?v=BvFzs76SJqc>). He rides a Harley (<https://www.youtube.com/watch?v=ZSHWd2N0Xfl>), was educated in the US and the UK and is a regular guest on US late-night TV. In fact, King Abdullah is the envy of US Republican media pundits for his tough stand on ISIS (<http://www.cc.com/video-clips/mtqomx/the-daily-show-with-jon-stewart-wish-you-were-him>). He has an uncanny ability to construct a persona of being the people's king, and the guardian of the nation, through his Jordan First programme (<http://kingabdullah.jo/index.php/en_US/initia tives/view/id/3.html>). His wife is beautiful, smart and a global advocate for women's rights.

The longevity of the monarchy can be attributed to a culture of cool constructed around the king. Tribal values, which run deep in the kingdom, weave webs of significance in a Weberian sense, to hold the fragile kingdom together. Jordan's relations with the US, Europe, the Gulf monarchies and Israel contribute, as well, to the kingdom's stability. A highly developed domestic intelligence service, along with a regime of fear, keeps public opposition relatively muzzled. Goods and services co-opt any sustainable opposition, which holds the state together. New media access and use play a role in power relations between ruler and ruled, balancing norm and norm violation, stability and change. Thus understanding what Jordanians do online and how cyber practices shape their lived experience in the kingdom is important in explaining the 2012 unrest, as well as the longevity of the monarchy.

In 2012, King Abdullah was interviewed about lessons learned during the first thirteen years of his reign. In response, he observed,

> I'd have to say the most important lesson I've learned has been from the resilience of Jordanians, their character and ability to succeed, against the odds and despite limited resources. I have seen Jordanians achieve impressive results. We are regional leaders in ICT, pharmaceuticals, education and health. We now create and manage 75 percent of all Arabic-language Internet content from the region – and that has happened even though we account for just two percent of the region's population! (AFP 2012)

One month after the king's observations, citizens in a mass demonstration in Haya Tefila, a neighbourhood in East Amman, used as their mobilising mantra 'Pack your clothes Abdullah' (Harikat al Ahrar, Street Protest, 8 September 2012, <https://www.youtube.com/watch?v=QP66Bn1fM9E>). These words reveal both an unprecedented verbal assault on the monarch and the degree to which the king may have underestimated the resilience of the Jordanian opposition. As suggested by University of Massachusetts professor Jillian Schwedler, Jordan's Arab Spring gathered steam through the micropolitics of repeated red-line breaches, accumulating beneath the surface of the status quo (Schwedler 2012).

Investigating the role that new media access and use played in transforming Jordanian society and politics is the goal of the following pages. While there are clearly many challenges and forms of misery in Jordan which give people something to grumble about, new media tools give the Jordanian public space to compare notes, to discuss strategy, to organise and breach social and political boundaries. As Daoud Kuttab observes, 'The Internet [is] a lifeline for freedom of expression' in Jordan (Kuttab 2012). The collective impact of discursive engagement online is an emboldened public sphere, more confident, more aware, more willing to mobilise for change, or so this chapter argues.

There is one big caveat, however, and that is that Jordan has not experienced an Arab Spring like Tunisia and Egypt, whereby the old regime is swept away (symbolically so in Egypt, given the persistence of the military's role in politics from behind the scenes). The closest Jordan has come so far is a series of street protests and 'corruption dances' (*Dabka al Fasad*) in front of government ministries and the palace gates. At some of these public protests, slogans including 'overthrow the regime' have been chanted. In response, the king has encouraged Jordanians to use the official channels for gradual political change, such as the January 2013 parliamentary elections, which the opposition boycotted, given electoral law reforms enacted by the king, which were designed, according to the opposition, to negate the emerging power of opposition parties (Ryan 2013, Seeley 2013). As the king has explained, in his response to the protesters in Haya Tefila,

> What is the regime? The regime is the state in all its institutions and agencies, under the umbrella of the Constitution. The regime is the values and the principles these institutions and agencies are founded upon. The regime is also the cadres who operate such institutions, which actually encompass all segments and components of our Jordanian society. No one has a monopoly over the components of the state. The regime is the organizations and citizens. Every individual in society is part of the regime. This country, which only relies on its people and their determination, has managed to overcome the impossible through unforgettable sacrifices. This Jordanian state is not the accomplishment of a single individual, or a single entity or party. It is the cumulative achievement of every Jordanian across the generations. (*Jordan Times* 2012a)

In this speech, delivered to a gathering of the Royal Court, but transmitted to society as a whole through the media, King Abdullah has embedded his rule within the Jordanian collective, to the degree that it cannot be overthrown without putting at risk the security and livelihood of all Jordanians. And this message resonates.

The 2012 street protests had only marginal appeal in Jordan; the silent majority considered security more important than challenging the status quo, even in the face of legitimate grievence. The survival of the Hashemite throne, its flexibility in making concessions in times of crisis, its emphasis on integrating and co-opting oppositional imaginations before they create damage to the regime, and the popular belief in the need for security, in a neighbourhood of refugee crises, civil war and instability, all attest to the regime's resilience (Greenwood 2003, Terrill 2009, Clark 2012).

The Hashemite throne has more legitimacy, less corruption, more freedom, more credibility and a longer track record of give and take with its public than less stable neighbours like Syria and Egypt (Burnell 2006, Terrill 2009). The public in Jordan is more timid in its opposition, more divided and more willing to compromise with the regime in the name of security, in order to avoid becoming the next Syria (Paul 2012). Thus Jordan is experiencing significant political and social change, but it is better managed, and the demands are for an eventual, gradual reduction of the role of the monarch in Jordanian politics, rather than the elimination of the throne. The fact that the most vocal demands for such changes are coming from Islamists, and the *hirak* street movements, means that wide swathes of Jordanian society are not interested in empowering Islamist opposition and poor, disenfranchised youths.

Still, the increasing boldness of the demands for change in 2012, and the degree to which economic hardship is on the rise, compounded by the Syrian refugee crisis, are causes for concern. The fact that 50% of young people are unemployed, and that, of those, more than 70% have some form of higher education, adds gravity to the possibilities for instability. The fact that increasingly broad swathes of Jordanian society have access to the Internet (86% of society by 2015) and social media tools (4,100,000 Jordanians use Facebook) with which to imagine and coordinate their demands for change means that Jordan is increasingly ripe for unrest. Also troubling is the fact that an estimated 1,800 Jordanians have gone to fight for the Islamic State and the Nusra Front, two militia groups active in the Syrian civil war (<https://freedomhouse.org/report/freedom-world/2015/jordan>). And yet, the resilience of the Hashemite throne in the face of past adversities means that explaining Jordanian politics past and future is not simple or straightforward. As the king observed on *The Daily Show*, 'monarchies have fared better than republics' (<http://www.cc.com/video-clips/ar2432/the-daily-show-with-jon-stewart-king-abdullah-ii-of-jordan-pt--1>), which provides one layer of interpretation, as does the kingdom's cool factor – one manifestation of which are the king's regular appearances on US late-night talk shows.

Indicators of Jordan's Ripeness for Change

If we look at the same indicators used for the Egyptian case study, a country that did experience a revolution, we see that Jordan is significantly better off in terms of corruption and freedom than Egypt, and considerably more wired communication-wise. A recent report ranked Jordan fifth out of nineteen MENA countries for press freedom (Jaques 2011). Jordan has never been listed as an 'Enemy of the Internet', whereas Egypt regularly makes the list. A clear downturn in both freedom and corruption ratings in Jordan, however, corresponds with street protests against unemployment and corruption, and demands for real democracy.

While these relative freedoms and good governance make Jordan a celebrated ally of the West, at home the Arab street remains potentially confrontational. While relatively free regionally, Jordan ranks 141 out of 196 countries worldwide in terms of press freedom, at the relative bottom globally (Jaques 2011). Jordan also has one of the highest rates of youth unemployment, estimated by the UN Economic and Social Commission for Western Asia in 2009 to be close to 50% (UN-ESCWA 2009, quoted in ibid.). From this perspective, it is possible to see why in 2012 people were on the streets demanding change, especially given the high degree of contact with the outside world enabled by the Internet, and supported by the testimonial data examined in the final section of this chapter.

Corruption

One of the most common calls for reform in Jordan is the demand that the king end corruption. While the figures in Table 3.1 show that Jordan ranks favourably among other developing countries, compared to international standards Jordan's corruption remains an area of concern. Corruption

Table 3.1 Corruption in Jordan 2001–2015

Year	Rank	Index score	Countries with same score
2001	37th	4.9	
2002	40th	4.5	South Korea, Mauritius, Costa Rica
2003	43rd	4.6	Cuba, Trinidad and Tobago
2004	37th	5.3	
2005	37th	5.7	Cyprus
2006	40th	5.3	
2007	53rd	4.7	Mauritius, Oman
2008	47th	5.1	Malaysia, Hungary
2009	49th	5.0	Poland, Bhutan
2010	50th	4.7	Saudi Arabia, Hungary
2011	56th	4.5	
2012	58th	48	Cuba, Namibia
2013	66th	45	
2014	55th	49	Bahrain, Lesotho
2015	45th	53	Mauritius, Namibia

Source: Transparency International. For the index score 10 is low corruption, 1 is highest corruption; the measurement changed for rankings between 2012 and 2015, with 0 being highly corrupt and 100 being very clean.

perceptions have a deep effect on foreign direct investment, and have been known to mobilise publics against the state. For example, the Institute for Economics and Peace has found that 'small increases in corruption can trigger large declines in peace' (Dawson 2015). If Jordan wants to be the 'Singapore of the Middle East', and to remain stable, the country will need to stamp out corruption, as Singapore ranks eighth in the world, even beating the US (sixteenth) and Canada (ninth) for being perceived as clean and transparent in governance (Transparency International 2014, <https://www.transparency.org/cpi2014/results>).

According to the figures in Table 3.1, corruption correlates with public protests in Jordan (Al-Qawam 2011), as street mobilisations occurred at the same time there was a sharp rise in corruption perceptions. Unrest among traditional forces, generally loyal to the regime, is stimulated by a perception that 'corrupt practices have become endemic in politics. Rumors run rampant about kleptocratic public figures enriching themselves through bribery, graft, and embezzlement while living standards recede for everyone else' (Yom and Khatib 2012). According to the Jordanian National Movement, the 'great majority of Jordanians – men and women, Bedouins, non-Bedouins and those of Palestinian origin – are dissatisfied with the corruption, flagrant misuse of authority, and lack of basic human rights that are a hallmark of the present regime in Amman' (Mualla 2012). Using the figures in Table 3.1, one might conclude that a decline in street protests is also linked with a marked decrease in corruption perception. At the height of the protests, Jordan had dropped twenty-six places in global rankings on corruption, a massive spiral downward. By 2015, Jordan leapt forward twenty-one places, evidence of a decline in perceived corruption.

Freedom

In addition to demands for crackdowns on corruption, public protests have also demanded political reform to allow greater freedom in Jordan. Again, Table 3.2 shows a worrying decline in freedom in the kingdom, and provides a partial explanation for public willingness to mobilise. The problem with a lack of freedom in Jordan is not new, although the level of public mobilisation and the overt demands for real change to empower Jordanian citizens are. As explored in this chapter, there are, increasingly, breaches of red lines in Jordan, and the regime is reluctant to crack down on protesters given the turn of events in Egypt, Tunisia and Yemen, when the state tried to use coercive powers to silence critique, and mobilisation subsequently increased.

Table 3.2 Freedom in Jordan 2002–2015

Year	Rating	Freedom	Civil liberties	Political rights
2002	Partly free	5	5	5
2003	Not free	5.5	5	6
2004	Partly free	5	5	5
2005	Partly free	4.5	4	5
2006	Partly free	4.5	4	5
2007	Partly free	4.5	4	5
2008	Partly free	4.5	4	5
2009	Partly free	5.0	5	5
2010	Not free	5.5	5	6
2011	Not free	5.5	5	6
2012	Not free	5.5	5	6
2013	Not free	5.5	5	6
2014	Not free	5.5	5	6
2015	Not free	5.5	5	6

Source: Freedom House (<www.freedomhouse.org>).

The range of tools to resist public demands for more freedom are dwindling in Jordan, especially as its twenty billion dollar deficit means the state lacks the financial resources to purchase submission.

The words of a Jordanian taxi driver recorded in my field notebook on 24 February 2004 provide insight into the freedom problem in Jordan:

> There is no freedom here. Our mouths are closed tight. We are suffering. There is no money and things are expensive. I had to quit school at 14 to start working and help my family. It was much better in the past. Now we are really suffering. The democracy talk is just talk. The government really doesn't want to know what we think or feel. They only put positive things in the newspaper; reality is not reported. (Field notebook entry, 24 February 2004, Amman)

Internet access

While feelings of helplessness and despair are not hard to locate in Jordan, what has made such voices louder is amplification online. As explored more carefully below, Internet access has empowered the Jordanian public. The king's drive to have a computer in every home, and the Internet easily accessible, to provide training and skills for the knowledge economy and to build new jobs has also given citizens tools with which to contest the regime and to push for change. As seen in the Egyptian case, authoritarianism, economic crisis, corruption and Internet access do not mix well. It is difficult to maintain the status quo and to limit freedoms when society is suffering and at the same time has the new media tools in hand to press for change.

In summarising the situation in Jordan, Ethan Bronner observes, during the peak of the Jordanian unrest,

Table 3.3 Internet access in Jordan 2000–2015

Year	Population	Internet users	% Internet penetration
2000	4,853,000	127,300	2.6%
2005	5,788,340	457,000	7.9%
2009	6,269,285	1,500,500	23.9%
2011	6,508,271	1,987,400	30.5%
2012	6,318,000	3,300,000	50%
2015	6,623,279	5,700,000	86.1%

Source: Internet World Stats.

Buffeted by the forces at play across the region – rising prices, a bulging underemployed youth population, the rapid spread of information and resentment, an unaccountable autocracy – Jordan is on edge. (Bronner 2011)

The following section examines the rapid spread of information, agency and civic engagement, through the use of new media tools.

Narratives of Change

If Internet statistics are to be trusted (note the scepticism), when this research took place in 2004, fewer than 10% of Jordanians had access to the Internet. In other words, it was far from a mass technology. This research was in part stimulated by a gap between the numbers documenting low connectivity and assumed lack of public awareness of the Internet, and clear ethnographic evidence to the contrary collected on the ground, in cafés, in community access points like Knowledge Stations, in the press, in public conversations and as revealed below, in the everyday lives of Jordanians. Most of those interviewed for this study also had a mobile phone (80%), and sending text messages was identified as common (78% sent text messages, on average nine texts a day – a supplement and substitute for email), more deeply connecting citizens to the emerging Jordanian information society.

The narratives of 200 Internet café users in Jordan attest to wide communications technology penetration. They also tell us that new communication practices are creating significant alterations in the politics and practices of everyday life. They tell us that even unemployed youths from non-elite families can spend up to forty hours a week in an Internet café. For those faced with a lack of employment, the Internet provides a path to some form of meaningful activity.

At a conference, when I was presenting these initial data, a colleague asked, 'how can someone who is unemployed afford to spend forty hours a week surfing the Web?' This is a very good question. Ethnographic research revealed that in order to build a bigger clientele, Internet cafés remain open 24/7, and offer patrons a discount if they surf from midnight to 8am. For this eight-hour block of Internet access, they would pay only 1 dinar ($1.25 at the time), the typical hourly rate during normal business hours. Strategies such as these gave even those with something to grumble about ample free time to explore new pathways out of misery, or at least a channel through which to connect with other disenfranchised youths.

In terms of documenting how widely spread new forms of information and communication were in Jordan in 2004, the following field notebook entry is illustrative:

> Even the falafel maker at our local sandwich shop has a mobile phone. Mobile technology is everywhere. Internet is also quite common in the form of cafés. Even in the poorest sections of East Amman, there are Internet cafés. Irbid [a city in northern Jordan] supposedly has the highest concentration of Internet cafés anywhere in the world. Satellite dishes are also ubiquitous. I have not found a building where people are living without one. Even the poorest of the poor neighbourhoods, filled with Iraqi refugees, have satellite. (Field notebook entry, 10 January 2004, East Amman)

Photographic evidence also captures a much wider presence of new communications technologies in everyday Jordanians' lives than might be assumed from afar, or from aggregate connectivity statistics based upon counting IP addresses. All neighbourhoods in 2004 had multiple Internet cafés. By 2016, seemingly ubiquitous smartphone availability made the cafés unnecessary. In 2015, it was estimated that more than 60% of Jordanians owned a smartphone, while mobile penetration was 147% (*Jordan Times* 2015). During my 2016 fieldwork, I did not find a single 'Internet café' sign in either Amman or Aqabah, two locations that in 2004 had had Internet cafés in every neighbourhood. When I asked Jordanians what had happened to the cafés, they said no one needed a dedicated Internet café as they got Internet from their phones. Figure 3.1, showing a billboard in Amman, illustrates the place of smartphone technology in everyday life. Figure 3.2 illustrates the ubiquity of smartphones, as each family member engages with the digital universe while they sit in a café together. What is most important about understanding the emergence of an information society in Jordan is not what the king, or ministers, or the queen, says about the goals of building wider information access and computer training in Jordan (Nagi and Hamdan 2009: 579), but rather how IT availability affects ordinary Jordanian lives.

Figure 3.1   Smartphone billboard, Amman, Jordan.
Photo: Deborah L. Wheeler, July 2016.

In 2004, Internet cafés throughout Amman and Zarqa, two cities where together three-quarters of the Jordanian public lives, provided ideal locations to collect data on Jordan's budding Internet cultures. This was not a random sample, although we did try to go to cafés in different neighbourhoods (upper class to working class) at different times of the day (morning, afternoon and evening) to interview half women and half men (to provide a gender balance), and to interview young and old (the eldest was forty-eight, the youngest was seventeen), educated and uneducated (those with less than a high school diploma to those with a BA or an MA). Participation in interviews was voluntary and anonymous. In general, through these interviews we found that most participants have a mobile phone and most read a daily newspaper. Most don't own a car and don't have Internet access at home. Most were trained to use

Figure 3.2   Now every café is Internet ready due to widespread smartphone access.
Photo: Deborah L. Wheeler, July 2016.

the Internet by a friend or family member, and many have returned the favour by sharing their knowledge with others (friends and family). While not a single person interviewed for this study in 2004 admitted to openly using the Internet to oppose the Jordanian regime, there are subtle signs of enhanced citizen voice and agency contained within their testimonies.

Within the interviews, when participants explain the impact of Internet use on their everyday lives, the four main effects are:

1. Wider access to information
2. Professional development/human capital accumulation
3. An escape from boredom
4. Social networking/civic engagement opportunities.

Two Internet café managers interviewed for this project provide a general summary of these impacts. A café manager in Abdoun, an upmarket neighbourhood in Amman, notes that 'the use of the Internet has changed people's mentalities . . . I think it changed their lives and ways of thinking' (interviewed April 2004, Amman). A second Internet café manager from Zarqa, a working-class suburb of Amman, notes that the Internet 'gave people access to unlimited information about everything, especially for news that is not covered well on TV or radio' (interviewed April 2004, Zarqa). The interview data reveal that even in the early stages of Jordan's information revolution, Jordanians' mentalities were changing; people were gaining wider access to information, and engaging with new sources of news beyond the state-controlled outlets of the press, TV and radio. Collectively, these micro-transformations were changing the way that Jordanian Internet users live and think. A more detailed examination of these processes follows.

Wider access to information

The information environment in Jordan is one where people are careful about what they say and read, given the highly active General Intelligence Directorate (*Muhabarat*), which monitors public discourse and watches for any signs of opposition. Breaches of red lines – including criticism of the regime and its allies and the spread of information which could be harmful to the state's security, economy and foreign relations – are illegal (USAID 2011). A very strict press law keeps journalists and publishers in check, and self-censorship is common, since the law also governs individual public expression, both online and off. One of my contacts in Jordan summarised the information and political environment as follows:

> Jordan has the structure of democracy (post 1989; pre 1956) but not the content of democracy. Compared to the period of martial law (1956–89) there is much freedom of speech and association. But compared to the UK or Israel, there is little. Ambiguities in the press law, restrictions on NGOs (can't be political) or on political parties (have to be registered to be legal) and so on keep people careful in their words and actions. In light of this context, people are careful; even among friends you have to be careful

what you say. The *Muhabarat* are everywhere. (Interviewed January 2004, Amman)

Although Jordan was rated as 'partially free' in 2004 when this study began, information environments at the time were still significantly constrained, especially in terms of news and political events. By 2010 Jordan had devolved into a 'not free' state, and these limitations on public expression remain as this book goes to press. Given these limitations, it is not surprising that a majority of those surveyed argued that Internet use was changing their lives by widening their access to uncensored news and information. Not only was the Internet giving them new knowledge, it was doing so without filters, faster and more economically (Open Net Initiative 2009).

For example, one café user states that Internet access 'made it easier for me to know about things quickly and all the info is available which saves me time in searching for it' (interviewed April 2004, Amman). Similarly, another Internet café user observes that 'the Internet made getting information a lot easier and faster for me. I can also find any info that I need that I wouldn't find in local newspapers. This gave me access to the world outside of Jordan' (interviewed April 2004, Amman). Another Internet café user notes that, by using the Internet, 'I got to know so many things about life and people that I didn't know before' (interviewed May 2004, Amman).

A recurring theme is that, with Internet access, Jordanians 'follow up on news' (interviewed April 2004, Amman). Again, stressing the power of expanding one's access to news, a Jordanian Internet café user observes, 'the Internet is an easy, fast source for information about any topic. It made things easier for me; also a good source for news, especially if a person wants to know more about news and events' (interviewed May 2004, Amman). The Internet allows another café patron to 'learn new things and info. It broadens one's mind and builds up one's capacities and eagerness to learn' (interviewed May 2004, Amman). The speed and ease issue is another recurring theme. For example, an Internet café user observes that, with the Internet, 'I can get any info I want, quickly and about anything' (interviewed April 2004, Amman). Another café user notes, the Internet allows me to 'talk freely' (interviewed May 2004, Zarqa). Another café user states that with the Internet he can 'know what is going on around in the world' (interviewed

May 2004, Amman). Another notes that, online, he 'likes to read news that are not covered enough or well on TV or newspapers' (interviewed May 2004, Amman).

What is most fascinating about Internet users in Jordan are the clear linkages they make between changing communication patterns online and spillover effects in their everyday life. For example, one male Internet café user claims that the Internet allows him to 'forget my troubles' (interviewed May 2004, Amman). A female Internet café patron notes that Internet use, especially chat, 'improved my discussion skills from discussion forums; we discuss many issues and voice one's opinions' (interviewed May 2004, Amman). Another female Internet café user notes that the Net allows people to 'exchange ideas and points of view' (interviewed May 2004, Amman). When describing the effect of Internet use she observes, 'I became more open minded and less conservative since I started talking with people in chat' (interviewed May 2004, Amman). One male Internet café user in his twenties notes that Internet use 'made other cultures closer to me' (interviewed April 2004, Amman). In summarising these impacts, an Internet café manager notes that, for his clients, Internet use 'generally advanced their minds, and added to their knowledge and info' (interviewed April 2004, Amman).

The process of obtaining new information online not only changes the way that Jordanians communicate, it also changes the way they live, making them more open minded and better educated, especially with wider access to uncensored news. It makes them more civically engaged by allowing them to interact with others, to develop and share opinions, to become less conservative and to make other cultures more familiar and closer to them. The fact that none of these acts are overtly threatening to the regime makes them hard to police or stop, and thus these transformations in the Jordanian citizenry accumulate, one click at a time, in an emerging micro-politics of change.

If we fast-forward to 2011, some have attributed increasing public opposition to Queen Rania as being linked with what the Jordanian public can observe uncensored online. For example, the journalist Mary Ann Sieghart observes of public attitudes towards the queen,

Queen Rania's mission [is] to bridge the growing gulf between East and West; to prove that Muslim countries could be moderate. But what she hadn't bargained for was the modern, global media. If she appeared on Oprah, millions of Jordanians watched it on YouTube. If she mingled at parties with Hollywood stars, her people read about it online. Given her countrymen's traditional hostility to the West, and particularly the US, this didn't go down well. Rania thought she was selling Jordan; many Jordanians thought she was selling out. Oprah introduced the queen as an 'international fashion icon'. Such an epithet was fine for Princess Diana. But in Jordan, I was told repeatedly, 'This is a poor country.' Jordan has no oil, the financial crisis has hit hard and food prices have soared. No wonder Jordanians resent what they see as the queen's profligacy. (Sieghart 2011)

With an increasingly global media-savvy public, the queen needs to be careful. In the increasingly free, networked media environment, the government of Jordan has struggled with finding a balance between civil rights and stability/security. The assumption is that 'increasing democratization and openness will unleash expressive activity . . . detrimental to Jordan's international relations, internal stability, and other interests' (USAID 2011: 17). Recent criticisms of both the king and the queen online, in the streets of Amman, and even by former supporters of the regime, including some members of the Jordan National Movement, the local tribes (Yom and Khatib 2012), the municipalities (Clark 2012), and labour unions (Adely 2012), all illustrate that the government's assumptions are correct. Increasing freedom of information by building an information society in Jordan, whether done for economic development or some other reason, has the effect of building more engaged citizens.

As illustrated in the 2012 uprisings in Jordan, these information-empowered citizens have become more expressive: some blog; some have created domestic unrest (Bronner 2011); others have called for drastic change in political relations between the king and his subjects/citizens (Sadiki 2012). Whether these are the growing pains of 'real' democracy, the beginnings of the end for the monarchy as we know it, or a temporary blip on the radar of authoritarian control will be determined both by citizen choices and by regime responses playing out their game on the streets, in elections, on screens (TV, computer, mobile), and in back-room negotiations. These are not only difficult times in Jordan, they are also interesting times, as citizens redefine their roles and expectations, as old traditions die, as new norms are defined, both within social practice and the exercise of power. This section suggests that one cause behind these new conversations is the emergence of a more digitally informed citizenry.

Professional development/human capital accumulation

How far do the government's IT initiatives trickle? Does IT figure in everyday life in Jordan? Are IT projects the best way to enable the Jordanian masses to live a better life? These questions were some of the most pressing behind this research. In my field notes, on 8 February 2004, I observed the following:

> The Internet café interviews, working in Jordan for the UNDP, and living in Amman have answered all of these questions. IT matters for all urban people; even poor ones. IT matters for rural people. It is viewed as a vehicle to employment; or better employment, even if not that many success stories exist right now. The few successes translate into BIG hopes and dreams. One of the main goals among Jordanians living outside the capital is to get trained locally, and remain employed locally. The real challenge at this stage in Jordan is not restructuring society for the knowledge economy. This is and will happen over the next five years through all the projects – Discovery Schools, Knowledge Stations, REACH initiative, E.Government initiatives, Intel Computer Clubhouses, and so on. The real problem is where to channel all this emerging talent. There are not enough opportunities to create a balance between training and jobs on the back end. (Field notebook entry, 8 February 2004, Amman)

With the goal of building new opportunities for the Jordanian people through IT diffusion, training and use, it is perhaps not by accident that Internet café users argue that one way access to the technology has changed their lives is by increasing their professional development and human capital. As the field notes above and the section on boredom below demonstrate, these new capabilities don't often translate into employment. Desires for employment and an end to corruption are two of the most powerful messages behind the 2012 street demonstration in Jordan.

Computer literacy, access to PCs and the Internet, and training for the knowledge economy are all goals of Jordan's IT strategy (ESCWA 2005). We see traces of these efforts in the narratives of Internet café users interviewed for this project. For example, one seventeen-year-old female from Zarqa notes that using the Internet at a café 'taught me how to type in Arabic' (interviewed May 2004, Zarqa). A twenty-three-year-old male states that 'Internet use improved my English through chat and added to my knowledge by talking to people' (interviewed May 2004, Amman). A twenty-six-year-old male who works as a maintenance engineer claims that using the Internet 'improved and advanced my academic level and my ability to do my job' (interviewed April 2004, Amman).

More directly linking IT and employment, many people interviewed for this project are looking for jobs online. One twenty-nine-year-old male notes, 'The Internet is good for looking for jobs outside Jordan. I also try to make a business through my relatives in Saudi Arabia and Qatar' (interviewed May 2004, Amman). As a general overview, a thirty-three-year-old manager of an import-export business notes, 'Internet technology has a positive effect on our work and mind' (interviewed April 2004, Amman). A twenty-two-year-old male from Zarqa notes, 'I didn't have the opportunity to study at university, but I learn many new things from the Net, especially related to my job, which make me do better at work' (interviewed May 2004, Zarqa).

While it is relatively easy to see people attempting to make themselves more marketable through their online activities, like improving their knowledge base, or polishing their English, their typing, their communication skills, it is difficult to link such activities with finding actual employment. While it is clear that those with jobs already use the tool to improve their job skills and knowledge, there is no real evidence that Internet use is a pathway out of unemployment, although many in this study stated that they were using the Net to try to find a job. Instead, what we find mostly is narratives like this one: 'The Internet fills my time and keeps me busy until I find a job. I made many good friends on the Net' (interviewed May 2004, Amman).

Unemployment is a major social issue in Jordan. A study of youths notes, 'The most important socio-economic problem refers to the gap between educational attainment and the labor market resulting in huge unemployment among university graduates and at the same time reluctance to accept low-skilled jobs' (Euro-Med Youth III 2005). Similarly, according to a 2011 study, 'despite high rates of growth in the early 2000s, the Jordanian economy created relatively few new productive jobs' (Rad 2011). In addition, those areas with job growth, including 'apparel manufacturing and construction, tend to be low-skilled and low wage', which explains high unemployment rates among Jordanians (they're educated and want 'good' jobs), and why 65% of all new job growth in the kingdom went to foreign labourers (Rad 2011, Brown et al. 2014: ix). One of the only viable solutions to this situation is to seek higher-skilled, higher-paid jobs abroad, thus the importance of the Internet to locating employment. Nearly 5% of the Jordanian population lives and works abroad (Rad 2011); 10% of the Jordanian population abroad lives or works in the Arabian Gulf countries (Brown et al. 2014).

Low wages, harsh working conditions and dissatisfaction among those who do work in Jordan spawned a new environment of protest among labour movement activists. A recent study notes that, 'In 2011 alone, Jordan Labor Watch, an initiative of the Amman-based Phoenix Center for Economics and Informatics Studies, documented over 800 labor actions' (Adely 2012). So whether the Internet is used to look for a job, to improve one's performance while on the job, to organise opposition to the state to contest a lack of good jobs, or to broadcast such opposition (<https://www.youtube.com/watch?v=QP66Bn1fM9E>), the Jordanian government will need immediate solutions to the problem of empowering their public. Giving them new powers of voice, while at the same time not providing solutions to economic hardships, in individual lives and the economy in general, is a recipe for unrest. The vastness of labour protests, geographically and across sectors, including workers such as 'Teachers, bank tellers, imams, phosphate and potassium workers, university employees, journalists, taxi drivers, nurses and doctors at state-run hospitals' and beyond (Adely 2012), suggests serious problems for the regime, as 'labor activists have been at the forefront of breaking the barrier of fear' (ibid.).

Labour movements, street protests, corruption dances and increasingly vocal critiques of the king and queen – all of these are the result of increasing hardship, civic awareness and voice among Jordanians. In response to a question about what role new media plays in this process of change, one Jordanian student observes,

Many of the protests that went on in the streets of Jordan were organized via Facebook, Twitter, and other social networks. In fact, many people are starting blogs and online groups to discuss up and coming issues and post articles, opinions, debates, etc about what is going on. It is interesting because you have people from all over Jordan and all over the world who all have different opinions who will not be penalized for saying whatever they think. They can actually say what they want to say and that is something that is unprecedented in Jordan, because media, and especially social media, did not used to be nearly as free and open as it is today. (*Politics and the New Media* 2011)

If you give people a voice, and they have something to grumble about, you remove the fear barriers to publicly grumbling and asking for change, then you change your public from a passive one to an active citizenry. Asef Bayat states, 'change in society's sensibilities is a precondition for far-reaching democratic transformations' (Bayat 2010: 248). This section shows that even through the simple act of trying to perform better on the job, to find a job, to entertain oneself until a job can be located, or to mobilise in protest when no jobs are in sight, we see Jordanian citizens 'discovering new spaces within which to make themselves heard, seen, felt, and realized' (ibid.: 249).

Boredom

One potential impetus for building an information-savvy public at the grass roots is boredom. A staggering 42% of those interviewed for this project stated that providing 'an escape from boredom' was one of the main impacts of the Internet in their lives. Boredom affects youths most significantly, especially with youth unemployment edging upwards of 33% in 2013 by World Bank estimates (<http://data.worldbank.org/indicator/SL.UEM.1524.ZS>) and ranging as high as 50% in other estimates (Mesiano 2012). When considered in light of the fact that youths make up more than 70% of Jordanian society, the problem and its significance grows. A study of boredom in Jordan notes that a 'large number of youngsters spend most of their free time in a café for *shisha* or just hanging out in their cars with their heads outside the windows' (Esmat 2008). In this context, it is easy to understand why young Jordanians are drawn to the Internet as a way to escape boredom. In fact, providing youths with Internet access and training is part of King Abdullah's National Youth Strategy (Euro-Med Youth III 2005: 19). The link between young people, grievances at being left out of Jordan's economic growth, Internet use, and demands for more accountable governance in Jordan is clarified by bored Internet users' testimonies. The narratives below reveal pent-up energy and talent and nowhere to go – except online.

Quite transparently, one twenty-five-year-old female from Amman notes, in response to whether or not the Internet has changed her life, 'Of course, if I don't go to the Internet café I'll die of boredom, especially [as] I'm not working lately and I have nothing to do' (interviewed April 2004, Amman). Another unemployed twenty-year-old female who is 'looking for a job' notes that the Internet 'is occupying my time. It's exciting and fun and keeps me busy' (interviewed May 2004, Zarqa). A twenty-four-year-old female from Zarqa exclaims, 'It's the best thing that ever happened to me. It's entertaining and especially now that I left my job two months ago and am still looking for a new one. It fills my time' (interviewed May 2004, Zarqa). A twenty-year-old male who is an accounting major at university notes that Internet use 'kills the emptiness of my free time' (interviewed April 2004, Amman). A seventeen-year-old male notes that because of Internet use 'I don't get bored anymore. When I get bored, I come here to the Internet café. I enjoy my time on the Net. It's better than walking around in the streets' (interviewed May 2004, Amman). A twenty-one-year-old male who is a marketing major at university notes that Internet use 'solved the problem of boredom and loneliness . . . I made many new friends on the Net. We exchange ideas' (interviewed April 2004, Amman). When asked if Internet use had changed his life in any way, one nineteen-year-old male responded, 'What life? I don't have one. Anyways, yes, it keeps me busy and occupies my time. I run away from thinking about my empty life. No job. No money' (interviewed May 2004, Zarqa).

These testimonials provide just a sample of the many 'boredom' narratives offered by Jordanians during our interviews. Collectively they provide images of the degree to which Jordan faces the problem of disenfranchised youths, many of whom are unemployed, and armed with Internet access. The processes of change sweeping through Jordan are in part caused by new media enabled youths, who are empowered by technology to find their voice and organise protests. 'Social media, cell phone cameras, satellite television, restive youth and years of pent-up anger are proving to be a toxic mix for authoritarian regimes in the Middle East' (Lefkow 2011). It is not surprising that less than a decade after these interviews were conducted, 'Protest movements from around Irbid and the towns of Dhiban, Jarash, Ajloun, Slat, Tafileh, Karak, Ma'an and Shobak, make great use of Facebook' (Yom and Khatib 2012; links to Facebook pages for these protest movements are provided by this source).

What is surprising is that by 2016, without a change in social and economic conditions, with a more wired kingdom (with Internet penetration rates nearing 90%) and persistently high youth unemployment, overt challenges to the regime are quieted. One clue as to why is a rapid slide downwards on the freedom index, and the resurgence of a more repressive state (as detailed in Chapter 6). The change in the Public Gatherings Law, however, which now makes demonstrations legal without prior permission from the state, would suggest more freedom to protest spontaneously (Freedom House 2015). More freedom to protest spontaneously, however, was contained by revised cyber- and counter-terrorism legislation which made it more dangerous to protest. Another possible explanation for the quieting of Jordan's Arab Spring is the failure of other Arab Springs (like those in Egypt, Libya, Syria, Bahrain and Yemen) to deliver positive results (Al-Samadi 2014). Jordanian youths, however, remain bored, wired and disenfranchised, and may become explosive with some encouragement from circumstances and friends. Moreover, how can the king create jobs when most youths interviewed for a RAND study want public-sector employment and the state is in fiscal crisis (Brown et al. 2014)? Thus pathways out of hopelessness with such a fragile economy, and a Syrian refugee crisis brewing, suggest that quick and sustainable solutions will be unlikely.

Knowing Jordan's history of surviving against steep odds, however, we will more than likely be surprised by the creativity and resilience of the monarchy and the loyalty of the Jordanian public. Enhanced repression, and a highly developed internal security network which even reaches into the university classroom, helps to contain unrest until jobs emerge (Freedom House

2015). World Bank youth unemployment data for Jordan (2016) show a slight improvement. Perhaps the aid money Jordan is receiving (although only part of what was pledged) for its role in efforts to stabilise Syria and host refugees might be providing some visible relief. Inflation in food, fuel and rent prices, however, does little to relieve the economic burdens of most citizens.

Social networking and civic engagement

One of the keys to building the foundations for change in any society is to mobilise a critical mass of citizens wanting change. Key to mass mobilisation in the twenty-first century is social media, for it allows the sharing of stories and misery, the pooling of micro-forms of power, the creation of solidarities and connections across sectors and social cleavages. In Jordan, this process of expanding social networks and civic engagement began relatively benignly, as citizens learned about the importance of the Internet from their king and embraced his vision of a new technologically advanced Jordan. Collectively, Jordanian citizens worked to be computer literate, fulfilling the king's mission for developing the knowledge economy, opportunities and hope. When promises tarnished over time, and opportunities failed to materialise for the masses, the Internet and social media provided the platform through which to organise opposition to the regime.

One of the overwhelming themes of the Internet café interviews conducted for this project is that the tool expands the boundaries of individual connections. For example, 62% of those interviewed stated that Internet use allowed them to expand their social networks. In the testimonies, we learn that one seventeen-year-old female 'has more friends' because of the Internet (interviewed May 2004, Zarqa). A twenty-four-year-old male observes that he uses the Internet to 'know about other countries' (interviewed April 2004, Amman). Illustrating the ways in which Internet use enables Jordanians to overcome barriers to civic engagement, a twenty-year-old female from Zarqa observes,

> I made friends with people in countries I know I can never travel to because
> of lack of money. Travelling is expensive. It's very interesting to know them
> and how they think. Some are strange and weird, but many are nice and

friendly and with big minds. I'm having a relationship with a man in Syria and he's coming in the summer to get engaged with me. (Interviewed May 2004, Amman)

These experiences of engaging with 'big-minded' people who are different but 'nice and friendly' are not just an exercise in virtual travel. Sometimes these forms of civic engagement lead to marriage proposals across national borders; on other occasions they lead to new conversations and debates. For example, a twenty-two-year-old female from Amman notes that, on the Internet, 'I enjoy talking with people from different countries, to exchange views with them and to learn about their culture and traditions' (interviewed April 2004, Amman). Similarly, a nineteen-year-old female from Zarqa states, 'I enjoy making friends with people from other countries in order to know how they live their lives' (interviewed May 2004, Zarqa). A twenty-year-old female from Amman notes that, with Internet use, 'I feel connected with the world outside' (interviewed May 2004, Amman). Similarly, a thirty-eight-year-old female notes that the Internet 'is a beautiful thing. By using it, I can see and know about the world outside' (interviewed April 2004, Amman). A twenty-two-year-old female states that 'especially chat' changed my life: 'I made many friendships and it's very nice to talk to people in other countries. We joke, argue and exchange thoughts and secrets. My best friend is now a woman I chatted with in Saudi Arabia' (interviewed May 2004, Zarqa).

These practices of engaging the global other are not overtly political practices. None of these testimonies about Internet use and its impact would be considered a threat to the state, even though such practices give Jordanians – especially women, whose lives are most constrained by the norms of traditional life in Jordan (Faqir 2001) – access to the outside world, new friendships, new ideas, and a willingness to explore, to risk (cyber-dating), and to grow. One young woman interviewed for this project links cyber-experimentation with a clear transformation in how she lives her life. She observes,

The Internet has changed my life in a positive way. It changed my character. I became more social and less reserved. My relationships with the other sex (males) became more relaxed. Before I used to feel shy. Chat teaches a person to be more relaxed and open with people. It's great. (Interviewed May 2004, Amman)

The point, then, is that what starts as a benign experiment results in life-changing, norm-defying impacts, both in the practice of everyday life and in the wider world of politics. The vehicle for such transformations is information technology, including new media tools like the Internet, which are a regular part of everyday life in Jordan. The IT industry contributes 14% of Jordan's GDP, as much as the tourism industry. Moreover, the IT sector is 'the fastest growing part of the economy' (Baker 2012). Even if the government wants to try to better police Internet-based opposition, as demonstrated by amendments to the Press and Publications Law (August 2012) to 'restrict Internet freedoms' (Tarawnah 2012), it's a little too late. Economic growth depends on the IT infrastructure, even if such infrastructure is a threat to 'business as usual' socially and politically.

Conclusion

This chapter illustrates that changing communication practices, new life patterns and, eventually, demands for more freedom and accountability in government are linked. One of the factors that has made revolutions in the region seem so sudden is that the most significant forms of change in norms and behaviours – civic engagement and awareness, training in using IT, developing a voice, risking letting it be heard – can begin, as illustrated in this chapter, as relatively benign experiments, with obvious long-term implications, from the household to the head of state. The accumulation of micro-changes in discourse and agency occurs beneath the surface of the status quo, working away at norms and power relations subtly until it is too late to contain.

The Jordanian case teaches us that although the process of transforming formal institutions of power is incomplete, we can anticipate continued micro-eruptions in the status quo as the public continues to breach red lines, and to leverage new media tools in the coordination of its demands. The government's extension of strict press laws to online activities reveals the state's fear of increased freedom of expression and, more specifically, increased public critique and demands for reform. But the information society in Jordan has progressed full throttle, to the degree that there is no way to 're-instill fear' without pushing the public further towards revolution (Sweis 2012). That is the lesson of the other Arab Spring revolutions in Tunisia and Egypt. Former MP Bassam Haddadin summarises the message of this chapter when he observes, 'the bottom line is that Jordanians no longer want to hear about reform – they want to see it implemented on the ground' (ibid.).

4

HURRY UP AND WAIT: OPPOSITIONAL COMPLIANCE AND NETWORKING AROUND THE STATE IN KUWAIT

The Internet made Arabs more active in reaching to others to find ways to express freedom . . . It taught Arabs a lot regarding the values of democracy and freedom. (Interviewed July 2009, Kuwait City)

Gulf leaders will have to show their subjects they have some say in their own governance: over time, the monarchs will not be able to avoid accelerating the pace of reforms, and they will have to respond to the pressures exerted from without and within by going beyond merely cosmetic change. (Guzansky, quoted in Kessler 2012)

Kuwait's ruling Al-Sabah family has issued a statement calling for obedience to the emir after rare public criticism of the ruler during opposition rallies. (Hall 2012: 2)

There's a saying in the military that has direct relevance to interpreting change in Kuwait: 'hurry up and wait'. In a military context, the phrase captures the urgency for readiness constrained by a plodding bureaucracy. In the Kuwaiti context, 'hurry up and wait' characterises the urgency and impatience for change (among some citizens) balanced by traditions and fears of disrespect and disruptiveness. Like the phrase, Kuwait is characterised by complex juxtapositions of hurry and wait. From a bird's eye view of the small Arabian Gulf country, we see, for example, rapid changes in styles of dress

compete with reinforced tradition in calls to respect the emir. We see globalised culture, in the form of restaurants like Cheesecake Factory and Texas
Road House, made local, by the absence of pork products and alcohol; and
the latest Hollywood films, severely edited, with any touching between the
sexes removed, while, ironically, gore, violence and foul language remain. In
terms of politics, we see 'oppositional compliant' behaviour in the practice of
everyday life, like participating in a youth movement for change while also
complying with a parent's wishes on choice of major at university, or career
and marriage decisions.

These competing narratives also influence Internet use and impact. For
example, stressing the transformative nature of Internet culture in Kuwait, a
2011 study argues that

> The technological revolution is changing modes of thinking and behavior,
> and governments that do not acknowledge and address such changes will
> be swept away by the waves of resentful citizens empowered by the various
> tools that the Internet offers. (Alqudsi-ghabra et al. 2011)

Four years later, however, in spite of increasingly common predictions for collapse (Davidson 2012), Arabian Gulf monarchies, including that of Kuwait,
persist while public opposition grows.

This chapter explores the diffusion, use and impact of the Internet in
Kuwait. It reveals changed modes of thinking and behaviour among citizens,
linked by participants in this study with new media use. This case study is
in part inspired by the small community of scholars who share interests in
the transformative power of new media use in the Gulf. The most notable
works on the subject include Tétreault (2011, 2012), Janardhan (2011),
Al-Nashimi et al. (2010), Nordenson (2010), Murphy (2009), Albloshi
and Alfahad (2009) and Albabtain (2010). My own research on Kuwaiti
new media use benefited from these scholars' interdisciplinary perspectives
(Wheeler 1998, 2000, 2001a, 2003a, 2006a; Wheeler and Mintz 2010).

This chapter also explores some explanations for the Sabah monarchy's
stability in spite of increasingly dangerous conditions, like an impending
budget crisis, an increase in perceived corruption, overt crackdowns on freedom of expression, an increase in Internet access and oppositional behaviour,
and a brutal terrorist attack on a Shi'i mosque during Ramadan 2015, which

threatened to escalate sectarian tensions in the emirate. Whereas a culture of cool keeps the Jordanian monarchy afloat, in Kuwait a culture of patriarchy, deference to elders and government subsidies keeps the Sabah monarchy surprisingly stable. Kuwait is characterised by a culture of 'oppositional compliance', whereby citizens challenge some norms, breach some red lines, but remain generally compliant enough to keep the status quo and longstanding social norms relatively intact. Thus we see an increase in opposition but a timidity, perhaps conditioned by a respect for patriarchy, that keeps such oppositional behaviour from affecting the Sabah family's dominance.

My research on Internet culture and politics in Kuwait began in 1996, when Internet use was first emerging. Research trips to Kuwait in 1996–7, 1998, 2009, 2010, 2011 and 2014 provided insights into the evolution of Kuwaiti Internet cultures and politics. The summer of 2014 provided the clearest evidence yet of how explosive oppositional politics has become in Kuwait, and as well revealed the presence of overt ISIS supporters in the emirate. A sharp decline in oil revenues, which provide more than 95% of the country's export revenue and more than 60% of its GDP, and subsequent proposed cuts in government subsidies and salaries puts at risk one of the regime's key tools for buying public loyalty and bolstering the Sabah family's legitimacy (OPEC 2015). A culture of deference to elders and especially patriarchs, however, keeps Kuwait in a state of oppositional compliance, for reasons explored throughout this chapter.

Initial Findings and Evolutions

When Internet culture was young and underdeveloped in Kuwait (late 1990s), information diffusion via new media use was viewed more as a potential threat than a means for individual empowerment. At the time, 'the desire to keep one's reputation protected' tamed Internet use, and kept the tool 'from registering significant political and social impacts' (Wheeler 1998: 366). When this observation was made, there were only an estimated 45,000 Internet users in Kuwait. In other words, around 2% of the population (ITU estimates, <http://www.itu.int/net4/itu-d/icteye/>) had access – too few to make much of an impact, especially if users were inhibited in how they used the tool, so as to protect their reputations.

By 2006, when the Kuwaiti 'Orange Revolution' emerged, it marked one of the first times in Kuwait's history that society mobilised in a mass, public way to directly confront the monarchy. The Orange Revolution energised oppositional politics by successfully pressuring the ruling family to change the emir and to redistrict voting procedures (Nordenson 2010). In 2006, 29% of the population had Internet access (ITU estimates, <http://www.itu.int/net4/itu-d/icteye/>). Is there a link between more widespread access to Internet technology and more widespread opposition to the Kuwaiti state? Moreover, are social norms being transformed by Internet use? My research in Kuwait was designed to answer these two questions.

Ethnographic research (1996–2014) and structured interviews conducted with the assistance of students at the American University of Kuwait (2009–11) suggest that new media tools are having a profound impact on social and political practices in the emirate (Wheeler and Mintz 2010). What we see over time is that Internet use removes inhibitions, gives the public a voice, encourages people to demand access to current, transparent news and information, and enables Internet users to become more engaged and active in the world. Evidence for these changes is provided by Internet user testimonials, as examined in this chapter.

Significant transformations linked with new media use coexist and compete with traditions and norms, what this chapter calls a culture of 'oppositional compliance'. Like Wittgenstein's duck-rabbit, Lloyd and Susanne Rudolph, reflecting on similar juxtapositions in Indian development, called the oppositional compliant behaviour they observed 'the modernity of tradition' (Rudolph and Rudolph 1967). The modernising of tradition in Kuwait is significantly affected by the diffusion, use and impact of new media technologies, even if transformations are mostly localised in the practice of everyday life, and oppositional behaviour at this stage mostly engenders a repressive response from the state, rather than sustainable reform.

Several observations are in order, to link the Kuwaiti case with the wider argument of this book – that changes in communication shape changes in living and ultimately affect the practice of politics. First of all, it should be no surprise that Kuwait, out of all the other Gulf monarchies, should be a harbinger of a new political culture of overt opposition. Kuwait, since the 1960s, has been a regional leader in political development in the Gulf, having a comparatively vibrant, relatively freely elected parliament, a relatively free press, and a lively associational culture, from *diwaniyya* social clubs to non-governmental organisations, political movements, professional societies and more. Even though political parties are illegal in Kuwait, as Mary Ann Tétreault observes, 'while some nations in the Middle East might well be described as lacking in "organized popular enthusiasm for democratic reform," Kuwait is not among them' (Tétreault 2011: 73). Similarly, Reporters without Borders notes that 'Kuwait holds first place among Gulf states in terms of respect for individual freedoms, and particularly in terms of press freedom' (Reporters without Borders 2012b).

As examined below, Kuwait also has the fourth highest Internet diffusion rate in the Middle East and North Africa, with more than 78.7% of society (see Figure 4.6) having access. This figure includes both Kuwaiti citizens and expat workers, the latter of which constitute two-thirds of Kuwait's population (Al-Jasser 2012). If the figure were limited to just Kuwaiti citizens, the access rate would probably be nearly universal. Kuwaitis have access to the Internet on their mobile phones, iPads, laptops, computers within the home and at school, and Wi-Fi is available, often for free, throughout the country. Prices for Internet access are relatively low, which has aided rapid diffusion. Age and gender barriers no longer significantly shape IT access in the emirate (Wheeler and Mintz 2012). Kuwaitis surf the Web in both English and Arabic. Facebook, YouTube, blogs and tweets are a regular part of everyday life in Kuwait. That the Internet would promote associational life and politics, increase civic engagement and enable demands for greater accountability in governance are all logical extensions of the politics of everyday life, what Tétreault calls 'bottom-up democratization' (Tétreault 2011: 73).

In spite of a high degree of Internet connectivity and use in Kuwaiti society, the country remains relatively stable, with an increasingly active and oppositional public sphere. The Kuwaiti case, like the two that preceded it, demonstrates once again that context and intervening variables matter. The Internet is just a tool. Its use may have cumulative (un)intended consequences, but contextual factors help to shape the meaning and form of accumulated impacts.

In order to better understand new media uses and the role of contextual variables in shaping meanings and impacts, fieldwork was necessary. In addition to my own participant observation (1996–14), structured interviews with Internet users were conducted by students at the American University of Kuwait as part of my Arab Human Development course (2009–11). Each student interviewed people both inside and outside their friend-and-family networks, asking the same questions posed in Jordan and Egypt several years earlier about Internet use in everyday life. The goal was to interview a broad range of Kuwaiti sources to see if the findings collected in 2004 in Egypt and Jordan held any comparative value. Between 2009 and 2011, AUK students interviewed more than 1,000 Internet users in Kuwait. The most important finding was that a majority of those interviewed stated that the Internet has had a definite impact on Arab politics. The narratives and ethnographic insights of Internet uses and impacts collected in Kuwait allow us to understand the context in which Kuwaitis have intensified their demands for a greater say in politics and resisted power relations at work in their lives, from the household to the state.

Kuwaiti citizens are more demanding, more assertive, less likely to quietly accept the inevitability of power relations at work in their lives. When this project began back in 1996, only about 2% of Kuwaiti society had Internet access; the most transformative impact at the time was that Kuwaitis could now get access to music, porn and 'any information they want' (interview with a Kuwait University staff member, January 1997). Over time, as access and use deepened, empowering more and more citizens, giving them wider access to uncensored information, allowing them to network and organise, impacts on politics and the distribution of power in Kuwaiti society also became increasingly visible. Still, at this moment, 'considerable wealth, high living standards, and traditions of quietism' have calmed the emergence of a full-scale Arab Spring in Kuwait (Maloney 2011: 180). Thus while we can document significant changes in life and politics in Kuwait (the oppositional side of the equation), at the same time, traditions of quietism and deference to societal norms keep most Kuwaitis compliant with expectations for good behaviour, in the home, at school, on the job, in social engagements and in the political arena (the compliant side of the equation).

This chapter represents a final attempt to make meaning out of interviews with Internet users, this time in the Gulf, where the Arab Spring has yet to result in a successful regime change (with the exception of Yemen, and a failed attempt in Bahrain). Our subject is Kuwait, and our question is how, if at all, is Internet use changing Kuwaiti society and politics? I have saved Kuwait for last, because this country is the alpha and omega of my investigations into the diffusion, use and impact of IT in the Arab world.

In a nutshell, this chapter argues that Kuwait is likely to experience a series of reforms by which power will be shared, over time, with an increasingly civically engaged public. One leading Kuwaiti with a long and distinguished career of government and private-sector service, whom I interviewed in 2011, was not so optimistic. He argued, 'In twenty years, Kuwait won't exist anymore. The country is falling apart. We are running out of water. We can't grow anything here. The government has not built a new hospital since the 1970s. The prime minister has been fired and rehired eight times; Kuwait is unlikely to survive' (interviewed July 2011, Kuwait City). This chapter provides insights into the wide range of possibilities awaiting Kuwait, from inevitable state collapse, to some kind of constitutional monarchical reform, to the status quo persisting, by considering grass-roots new media use and civic engagement.

Recent unrest, including the boycott of 2012 parliamentary elections by opposition politicians (for a video of the protests see <https://www.rt.com/news/kuwaiti-protests-opposition-march-012/>) and large protest rallies organised by the Kuwaiti opposition movements (including an odd mix of Islamists, liberals, tribalists and youth movements) against the prime minister, against authoritarian and arbitrary electoral reform, and against corruption (2006–14), attests to the explosiveness of Kuwait's public sphere. The arrest of journalists, bloggers and tweeters (including two members of the ruling family!) for insulting the emir and slandering the prime minister and the doling out of cash and free food for two years to citizens as a way to buy loyalty and stave off an Arab Spring rebellion in Kuwait (2011–13) demonstrate a state playing both offence and defence simultaneously. Mobilisation and repression/co-optation strategies reveal the fragility of relations between rulers and citizens in Kuwait. What role, if any, does new media use play in such explosiveness? This question is considered in the pages that follow.

Field Trips (2009–11, 2014)

For such a small country, Kuwait is an extremely complex place. Underneath its glamorous exterior of stability and prosperity resides a tempestuous mix of social and political problems. Drug addiction and communal violence, domestic abuse, extra-marital activity and a high divorce rate, economic hardship for some, guest-worker tensions and strong oppositional forces all weaken the Kuwaiti social fabric. Kuwait has many political and social cleavages, including divisions along sectarian, class, gender, tribal, ideological and generational lines, all of which test civic cohesion. The *bidoon*, stateless people, and frequent guest-worker abuses provide Kuwait with serious human rights challenges. Kuwait is a highly segmented, highly stratified society, with power and wealth heavily concentrated in the hands of a few leading families. Kuwait is a very traditional place, where honour, family and discretion characterise citizen behaviour (evidenced in the emir's call for 'obedience' quoted at the beginning of this chapter). Respect for Islam in the practice of everyday life, from dress to politics, is the norm. Economically, Kuwait is challenged by a dependence on oil revenue to run the country and a rapidly growing population conditioned to expect cradle-to-grave welfare support, in an era of shrinking returns on oil exports.

Part of what makes Kuwait so complex is that the country is changing rapidly, especially as younger generations enter the world as digital citizens almost from birth. It is common to see children in Kuwait younger than a year old tapping away on an iPad, to see toddlers dial a mobile phone, to have children surf the Web and teach their parents about computers, to have Facebook expand the boundaries of local communities, to have grown up on Al Jazeera news and satellite TV, to see the latest Hollywood films, sometimes opening in Kuwait before they do in the US. One seventeen-year-old Kuwaiti woman interviewed for this project notes, 'The Internet didn't really change my life, because I have used it ever since I was nine' (interviewed July 2010, Kuwait City). In the sections that follow, interviews and ethnographic data about new media use and impact reveal a conservative Islamic society and traditional, authoritarian monarchy in transition.

My first attempt at ethnographic research methods to better understand Kuwait's emerging Internet cultures began in 1996 and ultimately resulted in a book (Wheeler 2006a) in which I documented how, within the context of a high-tech conservative Islamic country, subcultures utilised new media tools to enhance agency and opportunity in the emirate. Research for the book identified women, youths and Islamists as the most active users of new media

Figure 4.1   Rolls-Royce driven by an American University in Kuwait student.
Photo: Deborah L. Wheeler, June 2014.

tools at the time. For example, women who used the Internet gained room to manoeuvre, interact and voice opinions in ways culturally prohibited in face-to-face engagement. Ultimately Kuwaiti women would use new media tools to gain their voting rights (2005), and even seats in parliament (2009). In the 2012 elections, no Kuwaiti women earned a seat, due to changes in the electoral laws which reduced the number of votes per citizen from four to one. As of 2016, Kuwaiti women are still struggling to have equal rights before the law, especially with regard to citizenship. For example, if a Kuwaiti woman marries a non-Kuwaiti, their children are denied Kuwaiti citizenship. Moreover, unmarried Kuwaiti women are unable to get housing loans and benefits from the government. Kuwaiti women also continue to experience a glass ceiling in terms of promotion within government and industry.

Youths were the next clearly identifiable subculture of new media activists in the early phases of this research. At the time, youths' new media activities were relatively benign, politically speaking, as experimentation expressed itself in challenges to patriarchy at work in their everyday lives, more so than in opposition to the state. In these early resistance practices, however, like gaining access to uncensored news, reading porn, joining chat rooms, debating social issues, and meeting people beyond their narrowly conscribed offline social networks, we see expressions of individual agency in their everyday lives. By 2006, youth activism in the Orange Revolution would help to challenge electoral law, to dismiss the prime minister, to demand more accountable governance, and to demand an end to corruption (Nordenson 2010). Even as early as 1997, when I guest-lectured at Kuwait University, students argued that 'the way power was structured was changing with the Internet'. The students 'were convinced that Internet use would make the world smaller and better' (field notebook entry, 18 March 1997).

Islamists were the most active users of the Internet during this initial phase of research. One liberal activist interviewed in 1997 called this, disparagingly, 'Shari'ah with electricity' (interviewed March 1997, Kuwait City). In my field notebook I noted that 'There is Shari'ah with electricity all over Kuwait – Quranic CD Roms, telephone hot lines for instant fatwas (24/7), T.V. shows on Shari'ah and basic life issues, computer data bases for Quran and Fiqh, websites for *dawah* [proselytising]' (field notebook entry, 17 March 1997). Liberals in Kuwait whom I interviewed were worried about the rise of Islamist influence in the country. Ironically, even when presented with a tool (the Internet) that could increase liberal power and voice, an editor I interviewed in Kuwait noted, 'the liberal attitude is generally one of defeat – they are afraid to offend the Islamists because of their power and influence – thus they say the best thing to do is to keep one's mouth shut' (interviewed March 1997, Kuwait City). One advisor to the emir whom I interviewed added, 'Political Islam should be stamped out, as in Egypt, immediately, before it is too late' (interviewed March 1997, Kuwait City). In 1997, however, 9/11 had not coloured our views of Islamists as a threat. Moreover, Islamist activism in Kuwait in the late 1990s was limited to increasing public observance of Islam in everyday life, such as creating legislation that would segregate university classrooms and campuses, end public gatherings like concerts where genders might mix, and make all Kuwaiti laws compatible with the Shari'ah. Since Islamists were loyal to the Sabah monarchy, the state was more than happy to 'Islamicise' public space and Kuwaiti law in exchange for their loyalty.

In 1997 Kuwaiti Internet culture was relatively benign. There were few signs of democratisation, opposition politics at the grass roots, or revolution. That Internet use is shaped by context; that users define the meaning and importance of the tool; that women, youths and Islamists were the most active users of the Internet; and that small changes in ways of communicating shape everyday life remain the most important lessons learned from this initial look at new media use and change in Kuwait.

The opportunity to return to Kuwait would not come until 2009, more than a decade from my initial journey. This time I would return for three summers in a row, to teach Arab Human Development courses at the American University of Kuwait. My initial impressions of what a twelve-year gap in fieldwork in Kuwait produces are captured by the following entry:

> So what has changed since my last visit 12 years ago? There is more building and development . . . more people too. There is more traffic, and more people are driving big F-150 pick-ups and Hummers . . . Kuwait still seems to be a large consumer of cheap labour . . . Also, Kuwait is way more wired than it was 12 years ago. Mobile phones are everywhere . . . we got our pay as you go for about 12 KD and that included 5 KD of minutes . . . Very cheap! So cheap, we got 4 lines. The buildings that were 'new' and fancy when we were here last are now very dirty and looking like they are not so trendy anymore. The new malls are trying to be Dubai . . . and succeeding to a degree. Health clubs are still for the rich and famous and/or foreign . . . One club wanted $1500 a month for a family membership . . . crazy. People seem fatter than my last visit. And for sure there are more women wearing abaya and hijab. I also see almost no other Americans. I saw a handful yesterday at the coffee house, and a few at the Sultan Center . . . but other than that . . . not as many as I remember in the past. (Field notebook entry, 20 June 2009)

A few days later, I would summarise my re-entry impressions as follows: 'Kuwaitis seem more liberal than before, and at the same time, more conservative too' (field notebook entry, 23 June 2009). Oppositional compliance at work.

One manifestation of the contest between liberal and conservative identities in the practice of everyday life occurs in the realm of clothing. For our household, the politics of dress started one week before departure, when I had an argument with my teenaged children about packing (May 2009). They insisted that they planned to dress in Kuwait as they do in the US: baseball caps, cargo shorts, surf tees for one son, black clothes of the 'emo' genre for the other son. (The youngest son let me pack for him!) Thinking about the anti-terrorist training I had had to take before getting clearance to travel to Kuwait, I knew that dressing like an American can be a security risk. I pleaded with my older sons to wear less identifiably American forms of dress. They argued, 'You want me to go on this trip to a desert hell-hole with ungodly summer weather, then let me dress as I please.'

The following field notebook entry reveals the ultimate end to our inter-generational conflict. My sons proved victorious when I observed,

> I am not used to seeing so many men wearing shorts. Especially at the new Marina mall . . . to see young Kuwaitis wearing shorts, baseball caps and surf t-shirts . . . like they were in the States . . . this is odd for me, but great for my boys, who fit right in. (Field notebook entry, 24 June 2009)

Kuwait's increased conservatism was observable in public as well. For example, many more women were wearing Islamic dress. There were also more men sporting beards and short *dishdasha*, both signs of religious conservatism. Traditional dress and Converse low tops reveal the hybrid nature of Kuwaiti culture – both globalised and local, Islamist and Western. The fact that the gentleman in the background of Figure 4.2 is about to go and see an IMAX film with his daughter, who sports matching Converse shoes, again shows mixed cultural practices in everyday life – which will also resonate in the oppositional compliant nature of Kuwaiti Internet practices examined in this chapter. Interestingly, however, young male dress as a predictor of future trends suggests a decline in Islamist dress over time. Most of the men wearing Islamist dress were in their thirties amd forties, while youths, part of a wired Facebook and Twitter generation, sported T-shirts that bordered on offensive. 'I-pood' (complete with toilet paper in case you missed the word play) and 'FBI – Female Body Inspector' were two of the most oppositional T-shirts I observed in my summer 2010 classes at the American University of Kuwait.

Dress is not disconnected from politics. Cargo short wearing, offensive

Figure 4.2   Dress as politics: Islamist *dishdasha* and Converse juxtaposition.
Photo: Deborah L. Wheeler, Kuwait Aquarium, 2009.

T-shirt sporting, iPhone and Blackberry (one of each) toting youths clearly understood the relationship between new media use and changing power relations. As early as 2009, perhaps inspired by the Green Revolution in Iran, the Orange Revolution in Kuwait (2006 onwards) and the Cedar Revolution in Lebanon (2005), I recorded my students reflecting on changing political environments in the region as follows:

> The students really think the Internet empowers women, changing power relations, transforming politics and society in the region, but that institutionalised power changes are slower to materialise. (Field notebook entry, 9 July 2009)

In addition to dress, YouTube is a site for the articulation of oppositional youth subculture and identity in Kuwait. In 2009 my students would teach me about youth resistance and new media use through the Umbrella movement, identified by AUK students as a sign of political development towards

Figure 4.3   Rebel dress and resistance of the Yellows.
Photo: Deborah L. Wheeler, Kuwait, June 2014.

inclusivity and freedom in Kuwait (see <http://www.youtube.com/watch?v=sUZK6pndTBA&list=PL921F36BD4B75D970&index=3>). In 2010 I learned 'how to be Kuwaiti' in a series of videos made by a Kuwaiti student studying abroad in Miami, with clear instructions for men (<http://www.youtube.com/watch?v=SoA-zAFB6HI>) and women (<http://www.youtube.com/watch?v=ESfHr3BlXvM>). In 2011 it was 'McChicken', a critique of Kuwaiti youth who have gone 'too global', with pink polo shirts (big emblem especially), madras shorts, iPhone, Blackberry and Ray-Bans, baseball cap turned rebelliously backwards, once again revealing a link between dress and identity in Kuwait.

Through the politics of dress, youth resistance and new media practices, as captured in the poster in Figure 4.3, we see 'the power of people acting in concert against official scripts' and, in the process, we see evidence of how 'political culture is reinvented in everyday life' (Goldfarb 2012: 107).

The Context: How Does Kuwait Compare with Egypt and Jordan?

In the previous case studies, we looked at indicators on corruption, freedom and Internet access to understand the context of Internet use. How does Kuwait look from these angles? As revealed below, Kuwait also experienced a sharp rise in corruption perceptions, which in part precipitated an increase in public opposition to the prime minister. Kuwait is also distinguished among the other cases for being one of the 'most free' societies in the region (partially free by Freedom House ratings). What is surprising, however, is that in the last few years, Kuwait has increasingly cracked down on citizens who breach red lines in their tweets, blogs and other forms of public discourse. The defensiveness of the regime in light of the sharp escalation of street protests and other forms of civic engagement, calling for concrete steps towards a constitutional monarchy, and a decreased role of the Sabah household members in leading cabinet positions, all reveal that Kuwait is ripe for change. The outspokenness of the narratives of Internet users, examined below, also reflect such changes in political consciousness, and action at the grass roots. Statistics and Internet user testimonials, in addition to overt civic engagement, including the election boycott by opposition politicians and citizens, escalating street protests and more intense public demands for change, across social sectors, reveal that Kuwait is a case to watch. Kuwait, like Jordan, is ripe for significant political change. As oil revenues decline, the population grows, climate change affects local weather negatively, by escalating temperatures and decreasing precipitation, public health, especially non-communicable diseases, reach crisis levels, and salaries and subsidies are cut to balance the state's budget, all combine to create a perfect storm in Kuwait (Wheeler 2015).

Corruption in Kuwait

Corruption is a perennial issue in Kuwait, and those who try to reform the culture of corruption face serious risks. For example, former MP Abdullah Nibari was chairman of the committee for the protection of public funds. In 1997, while en route to his beach chalet with his wife, their car was sprayed with bullets in an assassination attempt, which both of them miraculously survived. His oversight and investigation of corruption claims was linked

Table 4.1 Corruption in Kuwait 2003–2015

(Where in 2015 Denmark is ranked #1 least corrupt (score of 91), and Somalia is tied with North Korea at a rank of 167th (score of 8) as the most corrupt on the planet)

Year	Rank	Score	Countries with same score
2003	35th	5.3	Italy
2004	44th	4.6	Lithuania, South Africa
2005	45th	4.7	
2006	46th	4.8	Czech Republic
2007	60th	4.3	
2008	65th	4.3	Cuba
2009	66th	4.1	Georgia, Croatia
2010	54th	4.5	South Africa
2011	54th	4.6	Hungary
2012	66th	44	Romania, Saudi Arabia
2013	69th	43	Romania, Italy
2014	67th	44	South Africa
2015	55th	49	

Source: Transparency International. Note that the raw score system changed for the 2012–2015 data. Prior to 2012, the ranking was based upon a score between 1 and 10, with 10 being super clean and 1 being highly corrupt; beginning in 2012, the scale was 1–100, with 100 being the cleanest.

with the attack. In 2011, at his *diwaniyya*, Nibari was quoted as saying of the attack, 'it was probably related to opening the corruption files' (Calderwood 2011a). In response to this attack, Nibari ceased to wear Kuwaiti national dress. Mary Ann Tétreault sees Nibari's choice of dress post-attack as a form of resistance to 'a political and social order of which [he] disapproves' (Tétreault 2000: 27). The attack did not inhibit his efforts to make Kuwaiti politics more liberal and transparent. More than a decade and a half later, Nibari observes, in response to the attack, 'I didn't give up politics and I didn't change my attitude' (Calderwood 2011b). He still wears a suit, linking dress and politics. Since the assassination attempt, corruption perceptions have worsened, while opposition to Sabah rule has likewise intensified. The dissolution of the Kuwaiti cabinet and parliament in 2012, the firing and rehiring of the prime minister eight times over the last four years, and a steep increase in the number of public demonstrations in Kuwait are linked with questions of corruption and mismanagement of public funds. Over the past decade, we have seen a sharp drop in Kuwait's corruption perception index rating, which means that corruption is perceived to have significantly worsened over time. Improvements on the 2015 corruption ranking are promising, and may correlate with a decline in street protests.

Some attribute the rise in corruption to the rapid increase in the country's sovereign wealth (Calderwood 2011b). Over the past twelve years, the Kuwaiti government has amassed a 200 billion dollar government surplus, due to the surge in global oil prices (AFP 2011). Some of this surplus (an estimated 300 million dollars) has, according to a recent scandal, found its way into the bank accounts of at least nine Kuwaiti members of parliament, allegedly as a means to purchase loyalty to the Sabah leadership. Professor Shafiq al-Ghabra of Kuwait University calls this scandal 'Kuwait's Watergate' (Stack 2011). Especially within the current context, where significant budget deficits are projected, finding this squandered cash might help the government to keep citizens satisfied with the regime. Instead, however, budget cuts and austerity measures are expected to raise tensions (Asiya Research 2015).

What is most important for this analysis is that Internet use has increasingly given Kuwaitis a voice with which to express opposition to the regime; to spread information about corruption and bad governance; to mobilise resistance to the status quo. In Tétreault's words, 'new media are opening spaces for politics and social activism in Kuwait' (Tétreault 2011: 80). Fahad al-Somait, Professor of Media and Communications at Gulf University for Science and Technology in Kuwait, notes that 'such technologies open new pathways that are a necessary, if not sufficient, condition for political change' (Somait 2012: 1). He observes that especially 'traditionally marginalized groups, such as women, youths, and minorities, are at the forefront of utilising new media technologies to influence political discourse and action' (ibid.).

For example, we see this online participation in discourses about corruption in particular in the comments section on a recent Kuwaiti blog post (<http://248am.com/mark/interesting/kuwait-most-corrupt-country-in-the-world/>). TwoFortyEightAM, one of Kuwait's most widely read blogs, provided commentary on a study which correlated unpaid parking tickets with domestic corruption in a diplomat's home country. The study looked at the number of unpaid tickets in New York City accumulated over a five-year period by foreign diplomats taking advantage of their legal immunity to overtly break the law. The study found that in countries with high corruption at home there was a noticeably high number of parking violations by their diplomats in New York. The opposite was true for countries with low levels of corruption, where the number of unpaid parking tickets was also low. More specifically, the study notes that

> Kuwait blew away the competition with a whopping average of 246 unpaid parking tickets per diplomat over a 5-year period. Diplomats from countries famed for their good political behavior like Canada, Sweden, and Norway didn't have any unpaid tickets. (Dasgupta 2006)

The blog post, entitled 'Kuwait Most Corrupt Country in the World', garnered the following comment: 'Dude, is this supposed to be like news or something?' Another comment observes, 'At least who breaks a law gets punished in America in spite of nationality. In Kuwait the law is only for non-Kuwaiti. So strange and selfish in spite of being a Muslim society. They should learn something from the west besides adopting their life style.' Adding insult to injury, another commentator posts, 'A US official came to Kuwait a couple months ago working on a research of the country's corruption. The funny thing Kuwaiti officials tried to bribe her so she'd write good stuff about Kuwait! Well, of course the next day she got mad, left Kuwait and wrote the nastiest stuff about Kuwait.' Another posts sardonically, 'Great, so we are first at something :D.' Perhaps most transparently of all, one commentator responds, 'Fuck Kuwait.'

In all of these cyber civic engagements we observe participation in anti-corruption politics. Enhanced awareness of global perceptions, opportunities to vent about the ways in which *wasta* (using connections) in Kuwait leads to unevenness before the law, entitlements and bad driving are gained through these engagements. In the end, we glimpse in these transactions the ways in which cyber environments open new spaces for political engagement. Online political engagement as depicted in this blog post and discussion on corruption in Kuwait 'promote political participation and increase dialogue about political issues' (Albabtain 2010).

Freedom in Kuwait

Kuwait's openness is a source of national pride. Kuwaitis are articulate about the fact that their political environment is distinguished among Gulf societies, given Kuwait's long history of parliamentary politics, relatively free media and civic engagement. According to *New York Times* correspondent Liam Stack, Kuwait's 'political system has long been seen as one of the most freewheeling in the Persian Gulf, a region whose politics are dominated by absolute monarchs' (Stack 2011). But there are red lines, which limit Kuwaiti freedoms. Criticism of the ruling family is not allowed. Political parties are illegal. Public gatherings are not allowed without a licence. Discourse which harms national unity, insults Islam or defames Kuwait's national status or the country's allies are all potentially punishable with prison time.

Armed with new media tools, however, red lines are increasingly breached, the consequences of which are producing a series of institutionalised firsts (Nordenson 2010, Tétreault 2011, Somait 2012, Krauss 2011, BBC 2011, *The Telegraph* 2012), including the first public debates over succession (2006), the first women elected to parliament, in part because of their new media use (2009), the first multi-sector coordinated labour strikes in the public sector (2011), the first parliamentary grilling of the prime minister (2011), resulting in his ultimate resignation, and the first arrests of ruling family members for tweets critical of the emir (2012). In response to a more assertive public, and the clear institutional impacts on power in Kuwait, the government has responded with legal harassment of those who breach red lines.

The decline in civil liberties since 2007, and political rights since 2012, raises red flags, given Kuwait's unique political culture, which prides itself on being more democratic and free than that in neighbouring countries. Kuwait post-2012 more closely fits a regional pattern of repression. The arrest of bloggers, MPs, journalists, tweeters (including two younger members of the ruling family), the deportation of twenty Egyptians gathered to discuss presidential elections in Egypt – all of these are examples of a growing government crackdown on freedom of expression. In light of government repression, Kuwait's ruling family 'is growing increasingly willing to act in

Table 4.2 Freedom in Kuwait 2002–2015

(Where 1 means completely free, such as the US, and 7 indicates absence of freedom, such as North Korea)

Year	Freedom rating	Civil liberties	Political rights	Status
2002	4.5	5	4	Partly free
2003	4.5	5	4	Partly free
2004	4.5	5	4	Partly free
2005	4.5	5	4	Partly free
2006	4.5	5	4	Partly free
2007	4	4	4	Partly free
2008	4	4	4	Partly free
2009	4	4	4	Partly free
2010	4	4	4	Partly free
2011	4.5	5	4	Partly free
2012	4.5	5	4	Partly free
2013	5	5	5	Partly free*
2014	5	5	5	Partly free*
2015	5	5	5	Partly free*

Source: Freedom House (<www.freedomhouse.org>).

* The years 2013–15 have witnessed a sharp decline in political rights and civil liberties.

ways that belie the country's reputation for tolerating heated political debate' (Motaparthy 2010).

New media diffusion and use

Kuwait is the fourth most wired country in the Middle East. A high degree of Internet connectivity in Kuwait is both a reflection of cultural identity and a sign of security considerations, post-invasion (1990). Having the latest technology in the hands of citizens is a national source of pride. In recent years, the hyper-growth and modernisation of Dubai, Doha and Abu Dhabi has given Kuwait a run for its money development- and investment-wise, but Kuwait has remained distinguished in terms of its openness and democratic tendencies, which include the democratisation of information, and tools through which to spread Internet culture. Kuwait does not censor the Internet, never has, and hopefully never will. Over the last couple of years, the arrest of a few bloggers, a few tweeters and a few journalists is contrary to the Kuwaiti identity of openness and tolerance. Those who dis-tribute narratives that threaten national unity and the monarchy, crossing

Table 4.3 Internet access in Kuwait 2000–2015

Year	Population	Internet users	% of population with Internet access
2000	2,228,000	150,000	7%
2005	2,530,012	567,000	22.4%
2009	2,692,526	1,000,000	37.1%
2011	2,595,628	1,100,000	42.4%
2012	2,646,314	1,963,565	72.4%
2015	3,996,899	3,145,559	78.7%

Source: Internet World Stats. Note that the ITU estimates that only 75% of Kuwaitis have access.

red lines, are typically given warnings by the government. Several Kuwaitis who refused to self-censor recently received steep prison sentences and have had their Kuwaiti citizenship revoked (Freedom House 2015). These acts reveal that Kuwait is still a conservative Islamic society with a patriarchal social and political structure, in spite of widespread Internet diffusion and use.

But as explored in the section below, cultural and political norms are being transformed by new media use, one click at a time. An increasingly wired country may be less susceptible to invasion, a local theory argues, given the fact that fax machines, satellite phones and PCs helped to sustain underground resistance during the Iraqi occupation (Levins 1997). At the same time, such tools give citizens increased power over their own lives and political consciousness, or so their narratives argue. We find hints of such transformations in public protests, cargo short wearing youths, oppositional YouTube videos, blogs and tweets. The narratives of Internet users are another indicator of social and political disruption in Kuwait, for reasons explored more completely in the following section.

New Media and the Politics of Everyday Life in Kuwait

The previous sections reveal that Kuwait is a volatile context of social and political tensions, with an increasingly repressive government reining in an oppositional public sphere, in part enabled by new media access and use. As revealed in this case study, Kuwaitis offer similar assessments to those given by Jordanians and Egyptians about the role of Internet use in their everyday lives. What is perceived more overtly in the Kuwaiti case, however, is a direct link between new media use and political change.

The interview results show that Kuwaitis, like the Jordanians and Egyptians interviewed for this study, use the Internet for email, to download music, to aid with their studies, to chat, to access news, for shopping, to aid with their work, and to get wider access to information (Wheeler and Mintz 2010). Moreover, in terms of perceived impacts of Internet use, there are also transnational patterns. In all three cases, narratives of impacts clustered around a core of shared themes: expanding access to information, widening social networks, alleviating boredom, enhancing professional development, making life easier and, last but not least, changing power relations/enhancing civic engagement (political impact). What is unique in the Kuwaiti case, however, is a perceived direct link between Internet use and political change, as explored in more detail below.

Wider access to information

A total of 41% of those surveyed in Kuwait cited enhanced access to infor-mation as an impact of Internet use in their life. For example, one Kuwaiti woman who is in her forties notes that the Internet has changed her life because 'it's very informative. It provides me knowledge and options to find things. It's a good tool for communicating between people and it helps me a lot at work' (interviewed July 2009, Kuwait City). Similarly, a twenty-two-year-old Kuwaiti Muslim male who spends roughly fifteen hours a week on the Net notes that Internet use provides wider access to information 'because Internet use spreads news quickly' (interviewed June 2010, Kuwait City). Likewise, a twenty-two-year-old Kuwaiti woman observes, 'without the Internet I wouldn't have the world knowledge I have today' (interviewed June 2010, Kuwait City).

Some of the more interesting characterisations of Kuwaiti relationships with the Internet include the claim by a twenty-two-year-old Kuwaiti male, 'I'm an Internet addict' (interviewed June 2010, Kuwait City). Even more poignantly, a twenty-year-old Kuwaiti male who uses the Internet for email, chatting, gaming, music downloads, news, study and research states that the Internet 'is my "secret garden". I love to spend my time there' (interviewed June 2010, Kuwait City). Summarising the value of the Internet, one twenty-one-year-old Kuwaiti female observes, the Internet 'gives me more information about things; Google is like the brain I never had' (interviewed July 2010, Kuwait City). Emphasising the essentialness of the Internet to the practice of everyday life in Kuwait, one twenty-five-year-old Muslim female observes, 'Everything in my life depends on the Internet and there is no way to live without it' (interviewed July 2010, Kuwait City).

Freedom, social networking and changing communication patterns

A total of 28% of Kuwaitis surveyed stated that Internet use enabled new forms of social networking. For example, one Kuwaiti interviewed for this study notes, 'I am more connected with people now and I know more about the news by using the Net' (interviewed June 2009, Kuwait City). In the words of one fifty-five-year-old female Kuwaiti, the Internet 'opens the eyes of the younger generation, and because of this, they find more freedom to exercise and they can compare freedom in their countries to that in other countries' (interviewed July 2009, Kuwait City). A twenty-year-old Muslim female notes that Internet use is causing Arab culture and society 'to become very open' (interviewed June 2010, Kuwait City). Similarly, a twenty-five-year-old Muslim male notes that Internet access 'keeps me connected with people all around the world' (interviewed July 2010, Kuwait City).

Making life easier

Just over 46% of Kuwaitis surveyed cited ease-of-life factors as an impact of Internet use. For example, one Kuwaiti responds, 'Internet use made my life easier and I'm now more aware of what is happening worldwide and it has saved me time and money' (interviewed June 2009, Kuwait City). Another ease-of-life factor is that the Internet expands and speeds up communication. For example, one participant observes, 'The Internet is the same as SMS in mobile phones. When it was introduced, people learned a new way of sending information to multiple contacts and it arrives almost instantly' (interviewed July 2009, Kuwait City). Further illustrating changing communication patterns in the Arab world, a twenty-nine-year-old Kuwaiti female observes that Internet use 'speeds up the communication process' (interviewed June 2010, Kuwait City).

Many students observed that Internet use makes their research and studies easier by providing wider access to information. In the wider population, ease of access to information is also a key theme. For example, one twenty-eight-year-old Kuwaiti female observes, 'with the Internet I can get answers to questions that arise without having to wait too long' (interviewed July 2010, Kuwait City). One twenty-six-year-old Muslim male who surprisingly admits to 'surfing porn online' observes that Internet use makes his life easier because 'he can stay at home and be entertained' (interviewed June 2010, Kuwait City). Many interviewed for this study state ease of dating as a factor drawing them to the technology. For example, a twenty-five-year-old Kuwaiti woman notes, 'Internet use made my life easier. I met my fiancé through the Net' (interviewed July 2010, Kuwait City). In short, Internet use helps Kuwaitis satisfy basic needs, from access to information, to companionship, to entertainment; the tool makes it easier 'to find the things I want', states one twenty-two-year-old Kuwaiti male (interviewed July 2010, Kuwait City).

Escaping boredom

One thing that a handful of Kuwaitis interviewed for this study want is an escape from boredom. While only 9.4% of those surveyed in Kuwait used the Internet to escape boredom, this remains a shared pattern with Jordan and Egypt. For example, one Kuwaiti interviewed in 2010 notes, 'the Internet puts you in touch with any information you need, and kills boredom at work' (interviewed July 2010, Kuwait City). Similarly, a seventeen-year-old Kuwaiti male who taught himself to use the Internet and spends an estimated forty hours a week online notes that Internet use 'makes life less boring' (interviewed June 2010, Kuwait City). An eighteen-year-old Kuwaiti female concludes that Internet use 'makes life more interesting' (interviewed June 2009, Kuwait City). Showing that it's not just a young person's problem, a forty-nine-year-old Kuwaiti male notes, 'I use the Internet when I have nothing to do' (interviewed July 2010, Kuwait City). Similarly, one twenty-five-year-old Kuwaiti male who is employed in the oil industry notes, 'The Net gives me access to everything. Whenever I'm bored, I surf the Net and I get what I want' (interviewed July 2010, Kuwait City).

Political change

The most significant finding of this study was identifying perceived political impacts of Internet use. More than 80% of respondents stated that the Internet was having a major impact on politics. Internet users in Kuwait argue that new media are altering institutionalised power relations between rulers and ruled. For example, one person interviewed stated that 'The Internet is having an impact on politics in the Arab world because it has reached a level where it can make or break a country's politics such as revolution or evolution' (interviewed July 2010, Kuwait City). Another person interviewed addresses the differences in balance of power between ruler and ruled by noting that because of Internet use, citizens 'know more stuff about their government' (interviewed July 2010, Kuwait City). Another Kuwaiti interviewed for this study notes that because of Internet use, Arab countries 'go more towards freedom and democracy' (interviewed July 2010, Kuwait City). Because of Internet use, notes one person interviewed, 'people start thinking more about how their government compares with other governments' (interviewed July 2010, Kuwait City). Grounding such changes in individual forms of agency, one twenty-three-year-old Kuwaiti male observes, 'people actually have a voice while on the Internet and can actually be heard by others around the world' (interviewed July 2010, Kuwait City). Similarly, a twenty-four-year-old Kuwaiti male observes, 'Unofficial websites allow people to express their opinions and practise freedom of speech. Politicians take these opinions into consideration' (interviewed July 2010, Kuwait City).

Articulating a clear link between Internet use and institutionalisation of power, one person interviewed observes, 'women got into the Kuwaiti parliament, which is caused by globalisation and the Internet' (interviewed July 2010, Kuwait City). Another person interviewed just created a list of political impacts in the region, including 'women's empowerment, promoting human rights, changes towards democracy, political freedom is more than before' (interviewed July 2010, Kuwait City). A Kuwaiti male who is in his thirties summarises the political impact of the Internet in the region by observing, 'Recent developments in Iran prove that the Internet has a political impact. The government bans certain things, only to find the same banned thing propagated by media, among actors separated around the world, using

Twitter and other web-enabled platforms' (interviewed July 2009, Kuwait City).

Similar to the Egyptian and Jordanian cases, Kuwaitis argue that the Internet enhances the power of public opinion. For example, one Kuwaiti interviewed states that the Internet 'gives people a chance to express their political views' (interviewed June 2009, Kuwait City). Another notes that 'Internet use shows how the public of each country really thinks about their leaders and local and regional issues' (interviewed July 2010, Kuwait City). A twenty-one-year-old Kuwaiti male, when asked if Internet use was affecting Arab politics, notes, 'Yes. People can broadcast their voices on the Internet. If no one is listening in their country, they have more advantage by using Internet because now the audience is bigger' (interviewed July 2010, Kuwait City). Moreover, a twenty-five-year-old Muslim female from Lebanon (living in Kuwait) with 330 friends on Facebook notes that, online, 'people are able to express their views freely on political matters' (interviewed June 2010, Kuwait City). Likewise, a nineteen-year-old Muslim female from Kuwait who spends on average fifty-six hours a week online observes that Internet use gives people 'more freedom of expression and people can meet and share ideas' (interviewed June 2010, Kuwait City). Similarly, another nineteen-year-old Kuwaiti female observes that Internet use 'is teaching people how to become more open minded' (interviewed July 2009, Kuwait City).

One sign of becoming more open minded in Kuwait is linked with questions of sex and sexuality. For example, a number of males interviewed for this study stated that they regularly surf porn websites. This was an unusual response for an interview, considering that importing porn or viewing it online is illegal in Kuwait. Their comments reflect a new degree of openness in Kuwaiti cyber and offline environments, whereby citizens transgress Kuwait's laws and cultural norms. One twenty-four-year-old Kuwaiti male summarises the Internet's impact in Kuwait with two words: 'Yes, porn' (interviewed July 2010, Kuwait City).

Moreover, a surprising handful of those interviewed self-identify as 'gay' or 'lesbian' in the gender identification question, also highly unexpected, given the strict laws against homosexuality in Kuwait. These comments are both reflective and constitutive of new social and political relationships. New degrees of sexual openness and experimentation are in the same category as resistance through dress and physical appearance, increases in street activism, and more vocal public critiques of leaders. All of these practices reveal ways in which Kuwaitis are more politically engaged, and are using new media tools to confront traditions, norms and rules at work in their lives.

Demonstrating 'oppositional compliance' in Kuwaiti new media cultures, not everyone interviewed for this study considers increased openness enabled by Internet use a positive development. For example, a twenty-year-old Kuwaiti female states that Internet use 'is introducing the Arab world to the West and making it easier for communities with other ethnicities to interact and share ideas, and this interferes with our society' (interviewed July 2009, Kuwait City). Even more extreme, a Kuwaiti male who is forty-nine years old observes that 'political/religious websites brainwash youths online and Zionists control policies worldwide through the Net to negatively impact Arab politics' (interviewed July 2010, Kuwait City). A twenty-six-year-old Kuwaiti male provides further evidence of a concern with the negative impacts of Internet use when he observes that 'Internet use made people more open minded and accepting of change, which is leading to the loss of cultural values and traditions, and people are being corrupted' (interviewed June 2010, Kuwait City).

As illustrated by the advertisement for FAST Telco's high-speed Internet in Kuwait in Figure 4.4, new media use is creating rapid change in a conservative Islamic society. Yet as the interview data reveal, Internet use remains a deeply personal experience, with nuances shaped by everyday life situations, individual interests and perceptions. The cumulative effects, however, transform norms and behaviours within, upon and beyond the Kuwaiti state, producing hybrid Internet cultures and a politics of oppositional compliance.

Conclusion

The preceding pages have tried once again to make sense out of the transformative potential of new media uses, this time as reflected in the voices of new media participants in Kuwait. The most important finding of this case study is that as Internet use spreads, so too does the tool's impact on politics and the practice of everyday life. Kuwaitis are transparent about how Internet use is transforming relations between rulers and ruled. Some are optimistic

Figure 4.4 FAST Telco billboard, Salmiya, Kuwait. Photo: Deborah L. Wheeler, July 2009.

about the future of citizen empowerment, while others remain concerned about threats to Kuwaiti culture and authenticity. As reflected in new styles of dress, experimental and risky online social practices and intensified street protests against corruption, repression and authoritarianism, Kuwait is ripe for change. Where oppositional compliant behaviours will lead is something to watch, as some socially networked activists take on the state, while others remain passive and respectful of patriarchy and traditions of quietism (Maloney 2011: 180).

As I type these words I'm sitting in Kuwait (4 July 2014). On the surface, the country is deep in the Ramadan fast, and a strange brew of competing interests threatens to erupt. You can see these forces for change in the classroom, on college campuses, in the malls, in the press and on the streets. These disruptive forces include rising consumerism, overt expressions of sexual freedom, oppositional new media use, forces of globalisation, government repression, economic stagnation, the protests inspired by the youth bulge, ideological crisis (nationalism, Islamism and beyond) and women's empowerment. Add to these racism, public rage, protests against corruption, labour strikes, random acts of communal violence, drug abuse and trafficking, suicide, obesity, food, water and energy waste, growing tensions within the ruling family, increasingly overt corruption and questions of sustainability and a recipe for explosiveness emerges. In the face of these challenges, the social safety net provided to citizens by the government, with which to redistribute oil revenues, weakens. Strained by a population that is growing too rapidly, and diminishing returns on oil exports, the country's future seems rocky at best.

A 2010 assessment of Kuwait's future observes that 'revolution' is likely in Kuwait if the government is 'unable to provide the fiscal incentives to the population to stay quiet' and as a result 'is forced to make more and more concessions' (Business Monitor International 2010). While the world focuses on the threat of ISIS and the *Ikhwan* networks, the possibilities for terrorism, the spillover effects of the Arab Spring revolutions, and the refugee crises in Syria, Jordan, Turkey, Lebanon and Iraq, just beneath the surface a whole world of citizen empowerment, disruption and dissatisfaction with anachronistic patriarchal governance poses a more immediate and wider-spread threat to state and social stability in the Arabian Gulf. Citizens are stepping up to press for change in Kuwait, before the status quo squanders resources and sends the country backwards, not forwards.

5

THE MICRO-DEMISE OF AUTHORITARIANISM IN THE MIDDLE EAST: WORKING AROUND THE STATE IN COMPARATIVE PERSPECTIVE

This chapter provides comparative case-study evidence of the core argument of this book: that ordinary people can create change in small ways by leveraging new media tools to network around the state, and other structures of power at work in their lives. In the service of this argument, three types of digital resistance in authoritarian political contexts in the Middle East are examined: digital disclosure to confront bad governance; people-to-people diplomacy; and social media for social change. These examples of digital resistance are based upon new media campaigns against the Egyptian, Turkish, Kuwaiti, Israeli, Iranian and Saudi states. In each of these cases, citizens use new communication devices to resist bad governance, and to enhance agency and autonomy in their everyday lives.

The story of enhanced state power in the digital age, so-called 'repression 2.0' (Seib 2012: 97), is a common one, and yet not surprising (Kalathil and Boas 2003, Calingaert 2010, MacKinnon 2011, Morozov 2011b). Especially in authoritarian contexts, the Internet has been used by the state for 'propaganda purposes' and 'surveillance', by 'paying bloggers to spread propaganda and troll social networking sites looking for new information on those in the opposition' (Morozov 2011b: xiv, xv). What is surprising, however, is that citizens in authoritarian contexts have effectively used the Internet to enhance *their* political and social agency in spite of the risks. Why, when the chances of success are so limited, and the costs for taking on the authoritarian state are so potentially life threatening, do Middle Eastern citizens resist? As demonstrated vividly by the Arab Spring revolutions, and the case studies examined in this book, the Middle East is an increasingly oppositional space. Collectively examples of digital resistance present 'new avenues of political change, through autonomous capacity to communicate and organize' which take place 'beyond the usual methods of . . . political control' (Castells 2012: 21).

In other words, as argued in this chapter, people in the Middle East use social media to resist because they can, and because they have a great degree of dissatisfaction to express. Digital media multiply the forms in which resistance can occur, replicate the avenues through which resistance can be expressed, and pool and intensify the results of small acts of defiance into big, potentially transformative waves. With social media, a one-click raindrop can replicate, and turn into a Facebook like, a viral video, hashtag floods of resistance and change.

This chapter provides evidence with which to argue that communicative acts of opposition, occurring throughout the Middle East, are agentive. The enhanced sense of being effective that accompanies expressions of 'discontentment or grievance' replicates 'the attitude that people are able to change things if they become involved in politics' (Spaiser et al. 2012: 126). The end result is that 'political action becomes more likely' (ibid.). In other words, social media plays a role in mobilisation because 'it provides easier access to political action for . . . people who have reached the point of being motivated to act' (ibid.).

This analysis builds on the work of three scholars, each of whom examines micro-forms of political and social change. Jeffrey Goldfarb's *The Politics of Small Things* locates the groundwork for revolution in Poland within the oppositional imaginations and practices of the artist/theatre communities (Goldfarb 2006). Goldfarb's work encourages us to look for political resistance and change in unusual places, and also asks that we not underestimate the power of small forms of opposition. He encourages us to realise that 'there are smaller, less grand ways to combat powerful wrongs' (ibid.: 3). Asef Bayat's *Life as Politics: How Ordinary People Change the Middle East* highlights how just living, and refusing to be invisible, is a blow to the authoritarian state by fostering an active citizenry, even if this mobilised public is not collectively expressed, but rather exists in 'individual and quiet direct action' (Bayat 2010: 58). And last, but not least, this chapter builds on the groundbreaking work of *Small Media, Big Revolution* by Annabelle Sreberny-Mohammadi and Ali Mohammadi, which examines the role of new media tools in the Iranian revolution, and encourages scholars to think of revolutions 'in terms of communications' because of 'the amazing potential power of the media to foster change' (Sreberny-Mohammadi and Mohammadi 1994: xix). With these studies as inspiration, this chapter looks at small acts of opposition to authoritarian states, using social media as a new public sphere in which communicative acts strive to redefine power relationships and to encourage civic engagement in the service of better governance.

Why We Should Care about New Media

The three examples of 'networking around the state' analysed in this chapter highlight political engagement that is challenging power arrangements in the Middle East, albeit in subtle, individual and indirect ways. With these cases, scholars and policy makers are encouraged to consider the power and implication of new media practices in the Middle East. The main message of this chapter, and the book as a whole, is that new media micro-empowerments enable ordinary citizens to disrupt the status quo, thus neutralising the effects of authoritarian rule in small ways, even if the overall effects of such disruptions are hard to sustain and hard to measure, as explored more completely below.

Bottom line up front: the military has a firmer grip on Egyptian politics than ever before; Iran and Israel still sabre-rattle daily; women in Saudi Arabia still can't drive without risking punishment. But at the same time, the ability of citizens to work around such entrenched power structures, as examined below, suggests an enhanced citizen capacity for disruptive behaviour. Whether or not the status quo will be reshaped beyond individual life and digital practices is indeterminate, but we would be wise not to ignore individual acts of quiet new media resistance because they may be harbingers of change in the making.

Whistle blowing and resisting corruption in the digital age

The Middle East is not a region known for its transparency, but through the use of social media, citizens in the region are exposing corruption and bad governance in the quest for social and political change. According to Transparency International, 'Not a single country in the region figures in the top half of the world in terms of public accountability, as measured in terms of access to information or holding leaders accountable for their actions' (Transparency International, n.d.).

Social media usage is enabling Middle Eastern citizens to press for more accountable government by 'demanding reform through social empowerment' (Bertolt et al. 2010: 265). Social media gives citizens the power to disclose bad governance by leaking stealth video (Khalid Said, Egypt), leaking top-secret documents (Manning and Snowden; WikiLeaks has disclosed aspects of bad governance in the Middle East even if Snowden and Manning are not citizens of the region), conducting Twitter campaigns (Turkey), and mobilising public allegations and rallies (former Kuwait MP Barrak's mobilisations against corruption).

Turkey

In the words of Turkish Prime Minister Recep Erdogan, 'This thing called social media is currently the worst menace to society' (Vick 2014). Erdogan's words represent a state on the defensive and are uttered in response to two events: whistle blowers using social media tools to expose his alleged corruption (AP 2014) and leaking audio footage on YouTube which implicated Turkey in secret plans to attack Syria (Barden 2014).

In response to the public's critique, Erdogan shut down Twitter. And in response to the war plans leak, the prime minister shut down YouTube. The Freedom Foundation in response downgraded Turkey's media freedom to 'not free'. Efforts to control social media expression have tarnished Turkey's reputation abroad and have done little to calm public mobilisation. The Vice President of the European Commission called Erdogan's social media crackdown 'another desperate and depressing move' (Barden 2014).

The costs for Turkey could be high, for as former US Ambassador to Turkey James Jeffreys observes, 'By banning Turkish social media, the government is running the risk of exiling itself from the global economy' (quoted in Barden 2014). It's a risk Turkey cannot afford, since 'Turkey's success has been based on integrating into the global economy' (ibid.). By intervening in executive level politics, using social media disclosures, the Turkish public resists government policies – including corruption, and an unpopular proposed war against a neighbour. We see Turkish citizens, via social media use, become 'informed, participatory, critical, expressive, ethical, and creative', and through such practices 'individuals make democratic society a reality' (Simsek and Simsek 2013: 132).

Egypt

Likewise, the public campaign to resist bad governance and corruption has been highly animated in Egypt, before, during and after the Arab Spring revolution which deposed former President Husni Mubarak. For example, in the first week of October 2013, a citizen of Egypt 'networked around the state' to disclose a behind closed doors meeting with General Sisi's senior staff regarding the military government's emerging media strategy. During the meeting, an anonymous participant took a stealth video of Sisi admitting that new media tools were empowering citizens. After the meeting, the anonymous video was uploaded to YouTube (<http://www.youtube.com/watch?v=WB9MVTR02YE>). In the video, General Sisi instructs his officers to prepare for an increase in public and parliamentary oversight of the military. As Sisi states, 'The revolution has dismantled all the shackles that were present – not just for us, not just for the military, but for the entire state' (Kirkpatrick 2013). This disclosure reveals both public resistance to military oppression and the state's view of increased citizen empowerment.

Social media, which gives Middle Eastern citizens power to capture their states behaving badly, provides transparency where none is expected. Notable moments where Egyptian citizens worked around the state using social media include Khalid Said, who in 2010 videotaped – and posted online – 'Egyptian police officers sharing profits after a drug bust' (Eltahawy 2010b), an act of resistance for which Khalid Said paid with his life, being beaten to death while in police custody (Ungerleider 2010). David Faris highlights other social media disclosure campaigns to confront bad governance in Egypt, including analysis of 'the sexual harassment scandal of October 2006; the torture scandal of January 2007; the Sudanese refugee crisis of 2006; and the Al-Qursaya Island takeover attempt of 2007–8' (Faris 2013: 23). In all of these examples we see Egyptians using social media to expose bad governance. These examples illustrate what it means to 'experience the Middle Eastern state' (Rudolph and Jacobsen 2006: vii) at its worst, as a manifestation of 'pathology and failure' that 'direct attention to the possibilities of civil society' (ibid.: x). In the Middle East, resistance channels are multiplied and amplified through new media, and in this sense social media create 'new tools' that enable citizens 'to accomplish political goals that had previously been unachievable' (Howard and Hussain 2013: 18). In Egypt, a dictator was deposed, even if Sisi's Egypt calls into question the sustainability of citizen empowerment.

Kuwait

In the summer of 2014, a Twitter-wielding public bent on exposing bad governance besieged another Middle Eastern state – Kuwait. Mobilisations and citizen demands for more accountable governance in Kuwait stem from the 2006 campaign to oppose the appointment of an ailing emir. Public protests during these early stages of Kuwait's Orange Revolution, supported by both opposition politicians and youth movements, collectively called for political reforms and an end to corruption, and ultimately resulted in a change of head of state and a reform of Kuwait's electoral district lines (Nordenson 2010). Subsequent protests and mobilisations have resulted in increased government salaries, investigations of corruption, and even the dismissal and reappointment of a new prime minister eight times.

The most recent phase of Kuwait's political reform movement exploded with mass rallies in June 2014. The immediate cause of this round of Kuwait's protests was opposition to the government's detainment of outspoken critic and former MP Musallam al-Barrak. Barrak is a former member of parliament who obtained more votes for his seat than any other politician in Kuwait's history. He is the symbol and figurehead of a protest movement which demands an end to corruption and a constitutional monarchy to strengthen Kuwaiti democracy. Barrak is no stranger to the Kuwaiti justice and incarceration system. He is vulnerable, especially now that he and other opposition politicians boycotted the 2012 elections. The boycott was in response to the emir's use of emergency law to reform the election rules by reducing the number of votes per person from four to one. Opposition politicians claimed that this change was designed to undermine an opposition majority in parliament (Westall 2012). It was not only the opposition which was hurt by the change in electoral rules; women also lost all of their seats under the new system. Without parliamentary immunity, Barrak takes great risks to publicly protest and to voice concerns about government corruption.

In the summer of 2014, the presence of an active opposition, riot police, tear gas, rubber bullets, and revoked citizenship for some participants, including two former MPs, Abdullah al-Barghash and Ahmad Jabr al-Shemmeri, illustrate the degree to which Gulf countries are not immune to the political transformations sweeping the Middle East. Kuwait's active opposition movement, under the leadership of Barrak, worked collectively to expose an alleged 'coup plot that could implicate members of the ruling al-Sabah family of attempting to overthrow the monarchy's government' by assassinating the Crown Prince (Kholaif 2014).

Barrak also called into question the independence of the Kuwaiti judiciary, and risked jail time with his vocal opposition to several government officials, including the former speaker of the parliament Jassim al-Khorafi (now deceased) and another member of the ruling family, for alleged misuse of public funds, proof of which he threatened to leak (<http://fredw-cathar sisours.blogspot.com/2014/07/kuwait-joins-arab-spring-protests.html>). Barrak's detention in July 2014 led thousands of Kuwaitis to mobilise in protest. Public opposition led to Barrak's release from jail, in part because it was Ramadan, which encouraged the emir's pardon. The struggle to expose corruption through leaks of video and government documents continues, as does the Kuwaiti government's iron-fisted approach to calming the oppositional public. With each crackdown on citizens, Kuwait risks increased public explosiveness.

The Kuwaiti state has fostered a citizenry that expects a five-star lifestyle, and that was raised in a political culture that was distinguished among Gulf neighbours as being 'more democratic'. Regime loyalists label Barrak's actions, and the public opposition he encourages, as mobilisation against the constitution and Kuwaiti culture. Those who continue to benefit from regime patronage are unlikely to join the protest movement, and render Kuwait an increasingly divided society, with an uncertain future. In the words of Kuwaiti journalist Muna Al-Fuzai, 'Kuwait is passing through a very delicate time these days with regards to corruption and misuse of power. If the situation isn't controlled and resolved peacefully, consequences can be negative and unpredictable' (Al-Fuzai 2014). Reflecting on the summer 2014 protests, Al-Fuzai observes, 'when police began to use teargas . . . on the protesting civilians, we saw a new chapter in Kuwait's history' (ibid.). She predicts, 'I think more people will join the opposition – simply because the circle of corruption is becoming bigger and getting out of control' (ibid.). A recent Islamic State-inspired attack by a suicide bomber at a Shi'i mosque in Kuwait City, during Ramadan 2015, illustrates an escalation in security threats. This attempt to incite sectarian violence highlights one facet of the challenges ahead for Kuwait. Mobilised publics, active terrorist cells and repression to preserve the status quo all collide with a state increasingly under siege and less capable of quieting the public with handouts due to a loss of revenue from oil sales.

People-to-people social networking works around warmongering states: Israel Loves Iran

We see Middle Eastern citizens using social media to network around states when on 14 March 2012, tired of the threats and escalations to war, citizen diplomat Ronnie Edry, an Israeli graphic designer, shared a message on Facebook with the people of Iran: 'Iranians we will never bomb your country. We ♥ you' (<https://www.facebook.com/israellovesiran?ref=profile>). A letter, addressed to the Iranian public, accompanied the poster. The letter stated:

> To the Iranian people. To all the fathers, mothers, children, brothers and sisters. For there to be a war between us, first we must be afraid of each other, we must hate. I'm not afraid of you; I don't hate you. I don't even know you. No Iranian ever did me no harm. I never even met an Iranian . . . Just one in Paris in a museum. Nice dude.
>
> I see sometime here, on the TV, an Iranian. He is talking about war. I'm sure he does not represent all the people of Iran. If you see someone on your TV talking about bombing you, be sure he does not represent all

Figure 5.1 Ronny from Israel and Majid from Iran meet up (<https://www.facebook.com/israellovesiran/photos/>).

of us. I'm not an official representative of my country. I'm a father and a teacher. I know the streets of my town, I talk with my neighbors, my family, my students, my friends and in the name of all these people, we love you. We mean you no harm. On the contrary, we want to meet, have some coffee and talk about sports. To all those who feel the same, share this message and help it reach the Iranian people. (<http://www.youtube.com/watch?v=mYjuUoEivbE>)

With one simple poster, and message, Edry worked around the Israeli and Iranian states to make an effort at peace in the face of war. His efforts illustrate that 'The international, person-to-person relationships made possible by Web 2.0 technologies constitute, to a great degree, an increasing and substantial new domain for public diplomacy' (Payne, Sevin and Bruya 2011: 42).

And the message worked. Within days of the plea being posted on Facebook, citizen diplomats in Iran responded with their own cries for peace and cooperation. The return messages were equally transformative, enabling people-to-people peace opportunities one click at a time (Said 2012). In an interview with CNN, Ronnie Edry explained that he started this campaign 'to talk directly to Iranians to see whether there really was anything to fight about' (ibid.). A TED talk on Edry's Facebook movement has gone viral, with over 1.9 million views (<http://www.ted.com/talks/israel_and_iran_a_love_story>). One observer explains that the peace movement Ronnie Edry created illustrates 'a new dawn where individual people are forging friendships and alliances in the face of the politicians' (Hetzer 2013). Hetzer sees Edry's movement as part of the Arab Spring, because the Arab Spring 'is a movement based upon open communications among common people' whereby 'an opportunity to make changes at the grassroots level' emerges (ibid.).

Based on the success of the Facebook campaign, Ronnie and his team created a non-governmental organisation, the Peace Factory, to collect and channel the peace messages into action. The Peace Factory is a movement based upon the principle of working around the state to end war. Social media are the platform on which peace work takes place, under the slogan 'We make peace viral'. More specifically,

> Peace starts with the people, one person at a time. Today it's easier than ever to connect and reach out to one another. We can talk, we can meet, and we can start a new friendship without even leaving our homes just by the click of a button. One new person, one new connection. Peace is when we see and treat each other as people. All we have to do is talk. (<http:// thepeacefactory.org>)

An article in *The New Yorker* summarises the promise of working around the state with citizen-to-citizen social media tools. Ruth Margalit observes,

> The Israel-Iran group, apart from the colorful photos and catchy slogans, really hasn't *said* much so far; its organizers haven't put forth a cohesive agenda nor have they lobbied the Israeli or Iranian governments to tone down their threats. Yet to ignore the campaign would be to sadly, gravely miss the point: a new grassroots force seems to have found a unified voice in the unlikeliest of places. (Margalit 2012)

Since Margalit's 2012 observation, the Peace Factory has escalated its action agenda to work around the state of war in the Middle East by providing workshops, expanding social networks for peace, launching campaigns to encourage Israeli voters to 'vote for peace', and encouraging meetings between Israelis and Iranians in neutral locations. According to Edry, 'With every new person that joins our community we are moving one step forwards making the hope for peace in the Middle East a reality' (<http://thepeacefactory.org/ why-about-bepart/>). The Israel Loves Iran Facebook movement, as well as

Edry's Peace Factory efforts, demonstrates 'that people – citizens – today are increasingly driving global events' (Sonenshine 2013).

The Saudi women's driving campaign: 'No Woman, No Drive' no longer

A third case of using social media to work around the Middle Eastern state is unfolding in Saudi Arabia. The Saudi women's driving campaign is based upon a demand for increasing women's self-sufficiency. Transport for Saudi women costs large sums of capital, and reduces incentives for women to work outside of the home. Saudi Arabia is the only country in the world where women can't legally drive. One woman I interviewed in Riyadh in January 2014 noted that the cost of transportation (having to hire a driver) meant that she was 'actually paying to work' (interviewed January 2014 at the residence of the US Ambassador to Saudi Arabia).

With the 26 October women's driving campaign, and 'Women2Drive' (<https://www.facebook.com/SaudiWomenSpring/info>), we see Saudi women 'networking around the state' with the use of new media tools to publicise their defiance and demands for change. The 26 October Saudi women's driving campaign includes, in addition to women physically driving in the kingdom, a website, uploaded videos of women driving in the kingdom, photographs, an online petition and a comments board. The petition demands,

> In the midst of these regional and international developments and what is going on in the modern world of innovations in various fields of economics, society and culture, we as part of this total sum of humanity declare our ambition to develop and change for the betterment of ourselves and our homeland. As we find no clear justification for the government to ban adult female citizens who are able to drive a car from doing so, we call for the need to provide appropriate means to conduct driving tests for female citizens who want to be issued permits and that the government issue licenses for those women who do pass the driving test. And if female citizens do not pass the driving test then a driving license should not be issued to them, so that they are equal to men in this regard. Hence the ability to drive will be the only standard, regardless of the gender of the citizen. (<https://www.facebook.com/Women2DriveKSA/>)

By using the Internet to distribute their call for change, the Women2Drive movement has gained wide recognition in the global media (<http://www.youtube.com/watch?v=WcIojGwyZYo>) and has also garnered a complex web of supporters, crossing gender, social class and national boundaries. For example, in one video posted during the campaign, a woman driving in Saudi Arabia receives a 'thumbs up' from some male drivers that pass her (<http://www.huffingtonpost.com/2013/10/16/saudi-women-defying-drivi_n_4103375.html>). Women2 Drive makes active use of Twitter (<http://twitter.com/W2Drive/>) and Facebook (<http://www.facebook.com/SaudiWomenSpring>). One of the best-known responses to the campaign responsible for raising global awareness is the 'No Woman, No Drive' video. A satire by Hisham Fageeh, Fahad al-Butairi and Alaa Wardi, the YouTube video 'No Woman, No Drive' has gone viral (<http://www.youtube.com/watch?v=aZMbTFNp4wI>), achieving more than 14 million views since its posting on 26 October 2013. The video pokes fun at the driving law, to commemorate the Saudi women's day of resistance, and especially critiques a Saudi cleric's claim that women who drive put their reproductive organs in jeopardy. The video temporarily achieved 'top video' status on Reddit. In light of the social media campaign to support women's quest for change, *The Guardian* described the 26 October women's driving campaign as 'the best-organised social campaign ever seen in Saudi Arabia' (Black 2013).

While opposition to the Saudi state's driving laws by women is not new (the first public driving campaign occurred in 1990) and emerged prior to the country's first Internet connection (1994), public awareness of the movement both locally and globally has increased, given the amplification of calls for change online. Moreover, with global attention being paid to the issue, and increasingly widespread resistance within the kingdom, the Saudi state's willingness to crack down is on the wane. For example, one of the participants, Talama Alamiyi, expressed surprise and satisfaction at working around the state when she observed,

> One of the traffic policemen saw me and didn't stop me. I was scared, but when he just drove by and went away, I felt so happy, so reassured and more determined than ever to go out on the 26th. (Jamjoon 2013)

Figure 5.2   Committee for the Promotion of Virtue and Prevention of Vice headquarters, Riyadh, Saudi Arabia. Photo: Deborah L. Wheeler, 11 January 2013.

The cost of reimposing the status quo is high, perhaps impossible, as trumping state power increases citizen determination for change. New media practices and texts provide windows into political negotiations at the grass roots, on issues that matter both locally and globally, like the Saudi women's driving campaign. In January 2014, a Saudi colleague confided, 'I predict that women will be able to drive within the next five years' (conversation, 24 January 2014, Doha, Qatar). Moreover, one of the participants in the Women2Drive movement, Naseema al-Sada, observes, 'More people around the country seem to be warming up to the cause' (Byrnes 2014).

Women's use of social media for empowerment goes well beyond the Saudi driving campaign. For example, in 2012, a Saudi woman used YouTube to resist harassment by a *mutawah* (religious police working for the Committee for the Promotion of Virtue and Prevention of Vice) in a mall. The woman was wearing red nail polish, and the *mutawah* decided that this was considered sexually suggestive and a violation of public morality. The woman fought back, accusing him of sexual harassment and calling him a pervert for noticing her nail polish. She told him to leave her alone because she had rights, and King Abdullah had forbidden *mutawah* officers from harassing citizens in public. She threatened that if he didn't leave her alone, she was filming the whole encounter and the footage was going straight to the Internet. The encounter is available at <http://www.al-monitor.com/pulse/originals/2012/al-monitor/imagined-heroism-of-the-saudi-na.html>.

In the end, the Saudi government chastised the religious police officer, and the woman's act of defiance became one more sign of women's empowerment and change in the kingdom. One commentator observes,

> Saudi Arabia is not a country known for its women shouting 'I am free' and posting YouTube videos of themselves being assertive and defiant toward Committee members. The woman remained invisible in the clip while her phone camera followed the Haya agent and his comrades as they turned their backs and disappeared into the crowd of shoppers. Little did they know that the video of their encounter with this woman would draw hundreds of thousands of tweets and generate dozens of articles in the Arab and international press. The woman rocketed to fame as YouTube views topped one million. She is known now as the hero of the clip entitled '*Fatat al-Manakir*,' or 'The Nail Polish Girl.' (Al-Rasheed 2012)

A formal institutionalisation of women's empowerment in Saudi Arabia occurred in January 2013, when the late King Abdullah granted women one fifth of the seats in the Shura Council. The Shura Council acts in an advisory role to the king on issues of public policy and security. It is the highest political office the general public can achieve. The members of the assembly can propose draft laws to the king, but only the latter has the power to legislate. Represented in the Council are the nation's 'best and brightest', including doctors, lawyers, engineers, professors, retired civil servants, military officers and business leaders. Two of the women appointed are highly accomplished ruling family members. In the current Shura, 70% of members have PhDs, 50% of which are from US universities. While restrictions on women (including driving, and society telling them what they must or must not wear in public) remain severe, having women on the Shura Council may give women the opportunity to create change from within the government for the first time in the country's history. Some of the challenges which remain for women in Saudi Arabia include not being able to 'travel, work, study abroad, marry, get divorced or gain admittance to a public hospital without permission from a male guardian' (Al-Shihri 2013).

The Academy Award-nominated film *Wadjda*, made by a female Saudi filmmaker, and screened at embassies in Riyadh in order to qualify for the Academy Awards (2013), epitomises the situation of Saudi women. The film suggests that the bar is very high for women's empowerment, since institutions responsible for a woman's life and livelihood, all the way down to the family and primary school level, impose collective definitions of how a woman should act to guard her honour and reputation. Two of the rules depicted in the film are that women should not allow men to hear their voices, including laughter, and that girls are not allowed to ride bikes, to protect their virginity. The main character, Wadjda, however, uses a Quran recitation contest as a way to resist these conservative interpretations of women's public conduct. The film suggests that using Islam as a vehicle, women can carve out pathways to empowerment. In this same way, women in the Saudi Shura Council may find ways to use Islam in their redefinition of women's everyday life opportunities, from engaging in sport (Al Jazeera 2014), to working in retail shops (Wharton School of Business 2014), to driving a car (Byrnes 2014) and participating in governance (Al-Ahmedi 2014, Al-Shaqiran 2014). Social media gives Saudi women a public platform on which to organise, and with this tool they 'have become more engaged in political and civic actions, playing a critical, leading role in the rapid and historical changes sweeping the region' (Arab Social Media Report 2011).

Conclusion

While citizen resistance to bad governance intensifies with the diffusion and use of social media, the short- and long-term effects remain murky at best. Since, as Manuel Castells observes, 'few institutional systems can last long if they are predominantly based on sheer repression' (Castells 2007: 238), we may expect authoritarian states to be on the losing side of this battle with citizens, especially in an era of shrinking state resources, growing populations, global increases in the costs of grain and food imports, and volatility in oil markets, matched with explosive public spheres throughout the Middle East.

Civil wars, insurgencies, capital flight, refugee crises, terrorism and ecological breaches of sustainable food, water and energy demands all spell challenges for political stability in the region.

The contexts in which digital resistance occurs are increasingly fragile. As Howard and Hussain observe, however, 'it is not clear if the popular demand for change will result in new sustainable political institutions' (Howard and Hussain 2013: 3). In the meantime, we can watch the digital games people play and look for signs of lasting change, even in small forms. For what we could be witnessing is 'a zone of independent cultural and political action that is part of a society-wide reinvention of the political culture' of the Middle East, similar to what Jeffrey Goldfarb observed in Poland before the collapse of communism (Goldfarb 2012: 2). If so, social media may be the vehicle for increased resistance and greater effects on power relations over time, as more people obtain access, increased agency and voice. I feel privileged to have witnessed the historic transformation of Arab civic engagement and the subtle yet significant roles of new media technologies to encourage risk taking at the grass roots. I anticipate great disruptions to the status quo to continue as Middle Eastern citizens trade traditions of quietism for the power of voice.

6

FEAR THE STATE:
REPRESSION AND THE RISKS OF
RESISTANCE IN THE MIDDLE EAST

The element of fear is there. The people are afraid of the government, but the government is as afraid of the people. (Abdel Wahab el-Messery, Kefaya organiser, 6 April 2008, quoted in Slackman 2008)

Introduction

This chapter explores state responses to citizen empowerment in Egypt, Jordan and Kuwait in order to add a more complete analysis of the increasing costs of resistance in the Middle East. While a strong case has been made for the ways in which citizens in the Middle East leverage new media to create voice and agency to solve problems and promote opportunities in their everyday lives (society-centric cyber-optimism), what has yet to be explored in detail are the strategies Arab states use to discourage citizens from fully exercising their powers (state-centric cyber-pessimism). Whereas cyber-optimists stress the liberating effects of new media use for the marginalised (Shirky 2011), cyber-pessimists focus on the ways in which these same tools strengthen the coercive capacity of the state (Morozov 2011b). This chapter is a bow to the cyber-pessimists.

As a recent text on the ways in which digital power increases state surveillance capacity observes, 'before anybody can be disciplined and punished, they need to be identified and sorted' (Ansorge 2016). There is a lot of digitally

Figure 6.1   Jordanian Royal Guardsmen, Amman, Jordan.
Photo: Deborah L. Wheeler, July 2016.

enabled identifying, sorting and punishing going on in Egypt, Jordan and Kuwait, as explored in this chapter. The same digital media tools which help citizens to have a voice likewise empower the state to isolate these voices, and to police and punish those who dare to challenge the status quo. For example, reflecting on state responses to bloggers in Iran, Annabelle Sreberny and Gholam Khiabany argue that 'because the state is increasingly wary of losing control' it 'does its best to suppress the potential of new communications technologies' (Sreberny and Khiabany 2010: 86).

In spite of the disruptions people have caused in the region (or perhaps because of them?), the Arab state has leveraged digital tools to discourage oppositional behaviour, with great personal harm to individuals who rebel. For example, a digital surveillance tool called Scout 'uses about 60 algorithms and tracks a vocabulary list of about 10,000 words' in order to locate potential 'insider threats' (Parloff 2016). Companies and governments can use Scout to 'measure employees' [or citizens'] disgruntlement' by using 'an algorithm based on linguistic tells found to connote feelings of victimization, anger, and blame' (ibid.). While we don't know specifically which countries in the Middle East have used Scout, we do know that the company responsible for developing the program, Stroz Friedberg, has branch offices throughout the Middle East (Stroz Friedberg 2015a) and as recently as 2015 released a 'risk assessment' of Tunisia, UAE and Egypt (Stroz Friedberg 2015b).

Similarly, a company called Hacking Team delivers 'offensive intrusion software' with which to defend against insider threats and cyber-crime. With the company's main tool, Da Vinci, known to be in use by both the UAE and the Moroccan governments, states can 'monitor a suspect's cell phone conversations, emails, and Skype calls, and even spy on the target through his or her webcam and a microphone' (Jeffries 2013). Moreover, a piece of software called Stealth Falcon has been identified by Citizen Lab at the University of Toronto as a state-sponsored effort by the UAE to target journalists and dissidents (Marczak and Scott-Railton 2016). In addition, a leaked article in *Al-Watan*, an Egyptian newspaper, revealed that the Egyptian government had issued an open tender for 'real-time social media surveillance technology' that included a list of 'destructive ideas' the government sought to monitor (Radsch 2015). Under the state's firm grip, with the use of cyber tools, the marginalised can be sorted, and silenced, as the deep state discourages resistance through coercion (Filiu 2015).

Those who are caught resisting the Arab state face stringent counter-revolutionary strategies including torture (Human Rights Watch 2016), draconian changes to press and public gathering laws (Wilson 2014) and long prison sentences (Snyder 2014), often delivered by military courts (McRobie 2014). Some opposition members have lost employment (Huckabee 2015), including professors and journalists in Jordan and Egypt. Some opposition members have been stripped of their citizenship in Kuwait (Kholaif 2014). Others, found guilty of membership of the Muslim Brotherhood, have been sentenced to death in Egypt, sentenced to prison in the UAE and deported from Kuwait.

For example, as of November 2015, Egypt has sentenced 588 people to death, and in '72% of cases' the charge of death was linked with 'attending pro-democracy protests' (Green 2015). In Egypt under Sisi, it is illegal to protest, and just being present at a demonstration can result in significant jail time, or being shot to death. If arrested, citizens and foreigners are likely to be tortured (Kingsley 2014). In 2016 an Italian graduate student studying independent labour unions for his PhD died while in Egyptian custody after allegedly being arrested in Tahrir Square, Cairo, on the fifth anniversary of the Egyptian Arab Spring revolution, 25 January 2016 (Spencer 2016).

The Arab state faces an era of renewed challenges, and thus demands for change have been crushed swiftly. Efforts to maintain the status quo, however, have not improved the state's legitimacy. An authoritarian smack in the mouth for having a voice does not breed love and respect for the state, but rather enhances those conditions which encourage opposition in the first place. For example, recent protests in Madaba, Jordan, by unemployed youths were swiftly crushed by the regime with bullets, tear gas and arrests (Younes 2016). Repression might clear youths from the streets temporarily, but a coercive response does not breed loyalty to the regime, nor does it end the problem of youth joblessness. Rather it delays resolution, deferring dreams. As Langston Hughes aptly advises, dreams deferred are particularly explosive (Hughes 2004).

This chapter has three main messages. One is an argument that the Arab state is profoundly fearful of its digitally enabled public, as proven by the severity of repression post-Arab Spring. The second message is to not overestimate digital people power. As demonstrated in this chapter, the people's will to resist is easily crushed and punished by the recalcitrant state. Especially when opposition is expressed in collective movement or by formal organisations, the state is swift to act punitively. The authoritarian state, so long as it maintains a monopoly on coercive power, is unlikely to tolerate openly oppositional voices. The third argument, however, advises that we question the longevity of the coercive state because maintaining stability through brute force enhances desires to rebel.

History is full of examples of dictatorships falling when people lose their fear, and risk even life itself in attempts to regain their dignity. As so many political thinkers have stressed throughout the centuries, states that use violence to maintain stability show signs of increased fragility through a loss of legitimacy. Barrington Moore reminds us that there is a human 'right of resistance to unjust authority' (Moore 1966: 415). We saw such rights exercised in 2011, throughout the Arab world, and even if the results of resistance were disappointing in terms of solving problems (or perhaps because the returns for risk were so measly), these events are reminders of public explosiveness, not easily neutralised in the long term by increased repression.

The main conclusion of this analysis is that the increase in state repression is a sign of weakness and fear of the digitally enabled public. For every act of opposition there is a potential for state repression designed to intimidate those who would challenge the regime. With each act of repression, however, grievances and the will to resist also increase. Exploring that dynamic relationship is the main purpose of this chapter. I argue that the greater the public voice for change, the harder the crackdown by the state. The more brutal the state becomes, however, the less viable it remains. In all three countries, as explored below, states are fighting to secure an increasingly volatile public sphere, with increasingly draconian strategies, and uncertain futures, as discontent swells.

Characteristics of the Arab State

Kuwait, Jordan and Egypt, as Arab states, share some historical similarities. Darwish and Zartman highlight a series of general principles which characterise the Arab state. For example, the stability of Arab states is typically predicated on strongman rule. This is why the Arab Spring revolutions were so threatening to the states that remained. Strongmen fell in Tunisia, Egypt, Yemen and Libya in quick succession. 'Who would be the next ruler to fall?' was the sentiment that encouraged Arab heads of state to fight for the status quo through intimidation methods. Even under normal conditions, the political culture of the Arab world is based upon 'a politics of control in which there is no [or little] participation' (Darwish and Zartman 2015).

The strength and stability of the Arab state is based upon two factors, the strength or weakness of opposition forces within society balanced by the effectiveness of the state in responding to challenges, using both coercion and appeasement to maintain strongman rule (ibid.). What makes the stability of Arab countries so tenuous post-Arab Spring is that state effectiveness is weakened by budgetary crisis, regional instability and civil war or domestic unrest, all of which discourage tourism and foreign direct investment. So state effectiveness is declining. At the same time, opposition to the state has not been neutralised by repression. Opposition may be less overt, and organised, less present in the public squares, and riskier, but the desire for change, for a better life, and better governance, the hopes of the Arab Spring, are even more pronounced in the face of being so close to a better future for the region and losing it. As Marc Lynch observes, 'The Arab uprising failed primarily because the regimes they challenged killed it' (Lynch 2016: xviii). Even if stability can be temporarily regained through repression and strongman rule, this does not solve the problem of illegitimacy. Stability does not mean that Arab states 'govern well', nor is stability 'equated with legitimacy', as Darwish and Zartman appropriately observe (Darwish and Zartman 2015). Moreover, as Guazzone and Pioppi observe, even before the Arab Spring revolutions, Arab states faced 'internal challenges ranging from financial deficits to legitimacy crises and military interventions' (Guazzone and Pioppi 2009), and the instability that resulted from the popular uprisings has only increased the challenges. Such security challenges are leveraged to justify authoritarian rule. For example, Marc Lynch observes that, in efforts to diffuse future 'existential challenges' to the state as we saw during the Arab Spring uprisings, remaining leaders 'set out to ensure that it wouldn't happen again by doubling down or intensifying some of their worst practices' (Lynch 2015: 4). Such strong-arm tactics, however, indicate a loss of legitimacy more than they improve stability, making the future of state society relations in the Middle East explosive.

Of all the governments that have collapsed or succumbed to civil war, none of them are monarchies. This observation leads to the conclusion that Kuwait and Jordan are potentially more secure than Egypt is. Oil wealth also seems to be a stabilising factor for regimes blessed with the ability to offer enhanced services and benefits to create loyalty pacts between ruler and ruled, which would imply that Kuwait is more secure than Jordan or Egypt. The decline in the price of oil, in Kuwait's case, and the increase in fuel costs, in Jordan's case (subsidies have been lifted and taxes increased to bridge deficits), means that even monarchies are experiencing enhanced threats to their legitimacy. Given an increase in repression in all three countries, we can conclude that a shared authoritarian response reveals shared weakness. To test these hypotheses, we now turn to the case studies.

Egypt

To be a citizen in Sisi's Egypt (28 May 2014 to the present) means having few rights and much hardship, an especially demoralising state of being, after the Egyptian public made such collective sacrifices for change culminating in the overthrow of President Mubarak on 25 January 2011. Working collectively to replace strongman rule with democracy, the Egyptian public had many dreams about the country's future, including more equally distributed wealth, better rights for women, more inclusive democracy, rights for workers, and a political system that actually responded to people's needs (Mellor 2016).

While the first elections post-Arab Spring brought Muhammad Morsi to power, an astounding accomplishment when viewed in light of the persecuted past of the Muslim Brotherhood in Egypt, his presidency would be marred by inexperience, and derailed by continued SCAF (Supreme Council of the Armed Forces) manipulation of politics and the economy (Wickham 2013). A coup to remove Morsi from power, with quasi-public support from old-regime loyalists and some liberals, resulted in enhanced military control over public life, abruptly ending Egypt's democratic experiment. While those who opposed an encroachment of Islamist values into Egyptian everyday life with Morsi at the helm initially supported the reimposition of secular rule, no political activist has been spared the wrath of the new military dictatorship. As secular activist Ahmad Maher, co-founder of the April 6 Youth Movement, arrested in 2013 for violating Law 107 (no public gathering without a licence), noted from prison, 'everything we rose against in the January 25th revolution is back and worse than before' (Stork 2015).

Egypt currently has more than 40,000 people in jail for political crimes, and the economy continues to fail. Internal divisions have spawned new waves of domestic terrorism. While people fear the state, their hatred boils, promising future instability with each repressive act. A recent *Economist* article entitled, ominously, 'The Ruining of Egypt' observes, 'nowhere is the poisonous mix of demographic stress, political repression and economic incompetence more worrying than in Egypt under its strongman, Abdel-Fattah al-Sisi' (*The Economist* 2016).

Egypt's military dictator: not welcome here

Figure 6.2   Anti-Sisi poster of the Egypt Solidarity Initiative (<https://egyptsolidarityinitiative. files.wordpress.com/2015/07/sisi_notwelcome_7375501.png?w=1200>).

One of the powers of state is to legislate so as to regulate public life. While typically the concept of 'rule of law' implies the protection of citizens from what Weber labelled 'Qadi justice' (Deflem 2008: 37–58), in Sisi's Egypt, law serves the state and violates people's rights. As Dalia Fahmy, a member of the Egyptian Rule of Law Association, observes of Sisi's Egypt, 'the law here is a system that is not protecting the citizenry, but rather protecting the state' (Al Jazeera 2015a).

Use of the legislature to dissuade public unrest in Sisi's Egypt includes an anti-protest law passed in 2013 which makes it illegal to launch political demonstrations, even in places of worship, without permission from the police, obtained at least three days prior to any protest or demonstration. In addition, police are granted rights under the law to break up protests with force, including 'water cannon, tear gas, and birdshot' (Fick and Saleh 2013). Thus in Egypt, where five years ago men, women and children, young and old, rich and poor, Islamist and secular, Christian and Muslim, all poured into the public sphere to peacefully demand the end of the regime, today such actions could lead to arrest or, tragically, being legally shot on the spot by security forces. In effect, 'security forces have been given free rein to use excessive force, including live ammunition against demonstrators' (Samaan and Sanchez 2016). Expressing one's freedom might cost you your life. In fact, more than 1,000 people have died at peaceful protests as a result of police brutality since the 2011 uprising (Al Jazeera 2015b). Moreover, more than 120 people have died from torture while in police custody or in prison (Stevenson 2015).

The use of increasingly repressive methods to quiet public challenges to Sisi's regime resulted in the following violations, according to the US Department of State Human Rights Report:

> Excessive use of force by security forces, deficiencies in due process, and the suppression of civil liberties. Excessive use of force included unlawful killings and torture. Due process problems included the excessive use of preventative custody and pretrial detention, the use of military courts to try civilians, and trials involving hundreds of defendants in which authorities did not present evidence on an individual basis. Civil liberties problems included societal and government restrictions on freedoms of expression and the press, as well as on the freedoms of assembly and association. (Department of State 2015)

The resulting 'reign of terror' suggests the degree to which the state fears a new revolution (Al Jazeera 2016). As Egyptian human rights activist Gamal Eid argues, 'There is no law or power or tank that can stop the anger of the Egyptian people in the streets as long as the demands for the revolution are not met' (Fick and Saleh 2013).

In addition to an anti-protest law, an anti-terrorism law expands the state's legal right to spy on the public including what they say online. The law also limits journalists from publishing stories about terrorism which differ from the official state narrative. Terrorism as defined under the decree is so broad it includes any act of civil disobedience (Human Rights Watch 2016).

In a decree designed to give the government greater control over universities, Sisi can now appoint university presidents and deans. In addition, students' freedom of association and expression have been severely limited. Twenty students have been killed while protesting on university campuses,

790 students have been arrested, and more than 800 have been expelled (Ali 2016). Students who are arrested are often tortured in custody, and security forces increasingly patrol campuses to intimidate would-be protesters (Ismail 2016).

The severity of state repression suggests an uncertain future for Egypt. The more the state abuses citizens, especially those inspired by the short-term tastes of empowerment enabled by the 25 January revolution, the more the state encourages another revolution. Ushering in even more hardship for all Egyptians, and producing more animosity among citizens for the state, Sisi's strongman rule remains fragile. With tourism down, the pound losing value, foreign direct investment wary of making a bet on corruption and repression, and with more than a third of Egyptian youths out of work, including many who are educated, the authoritarian bargain, trading rights for stability and economic recovery, has not materialised. A recent Brookings report observes that 'Sisi came to power promising security, stability and economic prosperity in exchange for near total political control'; unfortunately, 'he failed to deliver on all three fronts' (Ghafar 2016). Perhaps Marc Lynch provides the most concise prediction of Egypt's future when he observes more generally, 'The Arab uprisings of 2011 were only one episode in a generational challenge to a failed political order' (Lynch 2016: 254). Thus, he predicts, and this author agrees, 'there will be more rounds of upheaval, more state failures, more sudden regime collapses, more insurgencies, and more proxy wars' (ibid.). Lynch advises us not to bet on the autocrats, but instead to go with the underdog, 'those Arabs seeking a more democratic future' (ibid.).

Jordan

Jordan has had a sharp downturn in freedom of expression and civil liberties post-Arab Spring. On a recent trip to the kingdom (summer 2016), however, I experienced citizens regularly expressing their willingness to suppress their desires for political change in exchange for stability (interviews conducted in July 2016). Gratitude to the king for making their country safe and secure in spite of regional turmoil was regularly expressed in interviews I conducted with everyday Jordanians. Several people I spoke to celebrated the king's altruism. In defending the king, they paraphrased their monarch, who in a speech said, 'the minute my people want me to step down, I am ready to give up the throne. This is a tough job, and I do it not for my own glory, but to serve my people. If they don't want me, I will leave' (interviews with two Jordanian citizens, July 2016, Amman).

The tools with which the Jordanian monarchy keeps its public safe, however, do not express altruism but rather authoritarianism, characteristic of most Arab states, whether run by monarchs or former generals. These tools include checkpoints, searches at hotels and malls, restrictions on freedom of expression, association and movement, and stiff punishments for those who breach red lines. The red lines have been drawn more boldly and enforced more readily since the Arab Spring unrest, and in the face of threats from an influx of over a million and a half Syrian refugees. Moreover, the fact that more than 2,000 Jordanians have travelled to Syria to join jihadist networks in the fight against Assad, and the discovery of ISIS cells in Jordan, has made the government proactively repressive towards Islamist activists, similar to security policies in Egypt. Thus in spite of liberalising legislation, such as electoral reform and lifting the penalties on unlicensed public gatherings, the Jordanian state has cracked down with new cyber laws and counter-terrorism legislation, both of which have been used to punish liberals and Islamists for confronting the regime and its allies, and to justify government crackdowns on protests.

As in Egypt, the more the Jordanian state fears the public, the more brutal it becomes. The legitimacy of the monarchy, however, makes Jordan's authoritarianism more benign, as the majority of the public is compliant to preserve state stability. As one observer notes, 'Even in its darkest hours, the Jordanian version of the security state never reached the level of authoritarian police state' characteristic of Sisi's Egypt (Ryan 2014: 52).

While it appears Jordan is more stable and legitimate than Egypt, evidence suggests that the two countries are more similar than they appear on the surface. Both operate using a wide range of police state tactics, because they fear the public and desire to maintain security. Both countries hold political prisoners, torture those in custody, imprison those who express opposition to the regime or the country's allies, and have used the legislature to protect the state at the expense of individual rights. In both countries people have died at protests through excessive use of force by security forces, and occasionally those arrested have died in police custody. Both countries are experiencing economic hardship, and have received refugees that place strain on existing resources. Both countries have severely limited freedom of speech and manage public information, including the use of cyber spy technologies. Both countries have an organised, vocal and oppositional Islamist movement, and have used counter-terrorism legislation to crush it (Egypt) or contain its spread and influence (Jordan).

The differences between Jordan and Egypt are matters of scale. Egypt is more than thirteen times the size of Jordan, geographically and demographically. And while there are some significant differences in political culture, in terms of police state tactics, frequency is the major difference, not type. If we control for relative population size, Jordan is not that different from Egypt. It could be that Jordan is simply a better police state, with better trained, more professional and less politicised security forces (Ryan 2014). This could explain why Jordan did not have a revolution in 2011 – and in fact has never experienced a revolution or a successful coup – while Egypt has experienced, in its modern history, two revolutions (1952 and 2011), a coup (2013) and a presidential assassination (1981). Maybe it is the skill of Jordan's security forces, the smaller size of the population and the more limited geographic reach, more than the leader's hereditary title, that explains why Jordan appears more stable.

Differences in political culture exist. In Jordan, leaders come to power through heredity and title, and rule until they die. In Egypt, following the abdication of King Farouk in 1953, rulers come to power mostly through their leadership in the military and as a result of their own cunning. In Jordan, leaders are born into the right to rule. In Egypt, right to rule has to be earned. Even if Jordan appears more stable because of the legitimacy awarded the monarchy, to see the state behave in ways patterning a military dictatorship is disturbing.

The fact that the US and Great Britain consider both countries and their leaders close allies, that we share intelligence, cooperate militarily and sell arms to both countries, makes the US and Great Britain complicit in the brutalities committed in the name of stability. This is especially ironic when those being tortured often are in prison for advocating Western-style democracy. Any foreign country that lends support to police states is partially responsible for the brutalities committed by these rulers in the name of security. This message is communicated by the poster of Sisi as 'not welcome in the UK' distributed by an Egyptian opposition group. If we wonder why people at the grass roots don't see countries like the US and the UK as 'friends', it is because of these countries' support of the people who are torturing, harassing and sometimes killing them, their friends and their family members.

So the differences in the practice of governance in Jordan are really matters of degree when compared with Egypt. For example, while Jordan has an estimated 180 Islamist prisoners, Egypt has more than 40,000 (Abuqudairi 2014). Whereas more than 1,000 have died at protests in Egypt through the excessive use of force by security forces, in Jordan only a handful of people have been killed at protests.

The human rights record of Jordan, as described by the US Department of State in 2015, reads similarly to the report on Egypt. For example, the report observes that Jordan has 'restrictions on the freedom of expression, including the detention of journalists' which 'limit the ability of citizens and the media to criticize government policies and officials' (Department of State 2015). There are also, according to the report, 'allegations of torture by security and government officials' (ibid.). Moreover, 'restrictions on freedom of association and assembly, poor prison conditions, arbitrary arrest and denial of due process' exist in both countries (ibid.).

If police state tactics and human rights violations are similar in Jordan and Egypt, this may indicate that the countries are equally vulnerable to mass mobilisation and fragility. According to one Jordanian journalist, who has been harassed by the Jordanian internal security forces, 'any type of reform and discussion about it has been stifled' (Radsch 2015) by police state tactics.

A conversation with a Jordanian taxi driver in the summer of 2016 illustrates that, in spite of state repression, animosity remains. He observes,

> We have no freedom here in Jordan; Rania is 'Ali Baba', her husband is 'Ali Baba'. He has ten palaces you know. We don't even have one. We can curse God and our neighbours, but curse the king and you go straight to prison. I am only talking to you openly because you are Americans. If you were Arab, I would have to keep my mouth shut. Freedom has never been here in Jordan, and it never will. The present is bad and the future will be

worse. I want to go to America to visit my uncle. He lives in Texas. He is a big business man, and my cousin is a doctor, but I can't afford to apply for a visa, and so many people who do apply don't get them. I didn't go to university; I couldn't, and there is no hope for me as I am already thirty-two, a grown man. I am even a 'real' Jordanian, not a Palestinian, not a Syrian, a 'real, original Jordanian', and look at my terrible life. No hope and no future. (Conversation with a Jordanian taxi driver, Amman, 10 July 2016)

With hope dying, and misery rising, the future of Jordan remains uncertain at best. When strong-arm tactics replace concessions in exchange for loyalty, potential for instability is the result. While Jordan is not Egypt, and the king has temporarily bought off or discouraged through repression any overt opposition to his rule (as detailed in Chapter 3), the country remains very fragile. Every act of oppression committed by the state in the name of security narrows the distance between Jordan and Egypt.

Kuwait

If Kuwait is potentially more stable than Jordan or Egypt, because of the monarchy and oil wealth, why do we see similar patterns of protest, and repression? If repression is a sign of state defensiveness and weakness in the face of more overt opposition, and a precipitating factor for decline in legitimacy, the presence of police state tactics in Kuwait is cause for concern, especially when the country prides itself on being regionally distinct for its relatively open political culture. Moreover, the national image of Kuwait is tarnished by police state tactics. Kuwaitis cast themselves as natural born leaders. They see their country as a light unto the other oil states in the neighbourhood, as a model of emerging democracy and stability to follow. National culture projects images of being reserved (except when road-raging or racing), rich, forward thinking, a place where buildings glitter and citizens sparkle with race cars and gemstones glitzing their lives.

So why are the leaders of Kuwait stripping citizens of parliamentary immunity, revoking citizenship of opposition members, changing legislation to limit freedom of expression and association, including online activities, and shutting down newspapers, including *Al-Watan*, a newspaper that until 2015 had been in print for more than thirty-five years? If Kuwait is so rich, and democratic, why is the state increasing commodities prices by eliminating state subsidies on food, water and energy, and arresting people for their tweets and protests? What will be the results in terms of public explosiveness? Do increases in repression indicate increasingly overt opposition to the Sabah monarchy? Does a terrorist attack on a Shi'i mosque by ISIS in June 2015, which killed twenty-six people, including children, indicate more widespread support for the Islamic State than was previously known? Do decreases in state-distributed oil wealth indicate that even Kuwait, both a monarchy and a petro-economy, is not stable?

The US Department of State 2015 Human Rights Report faults Kuwait for a similar pattern of repression as exists in Jordan and Egypt. For example, the Kuwaiti government is charged with limiting freedom of speech and assembly, not allowing citizens to change their government, prisoner abuse, arbitrary arrest and extra-judicial deportation (mostly of foreign labourers) (Department of State 2015). New cyber-legislation gives the state authority to block websites and to prosecute those who post things that threaten state security broadly defined. Cyber-crimes Law 63, which took effect in January 2016, in addition to the Press and Publications Law, revised in 2006, together give the state the right to punish anyone who, either online or off, says anything the state finds threatening.

Given the increase in state-insecurity in Kuwait, an increase in repressive behaviour is expected, given the argument of this chapter. But what is not expected is that Kuwait was hypothesised to be more stable than Jordan and Egypt because it has a monarchy and oil wealth. Overt increases in human rights violations, new legislation to protect the state at the expense of citizens' rights, and decreases in state distribution of oil wealth, in addition to budget deficits, make Kuwait look more similar to Jordan and Egypt sustainability- and security-wise than was predicted.

Thus what we see in Kuwait is 'something of an anomaly' (Freer 2015: 1). We see a country that is less liberal and rich than its national identity projects. We see a country that is richer and supposedly more liberal than Jordan and Egypt, and yet similar police state tactics and fiscal belt-tightening are found in Kuwait, suggesting that oil wealth and a political culture of liberalism are not enough to create stability in the current Arab regional environment. As a result, a resurgence of authoritarian responses is common throughout the case studies, regardless of differences in political culture and economic capabilities. Surprising indeed.

Conclusion

Ten years from now, when we read over this chapter, we will either see how good it was back then, that some states remained secure, or we will breathe a sigh of relief that enlightened leadership has returned calm to the majority of states. The challenges Arab states face, resource-wise, in a context of abundant oil and subsequently low prices, with the threat of climate change looming large, population growing out of control, sovereign wealth declining, unemployment rising, inflation rampant, women rising up, youths demanding change, Islamists weighing in on the best path forward, external powers using the region for proxy wars and self-interest, and states increasingly on the defensive, mean that the future of the region is not looking very rosy, for reasons explored in the preceding pages. The problems remain grand, public morale is low, the state is increasingly threatened by its own ineptitude, and the challengers to the status quo are many, even if partially repressed. The road ahead for the Middle East state is bumpy at best.

In defence of the state, we might agree that it is more desirable to visit Jordan, with its balmy beaches, beautiful reefs, bustling markets and relative stability, than to be a guest or citizen in Syria, a country with an absence of security, and much risk in everyday life. Tourism is up in Jordan and non-existent in Syria, and can serve as an indicator of why the state matters.

When faced with a choice between security and liberty, those in the Middle East are increasingly willing to accept the former and give up the latter, at least until things calm down a bit, especially when the sustained impacts of people's resistance in the Middle East are underwhelming. In most Arab countries, although opposition has been overt and potentially destabilising, the return for the risk has been paltry, except perhaps in Tunisia, where revolution has not led to counter-revolution or civil war, but rather to 'real' democratic change. In the wider Middle East, reforms are few, while crackdowns have been widespread.

A Moroccan blogger, Hisham al-Miraat, who works for the Association for Digital Rights in addition to being a physician, observes that the Arab Spring uprisings were a wake-up call for ossified regimes. They showed previously insulated leaders that the Internet could 'undermine the structures they had spent centuries building' (quoted in Radsch 2015). Most telling of all, he observes, 'But the Internet is ubiquitous; you can't just shut it down' (ibid.).

The contest between ruler and ruled will continue to animate unrest in the region. Many more people will die. Hundreds will go to prison and be tortured for having a voice. Some will be deported, or forced to flee to escape prosecution. These brave individuals will risk everything to stand up for their fellow citizens' rights. Future generations will inherit the small openings for change created by these rebels, even though the authoritarian state will suppress their will to resist, raising the costs of having a voice, but not silencing calls for a better, more dignified life.

CONCLUSION

Democracy will not come
Today, this year
Nor ever
Through compromise and fear.
(Langston Hughes)

Politics is the ability to foretell what is going to happen tomorrow, next week, next month and next year. And to have the ability afterwards to explain why it didn't happen. (Sir Winston Churchill)

When this book was conceived, sometime in 2003, the initial intent was to construct a series of case studies with which to provide comparative perspectives on transitions to the information age in authoritarian Middle Eastern countries. The goal was to investigate, using ethnographic methods, whether or not findings of a similar investigation, launched in 1997 in Kuwait, would have any meaning with the passage of time (and an increase in Internet diffusion rates) across national boundaries. Until 2011, the working title of this manuscript was 'Information (without) Revolution in the Middle East?'. The placement of the question mark at the end was important, as it indicated a growing concern that the changes in everyday life observed in my fieldwork would gather steam and explode. What began as relatively low expectations (1997–2004) for the political importance of people's resistance using new media tools intensified, leading to questions about regional stability as we barrelled towards the Arab Spring (2005–11), for reasons explored systematically in Chapter 1.

The initial indications in Egypt, Jordan and Kuwait were that something politically transformative was occurring (explored in Chapters 2 to 4) as a result of 'enhanced freedom and voice', linked with Internet use by those interviewed for this study. Two conversations in Cairo in 2004 (as analysed in the Introduction) were the first indicators of more enhanced civic engagement for this researcher. In 2004, I wondered if this discursive explosiveness would catch fire and spread, which with hindsight seems like a premonition. As I type these last words, the disappointment with the Arab state's counter-revolutionary efforts (as explored in Chapter 6) suggests the need for a new title. If this book were written today with evidence of new media resistance collected between 2011 and 2016, the title might be 'Revolution Undone: The Resurgence of Authoritarianism in the Middle East (except in Tunisia)'.

Do the findings of Chapter 6 mean that scholars of Middle East politics can expect stability to return, with the Arab police state as puppet-master, reminiscent of Saddam's Iraq, and Hafiz al-Assad's Syria? Are state-society relations in Sisi's Egypt prescriptive for other regimes struggling to reinstate the status quo? Or should we interpret such counter-revolutionary strategies, compounded by continued regional instability in Syria, Yemen and Libya, and sub-surface explosiveness in Saudi Arabia, Kuwait and Jordan, as indicators of more revolutions to come? I agree with Marc Lynch: we should see dictator-induced stability as an illusion, and vote for the regional democrats (whether Islamist, liberal or both; see Binder 1988), because the unravelling is just beginning (Lynch 2016). The problems that brought Middle Eastern citizens into the streets have not been solved but rather aggravated by the resurgent police state. Thus we can expect more unrest, more disgruntlement and enhanced opposition. With every act of torture, arbitrary arrest, or punishment for Facebook postings or tweets; for every stripped citizenship case, every violation of human rights; for every youth unemployed, or underemployed, empowered by extra access to time, technology and hopelessness; for every woman who wants to be respected and enabled to contribute to society's improvement, and every parent who worries about the next generation's future, we can expect demands for change. Moreover, an increase in state repression encourages subtle acts of resistance, as analysed throughout this text, as a means to have a voice while avoiding direct confrontation with the state.

Originally this manuscript included a case study on Tunisia, entitled 'Why Tunisia, Why Tunisia First?'. It reflected on the causes of an Arab Spring revolution in a state with an authoritarian leader and a highly repressive political environment, but a large middle class, progressive gender policies and beautiful beaches. Unfortunately, the data collected for the Tunisian case study had been gathered in 2000 (too dated to be credible) and did not include systematic interviews with Internet users (violating the criteria for systematic comparison with the other cases). The fact that in Tunisia alone the Arab Spring revolution has not devolved into greater authoritarian control or civil war, and melded a functioning coalition government, makes the country exceptional. In future research I plan to explore the Tunisian puzzle, to determine if the exception that is Tunisia might rather be the rule for the region with the addition of time. Since this is a big puzzle, I invite others to join me. Many hands make light work.

The words of Langston Hughes and Winston Churchill quoted at the beginning of this chapter highlight the main messages of this book. Don't give in and don't be afraid, because democracy will not come today from compromise (Kuwait and Jordan) or fear (Egypt). And unless circumstances become explosive again, creating a context in which people's voices overtly matter in the Middle East, democracy is not likely tomorrow either. Predictions that Internet use would lead to more open, democratic politics have failed to materialise, especially in Arab authoritarian contexts, again with the possible exception of Tunisia. Explaining why the democratic waves did not overcome the Arab state has become a more fruitful line of inquiry once again. Civil war eats away at Yemen, Syria and Libya; enhanced repression holds old infrastructures together in Bahrain and Egypt; and cosmetic reforms (and state retribution leveraged against rogue individuals) keep the status quo afloat in Kuwait, Jordan and other monarchies like Saudi Arabia, UAE and Morocco. Sir Winston Churchill challenges us to explain why predictions for a democratic wave, spreading in the Middle East with new media use, didn't prove sustainable.

Future scholarship will need to explain why participatory governance failed (or was temporarily uprooted) in spite of the most pronounced citizen demands for dignity, justice and bread ever witnessed. Moreover, scholars will have their gaze drawn to Tunisia, the puzzle. Tiny and relatively marginalised, Tunisia was the spark that started the current waves of unrest in the region. It's the country that provides hope for better governance in the future. Yet the fact that life inside the North African state remains difficult for most, that the country provides many foreign fighters for ISIS, and that jihadi violence has successfully targeted foreign tourists braving the instability to see such a beautiful country gives pause to optimism.

The authoritarianism and civil unrest that characterises the contemporary Middle East is not new, although the intensity and geography of these common traits have shifted. Egypt is more authoritarian under Sisi than ever; Syria and Libya have gone from stable police states to civil war; Iraq remains a mess; police state tactics have intensified in Kuwait, UAE, Saudi Arabia and Jordan; Yemen is closer to being a failed state than in the past. And access to the Internet continues to grow.

As I type these final words, the main message of this book remains the same: in spite of all the changes (or lack thereof) at the big institutional level in the region, new media tools are continuously leveraged, both before and after the Arab Spring, by citizens in the Middle East. With these tools, they carve out new spaces for agency and voice in spite of the risks (as explored in Chapter 5). Citizens use new media tools in the practice of everyday-life power struggles, and researchers are called to interpret the micro-political contests in which this resistance occurs, because mobilisation in the Middle East has its own trajectory. What begins as an exercise of voice online has a way of seeping through the power structures in the home, at work, in leisure practices, and on to the streets.

The harbingers of important political change, especially in authoritarian contexts, can emerge in unexpected or uncelebrated locations, with voices so quiet they almost are unheard. But these quiet voices are the most dangerous, because they are hard to police, nearly impossible to silence and, when they gather steam, highly explosive and damaging, given their widespread practice.

The best way not to miss the next revolution is to join the struggle through the use of ethnographic research methods, hanging out with the dispossessed and disgruntled, the aspirational, to watch their agency transformed by their use of new media tools. Some of this can be accomplished through virtual ethnography (Hine 2000), but there is no substitute for the insights gained while just living in a context – sitting in traffic, paying exorbitant prices for wilted produce, watching films heavily censored (and then feeling empowered by buying and streaming the full version to see what was missed), listening to taxi drivers diss the regime, having a young woman confide in you her aspirations to run for parliament, listening to the voices that drive the future of the Middle East in their own individual, idiosyncratic ways.

Like hot pita straight from the oven belt, lamb so fresh and tender that it melts in your mouth, and *kunafa* so sweet and syrupy that it sends your blood sugar soaring, there are many benefits to being a part of one's research context. Even if only because of the food, and the small voices of future opposition, I am optimistic about a new Middle East replacing the current season of discontent. One thing remains true: the Middle East will surprise you. Like a Cairo gun shop in Zamalek next to a cyber café (see front cover), democratic Tunisia next to police state Egypt, and a Guy Fawkes mask (resist) next to an 'I Love Jordan' T-shirt (comply), the Middle East is a context of strange juxtapositions, rewarding to explore.

Figure C.1 A call to resist, next to love for the state.
Photo: Deborah L. Wheeler, Amman, July 2016.

APPENDIX: INTERNET USER INTERVIEW QUESTIONS

1. Gender?
2. Age?
3. Religion?
4. Marital status?
5. Highest level of education obtained?
6. Age when started using the Internet?
7. Who taught you to use the Internet?
8. Have you ever taught anyone to use the Internet? If so, whom?
9. Do you have Internet access at:
    Home?
    Work?
    School/university?
10. Where are you most likely to use the Internet?
11. Are you employed?
12. Number of hours per week you use the Internet?
13. What do you use the Internet for?
    Email
    Chatting
    Gaming
    Health-related concerns
    To get advice

For religious purposes
Music downloads
News sites
For study/research
For work/business
For shopping
Other:

14. Has the Internet changed your life? If so, how?
15. Did you receive computer training at school, university or on the job?
16. Do you read a daily newspaper? If so, which one?
17. Are you comfortable using English?
18. Do you prefer to visit websites in Arabic or English?
19. Do your mum and/or dad use the Internet?
20. What are your favourite websites?
21. Have you ever made a friend online?
22. Were they the same gender?
23. Did you ever meet them in person?
24. Do you own a mobile phone?
25. Around how many text messages do you send per day?

Additional questions added to the Kuwait survey (2009 and 2010)
26. Do you think the Internet is having an impact on politics and society in the Arab world? Explain.
27. Do you have a Facebook page?
28. How many 'friends' do you have on Facebook?

BIBLIOGRAPHY

Aaronovitch, David (2002), 'It May Be a Holiday Paradise to You, But to the Locals It's a Place of Torture', *The Independent*, 22 August, <http://www.independent.co.uk/voices/commentators/it-may-be-a-holiday-paradise-to-you-but-to-the-locals-its-a-place-of-torture-5360282.html> (last accessed 3 January 2017).

Abdulla, Rasha A. (2007), *The Internet in the Arab World: Egypt and Beyond*, New York: Peter Lang.

Abo Alabass, Bassem (2012), '"I Am the Noblest Businessman on Earth": Egypt's Tycoon Abul-Einein', Ahram Online, 18 July, <http://english.ahram.org.eg/NewsContent/3/12/48107/Business/Economy/-I-am-the-noblest-business man-on-Earth-Egypts-bigg.aspx> (last accessed 3 January 2017).

Abuqudairi, Areej (2014), 'Jordan Prisoners Protest "Inhumane" Treatment', Al Jazeera, 21 May, <http://www.aljazeera.com/news/middleeast/2014/04/jordan-prisoners-protest-inhumane-treatment-20144182957556845.html> (last accessed 3 January 2017).

Adely, Fida (2012), 'The Emergence of a New Labor Movement in Jordan', MERIP (Fall), <http://www.merip.org/mer/mer264/emergence-new-labor-movement-jordan> (last accessed 3 January 2017).

AFP (2005), 'RSF Lists Egypt and Tunisia as Two of 13 "Enemies of the Internet" but Libya Removed from List', Balancing Act: Telecoms, Internet and Broadcast in Africa, <http://www.balancingact-africa.com/news/en/issue-no-331/internet/rsf-lists-egypt-and/en> (last accessed 3 January 2017).

AFP (2011), 'Kuwait Rally Demands PM Quit over Graft Scandal', 21 September,

<http://www.maannews.com/Content.aspx?id=422452> (last accessed 19 January 2017).

AFP (2012), 'Interview with His Majesty King Abdullah II', 12 September, <http://www.kingabdullah.jo/index.php/en_US/interviews/view/id/498/videoDisplay/0.html> (last accessed 3 January 2017).

African Development Bank (2012), *Jobs, Justice and the Arab Spring: Inclusive Growth in North Africa*, Tunis: AFDB; available at <http://www.afdb.org/fileadmin/uploads/afdb/Documents/Publications/Jobs%20and%20Justice%20-%20EN.PDF> (last accessed 3 January 2017).

Al-Ahmedi, Hanan Bint Abdel-Rahim (2014), 'Shura Council Membership Opened New Opportunities for Saudi Women', *Asharq Al-Awsat*, 12 July, <http://www.aawsat.net/2014/07/article55334168> (last accessed 3 January 2017).

Albabtain, Afraa Ahmed (2010), 'Downloading Democracy: Bloggers in the Gulf', World Security Institute, <http://democracyreviewforum.blogspot.com/2010/05/downloading-democracy-bloggers-in-gulf.html> (last accessed 19 January 2017).

Albloshi, Hamad, and Faisal Alfahad (2009), 'The Orange Movement of Kuwait: Civic Pressure Transforms a Political System', in Maria J. Stephan (ed.), *Civilian Jihad: Nonviolent Struggle, Democratization and Governance in the Middle East*, New York: Palgrave Macmillan, pp. 219–32.

Ali, Noura (2016), 'Sisi's Egypt Deprives University Students their Studying Rights', *Middle East Observer*, 11 July, <http://www.middleeastobserver.org/archives/15136> (last accessed 3 January 2017).

Alqudsi-ghabra, Taghreed M., Talal Al-Bannai and Mohammad Al-Bahrani (2011), 'The Internet in the Arab Gulf Cooperation Council (AGCC): Vehicle of Change', *International Journal of Internet Science*, 6.1, pp. 44–67, <http://www.ijis.net/ijis6_1/ijis6_1_alqudsi-ghabra_et_al.pdf> (last accessed 3 January 2017).

Alterman, Jon (1998), *New Media, New Politics? From Satellite Television to the Internet in the Arab World*, Washington, DC: Washington Institute for Near East Policy.

Alterman, Jon (2000a), 'Counting Nodes and Noses: Understanding New Media in the Middle East', *The Middle East Journal*, 54.3 (Summer), pp. 355–61.

Alterman, Jon (2000b), 'Middle East's Information Revolution', *Current History*, January, pp. 21–6.

Alterman, Jon (2011), 'The Revolution Will Not Be Tweeted', *Washington Quarterly*, 34.4 (Fall), pp. 103–16.

Anderson, Jon (1995), 'Cybarites, Knowledge Workers and New Creoles of the Information Superhighway', *Anthropology Today*, 11.4 (August), pp. 13–15.

Angrist, Michele Penner (2011), 'Morning in Tunisia: The Frustrations of the Arab World Boil Over', *Foreign Affairs*, 16 January, <https://www.foreignaffairs.com/articles/middle-east/2011-01-16/morning-tunisia> (last accessed 19 January 2017).

Ansorge, Josef Teboho (2016), *Identify and Sort: How Digital Power Changed World Politics*, Oxford: Oxford University Press.

Aouragh, Miriyam (2012), *Palestine Online: Transnationalism, the Internet and the Construction of Identity*, London: I. B. Tauris.

AP (2014), Opposition Leader Calls for Corruption Probe into Turkey PM Recep Tayyip Erdogan', 25 February, <http://www.cbsnews.com/news/opposition-leader-calls-for-corruption-probe-into-turkey-pm-recep-tayyip-erdogan/> (last accessed 3 January 2017).

AP (2015), 'Ancient Petra Sees Few Visitors as Jordan Tourism Declines', 30 March, <http://www.dailymail.co.uk/wires/ap/article-3017541/Ancient-Petra-sees-visitors-Jordan-tourism-declines.html> (last accessed 3 January 2017).

Al-Arabiya (2011), 'International Leaders Hail Qaddafi's Death as "Historic" for Libya', 20 October, p. 1; available at <http://english.alarabiya.net/articles/2011/10/20/172813.html> (last accessed 3 January 2017).

Arab Social Media Report (2011), 'The Role of Social Media in Arab Women's Empowerment', *Dubai School of Government: Arab Social Media Report*, November, <http://www.arabsocialmediareport.com/UserManagement/PDF/ASMR%20Report%203.pdf> (last accessed 3 January 2017).

Arab Social Media Report (2014), 'Citizen Engagement and Public Services in the Arab World: The Potential of Social Media', <http://www.mbrsg.ae/getattachment/e9ea2ac8-13dd-4cd7-9104-b8f1f405cab3/Citizen-Engagement-and-Public-Services-in-the-Arab.aspx> (last accessed 3 January 2017).

Arendt, Hanna (1963), *On Revolution*, New York: Viking Press.

Asiya Research (2015), 'Kuwait: Quarterly Monitor', <http://www.asiyainvestments.com/en/assets/reports/country-analysis/quarterly-monitor/gcc/kuwait/quarterly/country-analysis-quarterly-monitor-gcc-kuwait-q4-2015-10823.pdf> (last accessed 3 January 2017).

Assaad, Ragui (2011), 'How Will Tunisia's Jasmine Revolution Affect the Arab World?', Brookings, 24 January, <http://www.brookings.edu/research/opinions/2011/01/24-tunisia-assaad> (last accessed 3 January 2017).

Austin, Leila (2011), 'The Politics of Youth Bulge: From Islamic Activism to

Democratic Reform in the Middle East and North Africa', *SAIS Review*, 31.2 (Summer–Fall), pp. 81–96.

Al-Ayish, Muhammad (1998), 'Telecommunications Trends and Politics in the United Arab Emirates and their Implications for National Development', in Emirates Center for Strategic Studies and Research, *Information Revolution and the Arab World: Its Impact on State and Society*, Abu Dhabi: ECSSR, pp. 141–59.

Aziz, Sahar (2012), 'To Stop Corruption, Egypt Needs a Freedom of Information Law', *Huffington Post*, 23 May, <http://www.huffingtonpost.com/sahar-aziz/to-stop-corruption-egypt-_b_1538999.html> (last accessed 3 January 2017).

Baker, Stephanie (2012), 'Jordan Emerges as the Silicon Valley of the Arab World', *Washington Post*, 21 October, p. G04.

Bakr, Noha (2012), 'The Egyptian Revolution', in Stephen Calleya and Monika Wohlfeld (eds), *Change and Opportunities in the Emerging Mediterranean*, Malta: Mediterranean Academy of Diplomatic Studies, pp. 57–81, <http://www.um.edu.mt/medac/publications> (last accessed 3 January 2017).

Barden, Andrew J. (2014), 'Turkey Blocks YouTube after Syria Incursion Plans Leaked', Bloomberg, 28 March, <http://www.bloomberg.com/news/2014-03-27/turkey-blocks-youtube-after-leak-of-syria-incursion-planning.html> (last accessed 3 January 2017).

Baroi, Harold Sougato (2012), 'Peoples' Uprising in North Africa and the Middle East: Lessons Learnt and Challenges of Policy Implication – Egypt as an Illustrative Case', *Canadian Social Science*, 8.2, pp. 108–16.

Bassiouni, M. Cherif (2012), 'Corruption Cases against Officials of the Mubarak Regime', Egyptian American Rule of Law Association, 23 March, <http://www.earla.org/userfiles/file/Bassiouni%20Corruption%20Cases%20Against%20Mubarak_EARLA%20Letterhead%20(march%202012).pdf> (last accessed 4 October 2012).

Al-Bawaba (2000), 'Transforming Jordan into Singapore of the Middle East', 13 September, <http://www.albawaba.com/business/transforming-jordan-singapore-middle-east> (last accessed 3 January 2017).

Bayard de Volo, Lorraine, and Edward Schatz (2004), 'From the Inside Out: Ethnographic Methods in Political Research', *PS: Political Science and Politics*, April, pp. 267–71.

Bayat, Asef (2010), *Life as Politics: How Ordinary People Change the Middle East*, Stanford: Stanford University Press.

Baylouny, Anne Marie (2005), 'Jordan's New "Political Development" Strategy',

MERIP (Fall), <http://www.merip.org/mer/mer236/jordans-new-political-devel opment-strategy> (last accessed 3 January 2017).

BBC (2011), 'Kuwait's Prime Minister Resigns after Protests', 28 November, <http://www.bbc.co.uk/news/world-middle-east-15931526> (last accessed 3 January 2017).

Beardsley, Eleanor (2011), 'In Tunisia, Women Play Equal Role in Revolution', National Public Radio, 27 January, <http://www.npr.org/2011/01/27/133248219/ in-tunisia-women-play-equal-role-in-revolution> (last accessed 3 January 2017).

Bell, John (2014), 'The Age of Dissent: Why Are People Resorting to Street Politics across the Globe?', Al Jazeera, 11 February, <http://www.aljazeera.com/indepth/opinion/2014/02/age-dissent-20142115427346403.html> (last accessed 3 January 2017).

Bellin, Elizabeth (2004), 'The Robustness of Authoritarianism in the Middle East: Exceptionalism in Comparative Perspective', *Comparative Politics*, January, pp. 139–57.

Bellin, Eva (2011), 'Beyond the Arab Spring', *Brandeis Magazine* (Fall), pp. 1–3; available at <http://www.brandeis.edu/magazine/2011/fall/featured-stories/ arab.html> (last accessed 3 January 2017).

Ben Ali (2000), 'Sculpting a New Tunisia', *Pharaohs*, July, pp. 58–64.

Bennhold, Katrin (2011), 'Women's Rights a Strong Point in Tunisia', *New York Times*, 22 February, <http://www.nytimes.com/2011/02/23/world/middleeast/ 23iht-letter23.html> (last accessed 3 January 2017).

Berger, Lars (2011), 'The Missing Link? US Policy and the International Dimensions of Failed Democratic Transitions in the Arab World', *Political Studies*, 59.1 (March), pp. 38–55.

Berger, Lars (2015), 'Democratic Contagion versus Authoritarian Resilience: Jordan's Prospects for Change', in Fahed Al-Sumait, Nele Lenze and Michael C. Hudson (eds), *The Arab Uprisings: Catalysts, Dynamics, and Trajectories*, New York: Rowman and Littlefield, pp. 241–60.

Berger, Moore (1964), *The Arab World Today*, New York: Doubleday.

Bertolt, John C., Paul T. Jaeger and Justin M. Grimes (2010), 'Using ICTs to Create a Culture of Transparency: E-government and Social Media as Openness and Anticorruption Tools for Societies', *Government Information Quarterly*, 27, pp. 264–71.

Binder, Leonard (1988), *Islamic Liberalism: A Critique of Development Ideologies*, Chicago: University of Chicago Press.

Black, Ian (2013), 'Saudi Arabia's Women Hold Day of Action to Change Driving

Laws', *The Guardian*, 26 October, <http://www.theguardian.com/world/2013/oct/25/saudi-arabia-women-action-driving-laws> (last accessed 3 January 2017).

Bradley, John R. (2012), *After the Arab Spring*, New York: Palgrave Macmillan.

Brady, David (2009), *Rich Democracies, Poor People*, Oxford: Oxford University Press.

Braune, Ines (2012), 'The Middle East from Below: Dynamics of Subversion', *H-Net Reviews in the Humanities and Social Sciences*, February, pp. 1–3; available at <www.h-net.org/reviews/showrev.php?id=35388> (last accessed 3 January 2017).

Bronner, Ethan (2011), 'Jordan Faces a Rising Tide of Unrest, but Few Expect a Revolt', *New York Times*, 4 February, <http://www.nytimes.com/2011/02/05/world/middleeast/05jordan.html?pagewanted=all> (last accessed 3 January 2017).

Brown, Ryan Andrew, Louay Constant, Peter Glick and Audra K. Grant (2014), *Youth in Jordan: Transitions from Education to Employment*, Washington, DC: RAND; <http://www.rand.org/content/dam/rand/pubs/research_reports/RR500/RR556/RAND_RR556.pdf> (last accessed 3 January 2017).

Brownlee, Jason (2007), *Authoritarianism in an Age of Democratization*, Cambridge: Cambridge University Press.

Brynen, Rex, Bahgat Korany and Paul Nobel (1995), *Political Liberalization and Democratization in the Arab World*, vol. 1, Boulder: Lynne Rienner Publishers.

Burnell, Peter (2006), 'Autocratic Opening to Democracy: Why Legitimacy Matters', *Third World Quarterly*, 27.4, pp. 545–62.

Business Monitor International (2010), 'Democracy in Kuwait: No Turning Back', 1 May, <http://www.meamonitor.com/file/89155/democracy-no-turning-back.html> (last accessed 17 December 2012).

Byrnes, Mark (2014), 'Driving in Saudi Arabia as a Woman', *CityLab*, 1 April, <http://www.citylab.com/politics/2014/04/driving-saudi-arabia-woman/8771/> (last accessed 3 January 2017).

Calderwood, James (2011a), 'Kuwait Makes Stuttering Political Progress', *The National*, 24 February, <http://www.thenational.ae/news/world/middle-east/kuwait-makes-stuttering-political-progress> (last accessed 3 January 2017).

Calderwood, James (2011b), 'Kuwait MPs Want their Wealth Revealed amid Corruption Allegations', *The National*, 10 September, <http://www.thenational.ae/news/world/middle-east/kuwait-mps-want-their-wealth-revealed-amid-corruption-allegations> (last accessed 3 January 2017).

Calingaert, Daniel (2010), 'Authoritarianism vs. the Internet', *Policy Review*, May and April, <http://www.hoover.org/research/authoritarianism-vs-internet> (last accessed 3 January 2017).

Castells, Manuel (2007), 'Communication, Power and Counter-Power in the Network Society', *International Journal of Communication*, 1, pp. 238–66, <http://ijoc.org/index.php/ijoc/article/viewFile/46/35> (last accessed 3 January 2017).

Castells, Manuel (2012), *Networks of Outrage and Hope: Social Networks in the Internet Age*, London: Polity Press.

Charbel, Jano (2012), 'Workers Unite, Rally against Abuses', *Egypt Independent*, 19 July, <http://www.egyptindependent.com/news/workers-unite-rally-against-abuses> (last accessed 3 January 2017).

Chatham House (2012), 'Egypt: Defining and Tackling Corruption', 1 February, <http://www.chathamhouse.org/publications/papers/view/182782> (last accessed 3 January 2017).

Chayes, Sarah (2012), 'Corruption Is Still Tunisia's Challenge', *Los Angeles Times*, 10 June, <http://articles.latimes.com/2012/jun/10/opinion/la-oe-chayes-tunisia-corruption-20120610> (last accessed 3 January 2017).

Chebbi, Taoufik (2005), 'Tunisia Is Committed to Internet Expression', *USA Today*, 30 November, p. 10a.

Chen, Wenhong, Jeffrey Boase and Barry Wellman (2002), 'Global Villagers: Comparing Internet Users and Uses around the World', in Barry Wellman and Caroline Haythornthwaite (eds), *The Internet and Everyday Life*, Oxford: Blackwell, pp. 74–113.

CIA (2012), *The World Factbook*, <https://www.cia.gov/library/publications/the-world-factbook/> (last accessed 3 January 2017).

Clark, Janine A. (2012), 'Municipalities Go to Market: Economic Reform and Political Contestation in Jordan', *Mediterranean Politics*, 17.3 (October), pp. 358–75.

Clarke, Richard A., and Robert K. Kanke (2010), *Cyber War: The Next Threat to National Security*, New York: Ecco-HarperCollins.

CNN World (2011), 'How a Fruit Seller Caused Revolution in Tunisia', 16 January, <http://www.cnn.com/2011/WORLD/africa/01/16/tunisia.fruit.seller.bouazizi/> (last accessed 19 January 2017).

Cole, Juan (2011), 'New Wikileaks: US Knew Tunisian Gov. Rotten Corrupt, Supported Ben Ali Anyway', Informed Comment, 16 January, <http://www.juancole.com/2011/01/new-wikileaks-us-knew-tunisian-gov-rotten-corrupt-supported-ben-ali-anyway.html> (last accessed 3 January 2017).

Committee to Protect Journalists (2009), '10 Worst Countries to Be a Blogger', available online at <http://www.cpj.org/reports/2009/04/10-worst-countries-to-be-a-blogger.php> (last accessed 3 January 2017).

Coy, Peter (2011), 'Youth Unemployment Bomb', *Bloomberg Businessweek*, 3 February, <http://www.businessweek.com/magazine/content/11_07/b4215058743638.htm> (last accessed 3 January 2017).

Cunningham, Karla J. (2002), 'Factors Influencing Jordan's Information Revolution: Implications for Democracy', *The Middle East Journal*, 56.2 (Spring), pp. 240–56.

Darwish, Adeed, and I. William Zartman (eds) (2015), *Beyond Coercion: The Durability of the Arab State*, London: Routledge.

Dasgupta, Aditya (2006), 'Ticketing Corruption', *Foreign Policy*, 7 July, <http://blog.foreignpolicy.com/posts/2006/07/07/ticketing_corruption> (last accessed 3 January 2017).

Davidson, Christopher (2012), *After the Sheikhs: The Coming Collapse of the Gulf Monarchies*, London: Hurst.

Dawson, Stella (2015), 'Corruption Is Leading Indicator for Political Unrest, Study Finds', Reuters, 28 May, <http://www.reuters.com/article/us-corruption-peace-index-idUSKBN0OD23X20150528> (last accessed 3 January 2017).

Deflem, Mathieu (2008), *Sociology of Law: Visions of a Scholarly Tradition*, Cambridge: Cambridge University Press.

Department of State (2015), Country Reports on Human Rights Practices for 2015, <http://www.state.gov/j/drl/rls/hrrpt/humanrightsreport/#wrapper> (last accessed 3 January 2017).

Dhur, Agnes (2011), 'Secondary Data Analysis of the Food Security Situation in Tunisia', World Food Programme, Regional Bureau for the Middle East, April, <http://foodsecuritycluster.org/c/document_library/get_file?p_l_id=223390&groupId=120482&folderId=236523&name=DLFE-11417.pdf> (last accessed 3 January 2017).

Dickey, Christopher, and Babak Dehghanpisheh (2011), 'Tunisia's Message', *Newsweek*, 157.5 (31 January), pp. 40–2.

Dickinson, Elizabeth (2011), 'The First WikiLeaks Revolution?', *Foreign Policy*, 13 January, <http://wikileaks.foreignpolicy.com/posts/2011/01/13/wikileaks_and_the_tunisia_protests> (last accessed 3 January 2017).

Dreazen, Yochi (2012), 'United Arab Emirates: No Arab Spring in Sight', Pulitzer Center on Crisis Reporting, 27 January, <http://pulitzercenter.org/reporting/arab-spring-united-arab-emirates-uae-5-bin-ghaith-persian-gulf-states> (last accessed 3 January 2017).

Dubai School of Government (2011), Arab Social Media Report, 1.1, Dubai: Dubai School of Government, <www.arabsocialmediareport.com> (last accessed 3 January 2017).

Dubai School of Government (2014), 'The Arab World Online 2014: Trends in Internet and Mobile Usage in the Arab Region', <http://www.mbrsg.ae/getat tachment/ff70c2c5-0fce-405d-b23f-93c198d4ca44/The-Arab-World-Online-2014-Trends-in-Internet-and.aspx> (last accessed 3 January 2017).

Durac, Vincent, and Francesco Cavatorta (2009), 'Strengthening Authoritarian Rule through Democracy Promotion? Examining the Paradox of the US and EU Security Strategies: The Case of Ben Ali's Tunisia', *British Journal of Middle Eastern Studies*, 36.1 (April), pp. 3–19.

Earl, Jennifer, and Katrina Kimport (2011), *Digitally Enabled Social Change: Activism in the Internet Age*, Cambridge, MA: MIT Press.

Economist, The (1998), 'Be Happy and Shut Up: Tunisia', 31 January, p. 48.

Economist, The (2016), 'After the Arab Spring: The Ruining of Egypt', 6 August, <http://www.economist.com/news/leaders/21703374-repression-and-incom petence-abdel-fattah-al-sisi-are-stoking-next-uprising> (last accessed 3 January 2017).

ECSSR (Emirates Center for Strategic Studies and Research) (1998), *The Information Revolution and the Arab World: Its Impact on State and Society*, Abu Dhabi: ECSSR.

Eltahawy, Mona (2010a), 'Can Social Media Bring Democracy to Middle East?', Voice of America, 17 August, <http://www.voanews.com/content/will-new-media-bring-democracy-to-middle-east-100898544/124035.html> (last accessed 3 January 2017).

Eltahawy, Mona (2010b), 'Facebook, YouTube and Twitter Are the New Tools of Protest in the Arab World', *Washington Post*, 7 August, <http://www.washing tonpost.com/wp-dyn/content/article/2010/08/06/AR2010080605094.html> (last accessed 3 January 2017).

Eltantawy, Nahed, and Julie B. Weist (2011), 'Social Media in the Egyptian Revolution: Reconsidering Resource Mobilization Theory', *International Journal of Communication*, 5, pp. 1,207–24, <http://ijoc.org/index.php/ijoc/article/viewFile/1242/597> (last accessed 3 January 2017).

ESCWA (Economic and Social Commission for Western Asia) (2005), 'National Profile for the Information Society in Jordan', <http://isper.escwa.un.org/Portals/0/National%20Profiles/2005/English/JORDAN.pdf> (last accessed 3 January 2017).

Esmat, Ahmad (2008), 'Cultural Life in Amman – Is It Really Boring?', Goethe Institute Jordan: Euro-Mediterranean Academy for Young Journalists, <https://www.goethe.de/ins/jo/amm/prj/ema/far/cul/enindex.htm> (last accessed 3 January 2017).

Etling, Bruce, John Kelly, Rob Faris and John Palfrey (2009), *Mapping the Arab Blogosphere: Politics, Culture and Dissent*, Berkman Klein Center for Internet and Society, <https://cyber.law.harvard.edu/publications/2009/Mapping_the_Arabic_Blogosphere> (last accessed 3 January 2017).

Euro-Med Youth III (2005), 'Studies on Youth Policies in the Mediterranean Partner Countries: Jordan', <http://www.salto-youth.net/downloads/4-17-1866/> (last accessed 3 January 2017).

Fahim, Kareem (2011), 'Fighters from a Brutalized City Rejoice over a Tormentor's Fate', *New York Times*, 21 October, p. A 12.

Faqir, Fadia (2001), 'Intrafamily Femicide in Defense of Honor: The Case of Jordan', *Third World Quarterly*, 22.1 (February), pp. 65–82.

Faris, David (2008), 'Revolutions without Revolutionaries? Network Theory, Facebook, and the Egyptian Blogosphere', *Arab Media and Society*, 6 (Fall), pp. 1–11; available at <http://www.arabmediasociety.com/?article=694> (last accessed 3 January 2017).

Faris, David (2011), 'Mass Media: Faculty Essay', *Roosevelt Review*, Fall, 45–9; available at <http://sites.roosevelt.edu/dfaris/files/2010/09/rrarticle.pdf> (last accessed 3 January 2017).

Faris, David (2013), *Dissent and Revolution in a Digital Age: Social Media, Blogging and Activism in Egypt*, London: I. B. Tauris.

Fekete, Emily, and Barney Warf (2013), 'Information Technology and the Arab Spring', *Arab World Geographer*, 16.2, pp. 210–27.

Fick, Maggie, and Yasmeen Saleh (2013), 'Egyptian Government Bans Protests without Police Permission', Reuters, 24 November, <http://www.reuters.com/article/us-egypt-protests-idUSBRE9AN09C20131124> (last accessed 3 January 2017).

Filiu, Jean-Pierre (2015), *From Deep State to Islamic State: The Arab Counter-Revolution and its Jihadi Legacy*, Oxford: Oxford University Press.

Fleck, Fiona, and Anton La Guardia (2003), 'Internet a Tool of British Imperialism, Says Mugabe', *The Telegraph*, 11 December, <http://www.telegraph.co.uk/news/worldnews/africaandindianocean/zimbabwe/1449172/Internet-a-tool-of-British-imperialism-says-Mugabe.html> (last accessed 3 January 2017).

Foroohar, Rana (2003), 'A Country that Works', *Newsweek*, 26 May, p. 32.

Foucault, Michel (1998), *The History of Sexuality: The Will to Knowledge*, London: Penguin.

Fox, David Marshall (2012), '8 September 2012 Protest Statement, Haya al-Tafilah, Jordan', 25 September, <https://davidmarshallfox.wordpress.com/2012/09/25/full-translation-8-september-2012-protest-statement-haya-al-tafilah-jordan/> (last accessed 3 January 2017).

Freedom House (2010), *Policing Belief: The Impact of Blasphemy Laws on Human Rights*, October, <https://freedomhouse.org/sites/default/files/Policing_Belief_Full.pdf> (last accessed 19 January 2017); see especially pp. 21–34 for analysis on Egypt.

Freedom House (2013), Bahrain: Country Report, <https://freedomhouse.org/report/freedom-world/2013/bahrain> (last accessed 3 January 2017).

Freedom House (2015), Jordan: Country Report, <https://freedomhouse.org/report/freedom-world/2015/jordan> (last accessed 3 January 2017).

Freer, Courtney (2015), 'The Rise of Pragmatic Islamism in Kuwait's Post-Arab Spring Opposition Movement', Brookings: Rethinking Political Islam Series, August, <https://www.brookings.edu/wp-content/uploads/2016/07/Kuwait_Freer-FINALE.pdf> (last accessed 3 January 2017).

Friedman, Thomas L. (2013), 'The Other Arab Awakening', *New York Times*, 1 December, p. SR 11, <http://www.nytimes.com/2013/12/01/opinion/sunday/friedman-the-other-arab-awakening.html?_r=0> (last accessed 3 January 2017).

Al-Fuzai, Muna (2014), 'Freedom of Expression', *Kuwait Times*, 6 July, <http://news.kuwaittimes.net/freedom-expression/> (last accessed 3 January 2017).

Gause, F. Gregory III (2011), 'Why Middle East Studies Missed the Arab Spring: The Myth of Authoritarian Stability', *Foreign Affairs*, 90.4 (July/August), pp. 81–90.

Gazal, Mohammad (2015), '10 Years after Amman Bombings, War on Terror "Remains Our War"', *Jordan Times*, 9 November, <http://www.jordantimes.com/news/local/10-years-after-amman-bombings-war-terror-remains-our-war%E2%80%99%99> (last accessed 3 January 2017).

Gelvin, James (2012), *Arab Uprisings: What Everyone Needs to Know*, Oxford: Oxford University Press.

General Dynamics (2004), 'Sustainable Telecenter Development in Egypt: Current Status and a Model for the Future' (Information and Communications Technology Program, prepared for USAID mission to Egypt contract no: 263-C-00-02-00020-00).

George, Cherian (2005), 'The Internet's Political Impact and the Penetration Paradox in Malaysia and Singapore', *Media, Culture and Society*, 27.6, pp. 903–20.

Ghafar, Adel Abdel (2016), 'Youth Unemployment in Egypt: A Ticking Time Bomb', Brookings, 28 July, <https://www.brookings.edu/blog/markaz/2016/07/29/youth-unemployment-in-egypt-a-ticking-time-bomb/> (last accessed 3 January 2017).

Ghobashy, Mona (2012), 'The Praxis of the Egyptian Revolution', MERIP, 258 (Fall), <http://www.merip.org/mer/mer258/praxis-egyptian-revolution> (last accessed 19 January 2017).

Ghonim, Wael (2012), *Revolution 2.0: The Power of the People Is Greater than the People in Power: A Memoir*, New York: Houghton Mifflin Harcourt.

Gladstone, Rick (2014), 'Online Chats between Sexes Denounced in Saudi Arabia', *New York Times*, 29 May, <http://www.nytimes.com/2014/05/30/world/middleeast/online-chats-between-sexes-denounced-in-saudi-arabia.html?_r=0> (last accessed 3 January 2017).

Gladwell, Malcolm (2010), 'Small Change: Why the Revolution Will Not Be Tweeted', *The New Yorker*, 4 October, <http://www.newyorker.com/reporting/2010/10/04/101004fa_fact_gladwell?currentPage=all> (last accessed 3 January 2017).

Global Voices (2005), 'Zouhair Yahyaoui', Threatened Global Voices Online Project, <http://threatened.globalvoicesonline.org/blogger/zouhair-yahyaoui> (last accessed 3 January 2017).

Goldfarb, Jeffrey C. (2006), *The Politics of Small Things: The Power of the Powerless in Dark Times*, Chicago: University of Chicago Press.

Goldfarb, Jeffrey C. (2012), *Reinventing Political Culture: The Power of Culture versus the Culture of Power*, Malden, MA: Polity.

Goldstein, Eric (2011), 'A Middle-Class Revolution', *Foreign Policy*, 18 January, <http://foreignpolicy.com/2011/01/18/a-middle-class-revolution-2/> (last accessed 3 January 2017).

Goldstein, Eric (2012), 'Before the Arab Spring, the Unseen Thaw', *Human Rights Watch World Report 2012*, <http://www.hrw.org/world-report-2012/arab-spring-unseen-thaw> (last accessed 3 January 2017).

Goldstone, Jack (2011), 'Understanding the Revolutions of 2011', *Foreign Affairs*, 90.3 (May/June), pp. 8–18.

Good, Robin (2004), 'The Individual Is the Epicenter of the New Media Revolution', 26 April, <http://www.masternewmedia.org/2004/04/26/the_individual_is_the_epicenter.htm> (last accessed 3 January 2017).

Goodwin, Jeff (2011), 'Debate: Why We Were Surprised (Again) by the Arab Spring', *Swiss Political Science Review*, 17.4, pp. 452–6.

Gore, Albert (1994), 'Information Superhighways Speech', delivered 21 March 1994 at the International Telecommunications Development Conference, Sao Paolo, Brazil; available at <http://vlib.iue.it/history/internet/algorespeech.html> (last accessed 3 January 2017).

Green, Chris (2015), 'Egypt Executions: Figures Show Dramatic Rise . . .', *The Independent*, 13 November, <http://www.independent.co.uk/news/world/africa/egypt-executions-figures-show-dramatic-rise-in-death-sentences-and-mass-trials-under-presidency-of-a6733996.html> (last accessed 3 January 2017).

Greenwood, Scott (2003), 'Jordan's "New Bargain": The Political Economy of Regime Security', *The Middle East Journal*, 57.2 (Spring), pp. 248–68.

Grimaldi, James, and Robert O'Harrow (2011), 'Crony Capitalism with a US Root', *Washington Post*, 20 October, p. 1A.

Guazzoni, Laura, and Daniela Pioppi (eds) (2009), *The Arab State and Neo-Liberal Globalization*, Reading: Ithaca Press.

Guessoumi, Mouldi (2012), 'The Grammars of the Tunisian Revolution', *Boundary*, 2.39 (Spring), pp. 17–42.

Guzansky, quoted in Oren Kessler (2012), 'Arab Revolts Led to Islamization, Instability', *Jerusalem Post*, 12 March, <http://www.jpost.com/MiddleEast/Article.aspx?id=261557> (last accessed 3 January 2017).

Haddad, Saleem (2012), 'Jordan's Protests: Political Economy, Protest, and Empire', *Muftah*, 22 November, <http://muftah.org/jordans-protests-political-economy-protest-and-empire/#.VqZpbGSrSRZ> (last accessed 3 January 2017).

Hall, Camilla (2012), 'Kuwait Rulers Call for More Obedience after Rallies', *Financial Times*, 20 October, p. 2.

Hamilton, Nora, and Eun Mee Kim (1993), 'Economic and Political Liberalization in South Korea and Mexico', *Third World Quarterly*, 14.1, pp. 109–36.

Hanley, Delinda C. (1999), '"The Granary of Rome" Aims for Self-Sufficiency', *Washington Report on Middle East Affairs*, April/May, pp. 34–6; available at <http://www.wrmea.org/1999-april-may/the-granary-of-rome%C2%9D-aims-for-self-sufficiency.html> (last accessed 19 January 2017).

Hanley, Delinda C. (2011), 'The Jasmine Revolution', *Washington Report on Middle East Affairs*, 30.2 (March), <http://www.wrmea.org/2011-march/three-views-tunisia-s-jasmine-revolution.html> (last accessed 19 January 2017).

Heller, Nathaniel (2011), 'Corruption Risks in Egypt, Middle East Increased in Run-up to Revolutions, Study Finds', *Global Integrity*, 4 May; available at <http://pocerfacepage.blogspot.com/2012/02/corruption-risks-in-egypt-middle-east.html> (last accessed 19 January 2017).

Henry, Clement M., and Robert Springborg (2011), 'A Tunisian Solution for Egypt's Military: Why Egypt's Military Will Not Be Able to Govern', *Foreign Affairs* (February), <http://www.foreignaffairs.com/articles/67475/clement-m-henry-and-robert-springborg/a-tunisian-solution-for-egypts-military> (last accessed 3 January 2017).

Hetzer, Jim (2013), 'Power of One: Ronny Edry Creates Israel ♥ Iran Image', 18 February, <http://peaceworker.org/2013/02/power-of-one-ronny-edry-creates-israel-♥-iran-image/> (last accessed 19 January 2017).

Hine, Christine (2000), *Virtual Ethnography*, London: Sage.

Hoban, Russell (2002), *The Bat Tattoo*, London: Bloomsbury Publishers.

Hofheinz, Albrecht (2011), 'Nextopia: Beyond Revolution 2.0', *International Journal of Communication*, 5, pp. 1,417–34; available at <http://ijoc.org/index.php/ijoc/article/view/1186> (last accessed 3 January 2017).

Honwana, Alcinda (2011), 'Youth and the Tunisian Revolution', paper prepared for the Social Science Research Council Conflict Prevention and Peace Forum, <http://webarchive.ssrc.org/pdfs/Alcinda_Honwana,_Youth_and_the_Tunisian_Revolution,_September_2011-CPPF_policy%20paper.pdf> (last accessed 3 January 2017).

hooks, bell (1998), *Talking Back: Thinking Feminist, Thinking Black*, London: Sheba Feminist Publishers.

Howard, Philip N., et al. (2011), 'Opening Closed Regimes: What Was the Role of Social Media during the Arab Spring?', Project on Information Technology and Political Islam Data Memo 2011.1, <http://philhoward.org/opening-closed-regimes-what-was-the-role-of-social-media-during-the-arab-spring/> (last accessed 19 January 2017).

Howard, Philip N., and Muzammil M. Hussain (2013), *Democracy's Fourth Wave? Digital Media and the Arab Spring*, Oxford: Oxford University Press.

Huckabee, Charles (2015), 'Egypt Can Dismiss Professors for Political Activity under New Decree', *Chronicle of Higher Education*, 19 January, <http://chronicle.com/blogs/ticker/professors-in-egypt-can-be-dismissed-for-political-activities-under-new-decree/92433> (last accessed 3 January 2017).

Hudson, Michael (2000), 'A "Pan-Arab Virtual Think Tank": Enriching the Arab Information Environment', in *Middle East Journal*, 54.3 (Summer), pp. 362–77.

Hughes, Langston (2004), *Langston Hughes: Poems* (PoemHunter.com – The World's Poetry Archive), <http://www.black-success.com/langston_hughes_2004_9.pdf> (last accessed 3 January 2017).

Human Rights Watch (HRW) (2016), 'Egypt: Children Reported Tortured, "Disappeared"', <https://www.hrw.org/news/2016/04/21/egypt-children-repor ted-tortured-disappeared> (last accessed 3 January 2017).

Huntington, Samuel P. (1984), 'Will More Countries Become Democratic?', *Political Science Quarterly*, Summer, pp. 193–218.

Hussein, Abdullah Bin (2012), 'Interview', AFP, 12 September, <http://kingab-dullah.jo/index.php/en_US/interviews/view/id/498/videoDisplay/0.html> (last accessed 3 January 2017).

ICConline (2011), 'Bloody Repression in Tunisia and Algeria: The Bourgeoisie Is a Class of Assassins!', International Communist Current, 19 January, <http://en.internationalism.org/icconline/2011/tunisia-solidarity> (last accessed 3 January 2017).

Idiz, Semih (2014), 'Internet, Social Media a "Scourge" for Erdogan', *Al-Monitor*, 11 March, <http://www.al-monitor.com/pulse/originals/2014/03/erdogan-inter net-restrictions-social-media-control-cronyism.html#> (last accessed 3 January 2017).

IMF (2012), 'Jordan: Request for a Stand-By Arrangement', IMF Country Report No. 12/343, December, <https://www.imf.org/external/pubs/ft/scr/2012/ cr12343.pdf> (last accessed 4 January 2017).

IndexMundi (2012), 'Tunisia: Life Expectancy at Birth', <http://www.indexmundi. com/facts/tunisia/life-expectancy-at-birth> (last accessed 4 January 2017).

International Living (2009), Quality of Life Index 2009, <https://www.unc.edu/ courses/2009ss1/poli/472/001/472%20Summer%202009%20course%20CD/ Summer%202009%20Readings/Week%205/Quality%20of%20Life%20 Index%202009.htm> (last accessed 19 January 2017).

Ismail, Amina (2016), 'After University Crackdown, Egyptian Students Fear for their Future', Reuters, 1 June, <http://www.reuters.com/investigates/special-report/egypt-students/> (last accessed 4 January 2017).

Jahanbegloo, Ramin (2011), 'Reading Gandhi in Cairo', *New Perspectives Quarterly*, 28.2 (Spring), pp. 59–61.

Jamjoon, Mohammed (2013), 'Saudi Arabia Issues Warning to Women Drivers, Protesters', CNN, 24 October, <http://www.cnn.com/2013/10/24/world/ meast/saudi-arabia-women-drivers/> (last accessed 4 January 2017).

Janardhan, N. (2011), 'New Media in Search of Equilibrium', in Mary Ann Tétreault, Gwenn Okruhlik and Andrzej Kapiszewski (eds), *Political Change in the Arab Gulf States: Stuck in Transition*, Boulder: Lynne Rienner Publishers, pp. 225–45.

Jaques, Nick (2011), 'Jordan: Evolution or Revolution?', Transnational Crisis Project, 26 October, <http://crisisproject.org/jordan-evolution-or-revolution/> (last accessed 12 November 2012).

Jarjoura, Katia, Xavier Carniaux, Christophe Barreyre and Kim Tilbury (2011), *Goodbye Mubarak!*, Audiovisuel Multimedia International Production, ARTE France, Radio-télévision suisse, Icarus Films.

Al-Jasser, Hamad (2012), '2/3 of Kuwait Population Foreign, Half from Indian Subcontinent', *Al-Monitor*, 12 April, <http://www.al-monitor.com/pulse/busi ness/2012/04/two-thirds-of-the-kuwaiti-popula.html#> (last accessed 4 January 2017).

Al Jazeera TV (2012), 'Blogging in Jordan', 24 October.

Al Jazeera (2014), 'Saudi Arabia Moves to Allow Girls to Play Sports in School', Reuters, 9 April, <http://america.aljazeera.com/articles/2014/4/9/saudi-arabia-movestoallowgirlstoplaysportsinschool.html> (last accessed 4 January 2017).

Al Jazeera (2015a), 'Egypt Adopts Controversial Anti-Terrorism Law', 17 August, <http://www.aljazeera.com/news/2015/08/egypt-adopts-controversial-anti-terror-law-150817042612693.html> (last accessed 4 January 2017).

Al Jazeera (2015b), 'Protest Deaths Mark Anniversary of Egyptian Uprising', 25 January, <http://www.aljazeera.com/news/2015/01/protests-mark-fourth-anni versary-egyptian-uprising-150125100516885.html> (last accessed 4 January 2017).

Al Jazeera (2016), 'Is Another Revolution Brewing in Egypt?', 24 January, <http:// www.aljazeera.com/news/2016/01/160122114637805.html> (last accessed 4 January 2017).

Jdey, Ahmed (2012), 'A History of Tunisia, January 14, 2011: The End of a Dictator and the Beginning of Democratic Construction', *Boundary*, 2.39 (Spring), pp. 69–86.

Jeffries, Adrianne (2013), 'Meet Hacking Team, the Company that Helps the Police Hack You', *The Verge*, 13 September, <http://www.theverge. com/2013/9/13/4723610/meet-hacking-team-the-company-that-helps-police-hack-into-computers> (last accessed 4 January 2017).

Jordan Times (2012a), 'Next Parliament is the Gate to Comprehensive Reform', 23 October, <http://vista.sahafi.jo/art.php?id=e9767d3055e33c032ce615f30acb3 5946dff688d> (last accessed 19 January 2017).

Jordan Times (2012b), 'Registered Syrian Refugees Reach 100,000', 12 November, <http://jordantimes.com/registered-syrian-refugees-in-jordan-reach-100000> (last accessed 13 November 2012).

Jordan Times (2015), 'Majority of Smartphone Holders Use Messaging Apps', 15 April, <http://www.jordantimes.com/news/local/majority-smartphone-holders-use-messaging-apps——survey> (last accessed 4 January 2017).

Jourde, Cédric (2009), 'The Ethnographic Sensibility: Overlooked Authoritarian Dynamics and Islamic Ambivalences in West Africa', in Edward Schatz (ed.), *Political Ethnography: What Immersion Contributes to the Study of Power*, Chicago: University of Chicago Press, pp. 201–16.

Kalathil, Shanthi, and Taylor C. Boas (2003), *Open Networks, Closed Regimes: The Impact of the Internet on Authoritarian Rule*, Washington, DC: Carnegie Endowment for International Peace.

Kamalipour, Yahya R., and Hamid Mowlana (eds) (1994), *Mass Media in the Middle East: A Comprehensive Handbook*, Westport, CT: Greenwood Press.

Karam, Melhem (1999), 'An Arab with an Affinity for the Modern', *Jerusalem Post*, 9 November, p. 9.

Karimeh, Adnan (2014), 'Jordan Manages High Debt Burden', *Al-Monitor*, 29 June, <http://www.al-monitor.com/pulse/business/2014/06/jordan-economic-stability-high-public-debt-foreign-aid.html#> (last accessed 4 January 2017).

Keating, Michael, and Delinda Hanley (2007), '"The Change": Progress and Promise in Tunisia', *Washington Report on Middle East Affairs*, 26.9 (December), pp. 35–6.

Kepel, Gilles (1994), *The Revenge of God*, University Park: Pennsylvania State University Press.

Al-Khalidi, Suleiman (2012), 'Jordan Lifts Fuel Subsidies, Sparks Protests', Reuters, 13 November, <http://www.reuters.com/article/jordan-gasoline-prices-idUSL5E8MDCKK20121113> (last accessed 4 January 2017).

Khalifa, Reem (2012), 'Bahrain Protesters Boost Pressure with Huge Rally', Associated Press, 9 March, <http://www.sandiegouniontribune.com/sdut-bahrain-protesters-boost-pressure-with-huge-rally-2012mar09-story,amp.html> (last accessed 19 January 2017).

Kholaif, Dahlia (2014), 'Kuwait Strips Dissidents' Citizenship', Al Jazeera, 22 July, <http://www.aljazeera.com/news/middleeast/2014/07/kuwait-strips-dissidents-citizenship-201472211237525983.html> (last accessed 4 January 2017).

Kingsley, Patrick (2014), 'Egypt's Secret Prison: "Disappeared" Face Torture in Azouli Military Jail', *The Guardian*, 22 June, <https://www.theguardian.com/world/2014/jun/22/disappeared-egyptians-torture-secret-military-prison> (last accessed 4 January 2017).

Kirkpatrick, David D. (2011), 'Behind Tunisia Unrest, Rage over Wealth of Ruling

Family', *New York Times*, 13 January, <http://www.nytimes.com/2011/01/14/world/africa/14tunisia.html?pagewanted=all> (last accessed 4 January 2017).

Kirkpatrick, David D. (2013), 'In Leaked Video, Egyptian Army Officers Debate How to Sway News Media', *New York Times*, 3 October, <http://www.nytimes.com/2013/10/04/world/middleeast/in-leaked-video-egyptian-army-officers-debate-how-to-sway-news-media.html?_r=0> (last accessed 4 January 2017).

Kirkpatrick, David D. (2014), 'International Observers Find Egypt's Presidential Election Fell Short of Standards', *New York Times*, 29 May, <http://www.nytimes.com/2014/05/30/world/middleeast/international-observers-find-fault-with-egypt-vote.html?_r=0> (last accessed 4 January 2017).

Knudsen, Are, and Michael Kerr (2012), 'Introduction: The Cedar Revolution and Beyond', in Are Knudsen and Michael Kerr (eds), *Lebanon after the Cedar Revolution*, London: Hurst, pp. 3–22.

Kostial, Kristina (2012), 'Jordan Gets $2.0 Billion IMF Loan to Support Economy', IMF Survey, <http://www.imf.org/external/pubs/ft/survey/so/2012/int080312a.htm> (last accessed 4 January 2017).

Krauss, Clifford (2011), 'In Wave of Labor Unrest, Kuwait Customs Strike Halts Oil Shipments', *New York Times*, 10 October, <http://www.nytimes.com/2011/10/11/world/middleeast/customs-officers-strike-in-kuwait-halting-oil-shipments.html> (last accessed 4 January 2017).

Kubin, Jacquie (2011), 'Egypt: Pyramids and Revolution', *Washington Times*, 25 February.

Kuttab, Daoud (2012), 'Jordan's Bid to Muzzle Information', *Washington Post*, 7 October, p. A 25.

Lacroix, Stéphane (2011), 'Comparing the Arab Revolts: Is Saudi Arabia Immune?', *Journal of Democracy*, 22.4 (October), pp. 48–59.

LaTulippe, Steven (2011), 'The Internet and Muhammad Bouazizi', *Strike the Root*, 19 January, <http://www.strike-the-root.com/internet-and-muhammad-bouazizi> (last accessed 4 January 2017).

Lefkow, Chris (2011), 'Social Media, Cellphone Video Fuel Arab Protests', AFP, 22 February, <http://www.smh.com.au/technology/social-media-cellphone-video-fuel-arab-protests-20110222-1b3fw.html> (last accessed 19 January 2017).

Levins, John (1997), *Days of Fear: The Inside Story of the Iraqi Invasion and Occupation of Kuwait*, Dubai: Motivate Publishing.

Lewis, Aidan (2011), 'Why Has Morocco's King Survived the Arab Spring?', BBC News, 24 November, <http://www.bbc.co.uk/news/world-middle-east-15856989> (last accessed 4 January 2017).

Lewis, Bernard (1996), 'Islam and Liberal Democracy: A Historical Overview', *Journal of Democracy*, 7.2 (April), pp. 52–63.

List, Christian, and Kai Spiekermann (2013), 'Methodological Individualism and Holism in Political Science: A Reconciliation', *American Political Science Review*, 107.4, pp. 629–34.

Londono, Ernesto (2011), 'Egyptian Man's Death Became Symbol of Callous State', *Washington Post*, 9 February, <http://www.washingtonpost.com/wp-dyn/content/article/2011/02/08/AR2011020806360.html> (last accessed 4 January 2017).

Lulu, Tahiyya (2011), 'The Real Story of Bahrain's Divided Society', *The Guardian*, 3 March, <http://www.guardian.co.uk/commentisfree/2011/mar/03/bahrain-sunnis-shia-divided-society> (last accessed 4 January 2017).

Lynch, Marc (2006), *Voices of the New Arab Public: Iraq, al-Jazeera, and Middle East Politics Today*, New York: Columbia University Press.

Lynch, Marc (2012), *The Arab Uprising: The Unfinished Revolutions of the New Middle East*, New York: Public Affairs.

Lynch, Marc (2015), 'Introduction', in *The Arab Thermidor: The Resurgence of the Security State*, POMEPS Studies 11, 27 February, pp. 3–4; available at <http://pomeps.org/wp-content/uploads/2015/03/POMEPS_Studies_11_Thermidor_Web.pdf> (last accessed 4 January 2017).

Lynch, Marc (2016), *The New Arab Wars: Uprising and Anarchy in the Middle East*, New York: Public Affairs.

MacFarquhar, Neil (2004), 'Tunisia's Tangled Web Is Sticking Point for Reform', *New York Times*, 25 June, p. 3.

MacKinnon, Rebecca (2011), 'China's Networked Authoritarianism', *Journal of Democracy*, 22.2 (April), pp. 32–46.

McLuhan, Marshall (1965), *Understanding Media: The Extensions of Man*, Toronto: University of Toronto Press.

McRobie, Heather (2014), 'Military Trials in Egypt: 2011–2014', Chr. Michelsen Institute, December, No. 10.

Madar Research (2002), 'PC Penetration vs Internet User Penetration in GCC Countries', *Madar Research Journal: Knowledge, Economy and Research on the Middle East*, p. 1.

Maloney, Suzanne (2011), 'Kuwait, Qatar, Oman and the UAE: Nervous Bystanders', in *The Arab Awakening: America and the Transformation of the Middle East*, Washington, DC: Brookings, pp. 176–87.

Marczak, Bill, and John Scott-Railton (2016), 'Keep Calm and (Don't) Enable

Macros', 29 May, Citizen Lab, <https://citizenlab.org/2016/05/stealth-falcon/> (last accessed 4 January 2017).

Margalit, Ruth (2012), 'Israel Loves Iran (on Facebook)', *The New Yorker*, 23 March, <http://www.newyorker.com/online/blogs/culture/2012/03/israel-loves-iran-on-facebook.html> (last accessed 4 January 2017).

Mari, Marcello (2013), 'Twitter Usage Is Booming in Saudi Arabia', Global Web Index, 20 March, <http://www.globalwebindex.net/blog/twitter-usage-is-booming-in-saudi-arabia> (last accessed 4 January 2017).

Martinez, Michael (2015), 'Syrian Refugees: Which Countries Welcome Them, Which Ones Don't', CNN, 10 September, <http://www.cnn.com/2015/09/09/world/welcome-syrian-refugees-countries/> (last accessed 4 January 2017).

Marvin, Carolyn (1988), *When Old Technologies Were New: Thinking about Electronic Communication in the Late Nineteenth Century*, Oxford: Oxford University Press.

Marx, Karl (1885), *The Eighteenth Brumaire of Louis Bonaparte*, <https://www.marxists.org/archive/marx/works/download/pdf/18th-Brumaire.pdf> (last accessed 4 January 2017).

Marzouki, Moncef (2005), 'Tunisian Opposition Leader Says his Countrymen and Regime Are Hostage', *El-Khabar* (Algeria), 29 May.

Marzouki, Yousri, Ines Skandrani-Marzouki, Moez Bejaoui, Haythem Hammoudi and Tarek Bellaj (2012), 'The Contribution of Facebook to the 2011 Tunisian Revolution: A Cyberpsychological Insight', *Cyberpsychology, Behavior and Social Networking*, 15.5, pp. 237–44.

May, Christopher (2002), *The Information Society: A Sceptical View*, Oxford: Polity Press.

Mellor, Noha (2016), *The Egyptian Dream: Egyptian National Identity and Uprisings*, Edinburgh: Edinburgh University Press.

Mesiano, Riccardo (2012), 'Green Jobs for Youth Unemployment in the Arab Region', United Nations Economic and Social Commission for Western Asia, <http://www.ocemo.org/file/125829/> (last accessed 10 January 2016).

Microsoft (2002), 'Egypt's PC for Every Home Initiative', *Microsoft Unlimited Potential Magazine*; see <http://www.mcit.gov.eg/Publication/Publication_Summary/85> (last accessed 19 January 2017).

Miladi, Noureddine (2011), 'Tunisia: A Media Led Revolution?', Al Jazeera, 17 January, <http://www.aljazeera.com/indepth/opinion/2011/01/2011116142317498666.html> (last accessed 4 January 2017).

Miller, Daniel, and Don Slater (2001), *The Internet: An Ethnographic Approach*, Oxford: Berg Publishers.

Mintz, Steve (1998), *The Internet as a Tool for Egypt's Economic Growth*, Burke, VA: International Development Professionals Inc.

Mitha, Farooq (2009), 'Arab Information Revolution: Satellite and the Internet Have Brought Significant Changes', *Tampa Tribune*, 15 March, p. 8.

Moore, Barrington (1966), *Social Origins of Dictatorship and Democracy: Lord and Peasant in the Making of the Modern World*, Boston: Beacon Press.

Morozov, Evgeny (2011a), 'Facebook and Twitter Are Just Places Revolutionaries Go', *The Guardian*, 7 March, <http://www.guardian.co.uk/commentisfree/2011/mar/07/facebook-twitter-revolutionaries-cyber-utopians> (last accessed 4 January 2017).

Morozov, Evgeny (2011b), *The Net Delusion: The Dark Side of Internet Freedom*, New York: Public Affairs.

Motaparthy, Priyanka (2010), 'Operation Rollback Kuwaiti Freedom', *Foreign Policy*, 21 July, <http://www.foreignpolicy.com/articles/2010/07/21/operation_roll_back_kuwaiti_freedom> (last accessed 4 January 2017).

Mottahedeh, Negar (2015), *#iranelection: Hashtag Solidarity and the Transformation of Online Life*, Stanford: Stanford University Press.

Mualla, Abdal Salem (2012), 'Political Reforms and Current Monarchical System in Jordan: Talking Points', Press Conference at US Congress, 21 February, <http://www.jordannationalmovement.com> (last accessed 12 November 2012).

Murphy, Emma C. (2009), 'Theorizing ICTs in the Arab World: Informational Capitalism and the Public Sphere', *International Studies Quarterly*, 53.4, pp. 1,131–53.

Murray, Matt (2012), 'Ali Abdullah Saleh Forced from Power in Yemen', *Liberation*, 16 March, <https://www.liberationnews.org/ali-abdullah-saleh-forced-html/> (last accessed 19 January 2017).

Nagi, Iman, and Mohammad Hamdan (2009), 'Computerization and E-Government Implementation in Jordan: Challenges, Obstacles and Successes', *Government Information Quarterly*, 26 (July), pp. 577–83; available at <http://www.academia.edu/204101/Computerization_and_E-government_Implementation_in_Jordan_Challenges_Obstacles_and_Successes> (last accessed 4 January 2017).

Namatalla, Ahmad (2006), 'PC for Every Home Program Falls Short', *Daily News Egypt*, 15 August, <http://www.dailynewsegypt.com/2006/08/15/pc-for-every-home-program-falls-short/> (last accessed 19 January 2017).

Al-Nashimi, Eisa, Johanna Cleary, Juan-Carlos Molleda and Melinda McAdams (2010), 'Internet Political Discussions in the Arab World: A Look at Online Forums from Kuwait, Saudi Arabia, Egypt and Jordan', *The International Communication Gazette*, 72.8, pp. 719–38.

Noor, Naseema (2011), 'The Revolution that Started It All', *International Affairs Review*, 31 January, <http://www.iar-gwu.org/node/257> (last accessed 4 January 2017).

Nordenson, Jon (2010), 'We Want Five! Kuwait, the Internet and the Public Sphere', Master's Thesis in Arabic Language, Department of Culture Studies and Oriental Languages, University of Oslo, May 2010.

Northwestern University, Qatar (2013), *Media Use in the Middle East, 2013: An Eight-Nation Survey*, <http://menamediasurvey.northwestern.edu> (last accessed 4 January 2017).

Northwestern University, Qatar (2015), *Media Use in the Middle East, 2015: A Six-Nation Survey*, <http://www.mideastmedia.org/survey/2015/> (last accessed 4 January 2017).

Norton, R. Augustus (1999), 'New Media, Civic Pluralism and the Slowly Retreating State', in Dale Eickelman and Jon W. Anderson (eds), *New Media in the Muslim World: The Emerging Public Sphere*, Bloomington: Indiana University Press, pp. 19–28.

Al-Obaidi, Jabbar (2003), 'Communications and the Culture of Democracy: Global Media and Promotion of Democracy in the Middle East', *International Journal of Instructional Media*, 30.1, pp. 97–110.

Obama, Barack (2011), 'Speech on Middle East: Full Transcript', *The Guardian*, 19 May, <http://www.guardian.co.uk/world/2011/may/19/barack-obama-speech-middle-east> (last accessed 4 January 2017).

Obama, Barack (2014), 'Remarks by the President at the United States Military Academy Commencement Ceremony', 28 May, <https://www.whitehouse.gov/the-press-office/2014/05/28/remarks-president-united-states-military-academy-commencement-ceremony> (last accessed 4 January 2017).

OPEC (2015), 'Kuwait Facts and Figures', <http://www.opec.org/opec_web/en/about_us/165.htm> (last accessed 4 January 2017).

Open Net Initiative (2009), 'Country Profile: Jordan', <http://opennet.net/research/profiles/jordan> (last accessed 4 January 2017).

Osterman, Sharon (2007), 'Reality Silences Pro-Democracy Activist in Tunisia: Political Blogger, Family Harassed', *Washington Times*, 31 May, p. A15.

Oweidat, Nadia, Cheryl Benard, Dale Stahl, Walid Kildani, Edward O'Connell and Audra K. Grant (2008), *The Kefaya Movement: A Case Study of a Grassroots Reform Initiative*, Santa Monica, CA: RAND Corporation; <http://www.rand.org/pubs/monographs/MG778.html> (last accessed 4 January 2017).

Palmer, Brian (2011), 'Do Egyptians Have the Right to Free Speech?', *Slate*, 1 February, <http://www.slate.com/articles/news_and_politics/explainer/2011/02/do_egyptians_have_the_right_to_free_speech.html> (last accessed 4 January 2017).

Parloff, Roger (2016), 'Spy Tech that Reads your Mind', *Fortune*, 30 June, <http://fortune.com/insider-threats-email-scout/> (last accessed 4 January 2017).

Paul, Katie (2012), 'Will Amman's Polite Opposition Bring Arab Spring to Jordan?', *Al-Monitor*, 8 October, <http://www.al-monitor.com/pulse/originals/2012/al-monitor/jordanmarch.html> (last accessed 4 January 2017).

Payne, Gregory, Efe Sevin and Sara Bruya (2011), 'Grassroots 2.0: Public Diplomacy in the Digital Age', *Comunicação Pública*, 6.10, pp. 45–70; available at <http://cp.revues.org/422> (last accessed 4 January 2017).

Pezzini, Mario (2012), 'An Emerging Middle Class', *OECD Observer*, <http://www.oecdobserver.org/news/fullstory.php/aid/3681/An_emerging_middle_class.html> (last accessed 4 January 2017).

Pharaohs (2000), 'Word of Mouth', July, p. 16.

Politics and the New Media (2011), 'Interview by Zach with Jordanian Yale Undergrad', <http://politicsandthenewmedia.commons.yale.edu/2011/04/02/interview-with-jordanian-yale-undergrad-daughter-of-middle-eastern-diplomat/> (last accessed 21 November 2012).

Pollock, John (2011), 'Streetbook: How Egyptian and Tunisian Youth Hacked the Arab Spring', *Technology Review*, September/October, pp. 71–82.

Pratt, Nicola (2007), *Democracy and Authoritarianism in the Arab World*, Boulder: Lynne Rienner Publishers.

Prins, Gwyn (1990), 'Introduction', in Gwyn Prins (ed.), *Spring in Winter: The 1989 Revolutions*, Manchester: Manchester University Press, pp. xi–xxiv.

Al-Qawam, Nasr (2011), 'Ishrar Tjama'a Ibna' Jarash lil-Aslah' ('Sons of Jerash Call for Reform'), *A-Sabeel*, 3 July, <http://www.assabeel.net/local-news/local/46004-للإصــلاح-جرش-أبنــاء-تجمــع-إشـهار.html> (last accessed 12 November 2012).

Rad, Sahar Taghdisi (2011), 'Jordan's Paradox of Growth without Employment: A Microcosm of the Middle East?', *Viewpoint: Centre for Development and Policy Research*, School of Oriental and African Studies, University of London, No. 65 (August), <www.soas.ac.uk/cdpr/publications/dv/file70187.pdf> (last accessed 4 January 2017).

Radsch, Courtney (2015), 'Treating the Internet as the Enemy in the Middle East', Committee to Protect Journalists, 27 April, <https://cpj.org/2015/04/attacks-on-the-press-treating-internet-as-enemy-in-middle-east.php> (last accessed 4 January 2017).

Raghavan, Sudarsan (2012), 'In Yemen, Uncontested Presidential Vote on Feb. 21 Masks Tension over Salah Successor', *Washington Post*, 14 February, <http://www.washingtonpost.com/world/middle_east/in-yemen-uncontested-presidential-vote-on-feb-21-masks-tension-over-saleh-successor/2012/02/12/gIQA8PUqCR_story.html> (last accessed 4 January 2017).

Al-Rasheed, Madawi (2012), 'Imagined Heroism of the Saudi "Nail Polish Girl"', *Al-Monitor*, 30 May,<http://www.al-monitor.com/pulse/originals/2012/al-monitor/imagined-heroism-of-the-saudi-na.html> (last accessed 4 January 2017).

Reese, Bill (2015), 'Bridging the Hope Gap: Why Life Skills Matter', *Huffington Post*, 17 March, <http://www.huffingtonpost.com/bill-reese/bridging-the-hope-gap-why_b_6886728.html> (last accessed 4 January 2017).

Reporters without Borders (2005), 'The 15 Enemies of the Internet and Other Countries to Watch', 17 November, <http://en.rsf.org/the-15-enemies-of-the-internet-and-17-11-2005,15613.html> (last accessed 4 January 2017).

Reporters without Borders (2008), 'Tunisia: Country Continues to Be One of Region's Most Authoritarian', 12 November, <http://allafrica.com/stories/200811130043.html> (last accessed 4 January 2017).

Reporters without Borders (2010a), 'Web 2.0 versus Control 2.0', 18 March, <https://rsf.org/en/news/web-20-versus-control-20> (last accessed 19 January 2017).

Reporters without Borders (2010b), 'World Day Against Cyber Censorship', 12 March, <https://rsf.org/en/campaigns/world-day-against-cyber-censorship> (last accessed 19 January 2017).

Reporters without Borders (2012a), 'The Enemies of Internet Special Edition: Surveillance', <http://surveillance.rsf.org/en/> (last accessed 4 January 2017).

Reporters without Borders (2012b), 'World Report: Kuwait', <https://rsf.org/en/taxonomy/term/163> (last accessed 19 January 2017).

Reuters (2006), 'The United States expressed concern on Friday about the harassment of Tunisian activist Neila Charchour Hachicha and urged the Tunis government to allow its citizens to express opinions freely', 31 March, <http://forum-scpo.com/forum-scpo/topic3521-the-united-states-expressed-concern-about-neila-charchour-hachicha.html>(last accessed 4 January 2017).

Reuters (2011), 'UAE Police Hold Third Activist: Colleague', 10 April, <http://www.reuters.com/article/2011/04/10/us-emirates-arrest-idUSTRE7392W420110410> (last accessed 4 January 2017).

Rippin, Hannah (2005), 'The Mobile Phone in Everyday Life', *Fast Capitalism*, 1.1, <https://www.uta.edu/huma/agger/fastcapitalism/1_1/rippin.html> (last accessed 4 January 2017).

Ritzer, George (2002), 'An Introduction to McDonaldization', in George Ritzer (ed.), *The McDonaldization Reader*, Thousand Oaks, CA: Pine Forge Press, pp. 7–23.

Ritzer, George (2012), *The McDonaldization of Society: 20th Anniversary Edition*, Thousand Oaks, CA: Sage.

Rotberg, Robert (2007), 'Repressive, Aggressive and Rogue Nation States: How Odious, How Dangerous?', in Robert Rotberg (ed.), *The Worst of the Worst: Dealing with Repressive and Rogue Nations*, Washington, DC: Brookings, pp. 1–39, <https://www.brookings.edu/book/worst-of-the-worst/> (last accessed 4 January 2017).

Roy, Arundhati (2004), 'The 2004 Sydney Peace Prize Lecture', 4 November, <http://sydney.edu.au/news/84.html?newsstoryid=279> (last accessed 4 January 2017).

Rudolph, Lloyd, and John Kurt Jacobsen (eds) (2006), *Experiencing the State*, Oxford: Oxford University Press.

Rudolph, Lloyd, and Susanne H. Rudolph (1967), *The Modernity of Tradition: Political Development in India*, Chicago: University of Chicago Press.

Rugh, William (2004), *Arab Mass Media: Newspapers, Radio, and Television in Arab Politics*, Westport, CT: Praeger Publishers.

Ryan, Curtis R. (2013), 'Jordan's Unfinished Journey: Parliamentary Elections and the State of Reform', POMED Policy Brief, March, <http://pomed.org/wp-content/uploads/2013/03/POMED-Policy-Brief-Ryan.pdf> (last accessed 4 January 2017).

Ryan, Curtis R. (2014), 'Security Dilemmas and the "Security State" Question in Jordan', <http://pomeps.org/2014/12/29/security-dilemmas-and-the-security-state-question-in-jordan/> (last accessed 4 January 2017).

Ryan, Yasmine (2011), 'How Tunisia's Revolution Began', Al Jazeera, 26 January, <http://english.aljazeera.net/indepth/features/2011/01/2011126121815985483.html> (last accessed 4 January 2017).

Sadiki, Larbi (2012), 'Jordan's Arab Spring: To "Spring" or Not to "Spring"?', Al Jazeera, 25 February, <http://www.aljazeera.com/indepth/opinion/2012/02/2012217141945258425.html> (last accessed 4 January 2017).

Said, Samira (2012), 'Peace-Minded Israeli Reaches Out to Everyday Iranians via Facebook', CNN, 21 March, <http://edition.cnn.com/2012/03/19/world/meast/israel-iran-social-media/index.html?hpt=hp_c1> (last accessed 4 January 2017).

Sakr, Naomi (2001), *Satellite Realms: Transnational Television, Globalization and the Middle East*, London: I. B. Tauris.

Samaan, Magdy, and Raf Sanchez (2016), 'Egypt: Protests against President Fattah el-Sisi . . .', *The Telegraph*, 25 April, <http://www.telegraph.co.uk/news/2016/04/25/egypt-braces-for-mass-protests-against-president-fattah-el-sisi/> (last accessed 4 January 2017).

Al-Samadi, Tamer (2014), 'Jordan's Economic Crisis Worsens, Protests Subside', *Al-Monitor*, 12 January, <http://www.al-monitor.com/pulse/security/2014/01/jordan-economic-crisis-protests-subside.html> (last accessed 4 January 2017).

Sanchez, Alejandro (2009), 'Tunisia: Trading Freedom for Stability May Not Last – An International Security Problem', *Defense Studies*, 9.1 (March), pp. 85–92.

Saunders, Doug (2004), 'What Changed Libya? Not Iraq, but IRC', *The Globe and Mail* (Canada), 11 December, p. F3.

Schatz, Edward (2009), 'What Kind(s) of Ethnography Does *Political Science Need?*', in *Edward Schatz (ed.), Political Ethnography: What Immersion Contributes to the Study of Power*, Chicago: University of Chicago Press, pp. 303–18.

Schwedler, Jillian (2012), 'Al-Qaeda's Gift to Jordan's King Abdullah', Al Jazeera, 29 October, <http://www.aljazeera.com/indepth/opinion/2012/10/20121028132643365347.html> (last accessed 4 January 2017).

Scott, James (1987), *Weapons of the Weak: Everyday Forms of Peasant Resistance*, New Haven: Yale University Press.

Scott, James (1990), *Domination and the Arts of Resistance: Hidden Transcripts*, New Haven: Yale University Press.

Scott, James (2012), *Two Cheers for Anarchism*, New Haven: Yale University Press.

Seeley, Nicholas (2013), 'The Jordanian State Buys Itself Time', MERIP, 12 February, <http://www.merip.org/mero/mero021213> (last accessed 4 January 2017).

Seib, Philip (2012), *Real-Time Diplomacy: Politics and Power in the Social Media Era*, New York: Palgrave Macmillan.

Shane, Scott (2011), 'Cables from American Diplomats Portray U.S. Ambivalence on Tunisia', *New York Times*, 16 January, p. 14.

Sharabi, Hisham (1992), *Neo-Patriarchy: A Theory of Distorted Change in Arab Society*, Oxford: Oxford University Press.

Al-Shaqiran, Fahid Bin Suleiman (2014), 'Shura Council Membership Did Not Open New Opportunities for Saudi Women', *Asharq Al-Awsat*, 12 July, <http://www.aawsat.net/2014/07/article55334169> (last accessed 4 January 2017).

Sharp, Gene (1973), *The Politics of Nonviolent Action, Part 1: Power and Struggle*, Boston: Porter and Sargent.

Shehata, Dina (2011), 'The Fall of the Pharaoh: How Hosni Mubarak's Reign Came to an End', *Foreign Affairs*, May/June, <http://www.foreignaffairs.com/articles/67687/dina-shehata/the-fall-of-the-pharaoh> (last accessed 4 January 2017).

Al-Shihri, Abdullah (2013), 'Saudi King Grants Women Seats on Advisory Council', Associated Press, 11 January, <http://bigstory.ap.org/article/saudi-king-grants-women-seat-top-advisory-council-first-time> (last accessed 4 January 2017).

Shirky, Clay (2011), 'The Political Power of Social Media: Technology, the Public Sphere and Political Change', *Foreign Affairs*, 90.1 (February), pp. 28–41.

Sieghart, Mary Ann (2011), 'Queen Rania of Jordan: The New Marie Antoinette?', *The Spectator*, 5 March, <http://www.maryannsieghart.com/uncategorized/queen-rania-of-jordan-the-new-marie-antoinette/> (last accessed 4 January 2017).

Simsek, Eylem, and Ali Simsek (2013), 'New Literacies for Digital Citizenship', *Contemporary Educational Technology*, 4.2 (April), pp. 126–37.

Slackman, Michael (2008), 'In Egypt, Technology Helps Spread Discontent of Workers', *New York Times*, 7 April, p. A6; available at <http://www.nytimes.com/2008/04/07/world/middleeast/07egypt.html?_r=0> (last accessed 4 January 2017).

Slackman, Michael (2011), 'A Brittle Leader, Appearing Strong', *New York Times*, 11 February, <http://www.nytimes.com/2011/02/12/world/middleeast/12mubarak.html?_r=1&ref=hosnimubarak> (last accessed 4 January 2017).

Slama, S. A. (1998), 'Inta fil Internet ithan fa inta maojoud' ('If you are on the Internet, then you exist'), *Al Ahram*, 27 July, p. 10.

Snyder, Peter (2014), 'Kuwait Top Court Upholds 10-Year Sentence for Twitter User', Jurist, <http://www.jurist.org/paperchase/2014/07/kuwait-top-court-upholds-10-year-sentence-for-twitter-user.php> (last accessed 4 January 2017).

Somait, Fahad (2012), 'Kuwaiti Perspectives on New Media, Democratization, and the Arab Spring', paper presented at the International Studies Association meeting, 1–4 April 2012, San Diego, California.

Sonenshine, Tara (2013), 'People-to-People Engagement: Cultures, History, and Mutual Understanding through Public Diplomacy', remarks at the

U.S.-Islamic World Forum, Doha Qatar, 9 June, <http://www.state.gov/r/remarks/2013/210431.htm> (last accessed 4 January 2017).

Sorensen, Juliet (2012), 'Ideals without Illusions: Corruption and the Future of a Democratic North Africa', *Northwestern University Journal of International Human Rights*, 10.4 (Spring), <http://www.law.northwestern.edu/journals/jihr/v10/n4/3/index.html> (last accessed 4 January 2017).

Spaiser, Viktoria, Luis Luna-Reyes and Soon Ae Chun (2012), 'Empowerment or Democratic Divide? Internet-Based Political Participation by Young Immigrants and Young Natives in Germany', *Information Polity: The Journal of Government and Democracy in the Information Age*, 17.2, pp. 115–27.

Spencer, Richard (2016), 'New Claims that Murdered Cambridge Student Giulio Regeni Was Arrested by Egyptian Police', *The Telegraph*, 21 April, <http://www.telegraph.co.uk/news/2016/04/21/new-claims-that-murdered-cambridge-student-giulio-regeni-was-arr/> (last accessed 4 January 2017).

Sreberny, Annabelle, and Gholam Khiabany (2010), *Blogisan: The Internet and Politics in Iran*, London: I. B. Tauris.

Sreberny-Mohammadi, Annabelle, and Ali Mohammadi (1994), *Small Media, Big Revolution: Communication, Culture, and the Iranian Revolution*, Minneapolis: University of Minnesota Press.

Stack, Liam (2011), 'Corruption Inquiry Rocks Kuwait', *New York Times*, 21 September, <http://www.nytimes.com/2011/09/22/world/middleeast/corruption-inquiry-rocks-kuwait.html?adxnnl=1&adxnnlx=1354888906-7ZA3cZvWLQNbGFHwi3gyFg> (last accessed 4 January 2017).

Stevens, Karen (2012), 'Political Scientists are Lousy Forecasters', *New York Times*, 23 June, <http://www.nytimes.com/2012/06/24/opinion/sunday/political-scientists-are-lousy-forecasters.html?pagewanted=all> (last accessed 4 January 2017).

Stevenson, Tom (2015), 'New Accounts Suggest Severe Torture in Egypt Is Ongoing', *Middle East Eye*, 23 May, <http://www.middleeasteye.net/in-depth/features/new-accounts-suggest-severe-torture-egypt-ongoing-not-decreasing-92831992> (last accessed 4 January 2017).

Stork, Joe (2015), 'Egypt's Political Prisoners', Human Rights Watch, 6 March, <https://www.hrw.org/news/2015/03/06/egypts-political-prisoners> (last accessed 4 January 2017).

Stroz Friedberg (2015a), 'Press Release: Insider Threat Detection Tool Scout', 19 June, <https://www.strozfriedberg.com/press-release/stroz-friedberg-announces-insider-threat-detection-tool-scout/> (last accessed 4 January 2017).

Stroz Friedberg (2015b), 'MENA Risk Outlook 2015: A Focus on UAE, Egypt and Tunisia', 1 April, <https://www.strozfriedberg.com/client-advisory/mena-risk-outlook-2015-a-focus-on-uae-egypt-tunisia/> (last accessed 4 January 2017).

Sunstein, Cass (2001), *Republic.com*, Princeton: Princeton University Press.

Al-Suwaidi, Jamal (1998), 'Introduction', in Emirates Center for Strategic Studies and Research, *Information Revolution and the Arab World: Its Impact on State and Society*, Abu Dhabi: ECSSR, pp. 1–10.

Sweis, Rana F. (2012), 'Jordan Tries to Hold Back Protests and Online Media', *International Herald Tribune*, 20 September, <https://www.questia.com/news paper/1P2-36291618/jordan-tries-to-hold-back-protests-and-online-media> (last accessed 4 January 2017).

Taborda, Joana (2015), 'Egypt Inflation Rate at 6-Year High', Trading Economics, 12 June, <http://www.tradingeconomics.com/articles/06102015144722.htm> (last accessed 4 January 2017).

Taleb, Nassim Nicholas, and Mark Blyth (2011), 'The Black Sway of Cairo: How Suppressing Volatility Makes the World Less Predictable and More Dangerous', *Foreign Affairs*, 90.3 (May/June), pp. 33–9.

Tarawnah, Naseem (2012), 'Jordan's Internet Goes Dark', *Foreign Policy: The Middle East Channel*, 31 August, <http://mideast.foreignpolicy.com/posts/2012/08/31/jordans_internet_goes_dark> (last accessed 4 January 2017).

Telegraph, The (2012), 'Kuwaiti Royals Arrested for Critical Government Tweets', 9 November, <http://www.telegraph.co.uk/news/worldnews/middleeast/kuw ait/9666989/Kuwaiti-royals-arrested-for-critical-government-tweets.html> (last accessed 4 January 2017).

Tenner, Edward (1997), *Why Things Bite Back: Technology and the Revenge of Unintended Consequences*, New York: Vintage.

Terrill, W. Andrew (2009), *Global Security Watch – Jordan*, Westport, CT: Praeger Publishers.

Tétreault, Mary Ann (2000), *Stories of Democracy: Politics and Society in Contemporary Kuwait*, New York: Columbia University Press.

Tétreault, Mary Ann (2011), 'Bottom-Up Democratization in Kuwait', in Mary Ann Tétreault, Gwenn Okruhlik and Andrzej Kapiszewski (eds), *Political Change in the Arab Gulf States: Stuck in Transition*, Boulder: Lynne Rienner Publishers, pp. 73–98.

Tétreault, Mary Ann (2012), 'Looking for Revolution in Kuwait', MERIP, 1 November, <http://www.merip.org/mero/mero110112> (last accessed 4 January 2017).

Theodoulou, Michael (2003), 'Proliferating Iranian Weblogs Give Voice to Taboo Topics', Christian Science Monitor, 23 June, <http://www.csmonitor.com/2003/0623/p07s02-wome.html> (last accessed 4 January 2017).

Thurow, Lester (1998), 'Information-Communications Revolution and the Global Economy', in Emirates Center for Strategic Studies and Research, *Information Revolution and the Arab World: Its Impact on State and Society*, Abu Dhabi: ECSSR, pp. 11–35.

Transparency International (no date), 'Middle East and North Africa: Archive Site', <https://issuu.com/cmi-norway/docs/expert-helpdesk-151> (last accessed 19 January 2017).

Transparency International (2011), 'What Is the Corruption Perceptions Index?', <http://cpi.transparency.org/cpi2011/in_detail/> (last accessed 4 January 2017).

Tufekci, Zeynep, and Christopher Wilson (2012), 'Social Media and the Decision to Participate in Political Protests: Observations from Tahrir Square', *Journal of Communication*, 62.2, pp. 363–79.

UNDP (2012), Arab Development Challenges Report 2011, <http://www.undp.org/content/undp/en/home/librarypage/hdr/arab-development-challenges-report-2011.html> (last accessed 4 January 2017).

Ungerleider, Neal (2010), 'Egyptian Cops Kill Internet Café Patron', True/Slant, 14 June, <https://womenslens.blogspot.com/2010/06/egyptian-cops-kill-internet-cafe-patron.html> (last accessed 19 January 2017).

USAID (2011), 'Introduction to News Media Law and Policy in Jordan: A Primer Compiled as Part of the Jordan Media Strengthening Program', May, <http://www.global.asc.upenn.edu/fileLibrary/PDFs/revisedjordanprimer_eng.pdf> (last accessed 4 January 2017).

Vargas, Jose Antonio (2012), 'Spring Awakening: How an Egyptian Revolution Began on Facebook', *New York Times*, 17 February, <http://www.nytimes.com/2012/02/19/books/review/how-an-egyptian-revolution-began-on-facebook.html> (last accessed 4 January 2017).

Vick, Karl (2014), 'Turkey's Erdogan Turns off Twitter, Turns up the Nationalism', *Time*, 21 March, <http://time.com/33393/turkey-recep-tayyip-erdogan-twitter/> (last accessed 4 January 2017).

Wavell, Stuart (1995), 'Closed Societies Opened by Internet Genie', *The Sunday Times*, 3 September, p. 1.

Weber, Max (1946), 'Science as a Vocation', in H. H. Gerth and C. Wright Mills (eds), *From Max Weber: Essays in Sociology*, Oxford: Oxford University Press.

Wedeen, Lisa (2010), 'Reflections on Ethnographic Work in Political Science', *Annual Review of Political Science*, 13, pp. 255–72.

Wellman, Barry, and Caroline Haythornthwaite (2002), '*The Internet and Everyday Life*: An Introduction', in Barry Wellman and Caroline Haythornthwaite (eds), The Internet and Everyday Life, Oxford: Blackwell, pp. 3–41.

Westall, Sylvia (2012), 'Opposition Boycott, Protests Hit Kuwaiti Election', Reuters, 1 December, <http://www.reuters.com/article/us-kuwait-election-idUSBRE8B004E20121201> (last accessed 5 January 2017).

Weymouth, Lally (2012), 'Regimes Which Persecute Do Not Remain Standing: Interview with Turkey's Prime Minister about the Syrian Revolution', *Washington Post*, 23 September, p. B1.

Wharton School of Business (2014), 'Women Employees Reshape Saudi Arabia's Labor Market', 3 February, <http://knowledge.wharton.upenn.edu/article/women-employees-reshape-saudi-arabias-labor-market/> (last accessed 5 January 2017).

Wheeler, Deborah L. (1995), 'In Praise of the Virtual Life: New Communications Technologies, Human Rights, Development and the Defense of Cultural Space – Views from the Middle East', *Monitors: A Journal of Technology and Human Rights*, 1.1.

Wheeler, Deborah L. (1998), 'Global Culture or Culture Clash: New Information Technologies in the Islamic World – A View from Kuwait', *Communication Research*, 25.4 (August), pp. 359–76.

Wheeler, Deborah L. (2000), 'New Media, Globalization and Kuwaiti National Identity', *Middle East Journal*, 54.3 (Summer), pp. 432–44.

Wheeler, Deborah L. (2001a), 'The Internet and Public Culture in Kuwait', *Gazette: International Journal for Communications Studies*, 63.2–3 (May), pp. 187–201.

Wheeler, Deborah L. (2001b), 'Beyond Global Culture: Islam, Economic Development and the Challenges of Cyberspace', *Digest of Middle East Studies*, 10.1 (Summer), pp. 1–26.

Wheeler, Deborah L. (2001c), 'Islam, Technology and Community: September 11th and its Global Meaning', *Interface: The Journal of Education, Community and Values*, 1.1 (October), <http://commons.pacificu.edu/inter01/4/> (last accessed 31 January 2017).

Wheeler, Deborah L. (2002), 'Islam, Community, and the Internet: New Possibilities in the Digital Age', *Interface: The Journal of Education, Community and Values*, 2.2 (March), <http://commons.pacificu.edu/inter02/11/> (last accessed 5 January 2017).

Wheeler, Deborah L. (2003a), 'The Internet and Youth Subculture in Kuwait', *Journal of Computer-Mediated Communication*, 8.2 (January), <http://onlinelibrary.wiley.com/doi/10.1111/j.1083-6101.2003.tb00207.x/full> (last accessed 19 January 2017).

Wheeler, Deborah L. (2003b), 'Living at E.Speed: A Look at Egypt's E-Readiness', in Imed Limam (ed.), *Challenges and Reforms of Economic Regulation in MENA Countries*, Cairo: Economic Research Forum, pp. 129–57.

Wheeler, Deborah L. (2003c), 'Egypt: Building an Information Society for International Development', *Review of African Political Economy*, 30.98 (December), pp. 627–42.

Wheeler, Deborah L. (2004), 'Blessings and Curses: Women and the Internet in the Arab World', in Naomi Sakr (ed.), *Women and the Media in the Middle East*, London: I. B. Tauris, pp. 138–68.

Wheeler, Deborah L. (2005), 'Gender Matters in the Internet Age: Voices from the Middle East', in May Thorseth and Charles Ess (eds), *Technology in a Multicultural and Global Society*, Trondheim: NTNU, pp. 27–42.

Wheeler, Deborah L. (2006a), *The Internet in the Middle East: Global Expectations and Local Imaginations in Kuwait*, Albany: SUNY Press.

Wheeler, Deborah L. (2006b), 'Empowering Publics: Information Technology and Democratization in the Arab World – Lessons from Internet Cafes and Beyond', OII Research Report No. 11, 1 July, <http://papers.ssrn.com/sol3/papers.cfm?abstract_id=1308527> (last accessed 5 January 2017).

Wheeler, Deborah L. (2007a), 'Digital Governance and Democratization in the Arab World', in Ari Veikko Anttiroiko and Matti Malkia (eds), *Encyclopedia of Digital Government*, London: Idea Group Reference, pp. 327–35.

Wheeler, Deborah L. (2007b), 'Empowerment Zones? Women, Internet Cafes and Life Transformations in Egypt', *Information Technologies and International Development*, 4.2 (Winter), pp. 89–104.

Wheeler, Deborah L. (2009), 'Working around the State: Internet Use and Arab Identity in the Arab World', in Andrew Chadwick and Philip N. Howard (eds), *Routledge Handbook of Internet Politics*, London: Routledge, pp. 305–20.

Wheeler, Deborah L. (2011), 'Freedom from Want, and Freedom from Fear: A Human Security Approach to a New Middle East?', *Journal of Human Security*, 7.1 (January), pp. 37–52.

Wheeler, Deborah L. (2012), 'Information (without) Revolution? Ethnography and the Study of New Media-Enabled Change in the Middle East', in Sean S.

Costigan and Jake Perry (eds), *Cyberspaces and Global Affairs*, Burlington, VT: Ashgate Publishing, pp. 155–72.

Wheeler, Deborah L. (2015), 'Food Security, Obesity and the Politics of Resource Strain in Kuwait', in *World Health and Medical Policy – Special Issue on Global Food Security and Health*, ed. Bonnie Stabile, 7.3 (5 September), pp. 255–77.

Wheeler, Deborah L. (2016), 'Working around the State: The Micro-Demise of Authoritarianism in a Digitally Empowered Middle East', in Noha Mellor and Khalil Rinnawi (eds), *Political Islam and Global Media: The Boundaries of Religious Identity*, London: Routledge, pp. 122–37.

Wheeler, Deborah L., and Lauren Mintz (2010), 'The Internet and Political Change in Kuwait', *Foreign Policy: The Middle East Channel*, 15 April, <http://mideast. foreignpolicy.com/posts/2010/04/15/the_internet_and_political_change_in_ kuwait> (last accessed 5 January 2017).

Wheeler, Deborah L., and Lauren Mintz (2012), 'New Media and Political Change: Lessons from Internet Users in Jordan, Egypt and Kuwait', in Richard Fox and Jennifer Ramos (eds), *iPolitics: Citizens, Elections and Governing in the New Media Era*, Cambridge: Cambridge University Press.

Wickham, Carrie R. (2002), *Mobilizing Islam: Religion, Activism and Political Change in Egypt*, New York: Columbia University Press.

Wickham, Carrie R. (2013), *The Muslim Brotherhood: Evolution of an Islamist Movement*, Princeton: Princeton University Press.

Widdershoven, Cyril (2000), 'Mediterranean Development Forum: Voices for Change, Partners for Prosperity', *Pharaohs*, April, pp. 50–1.

Williams, Raymond (1961), *The Long Revolution*, London: Chatto & Windus.

Willis, Paul (2008), 'Queen Rania of Jordan: A Beautiful Paradox', CNN, 15 July, <http://edition.cnn.com/2008/WORLD/meast/07/11/queen.rania/index.html> (last accessed 5 January 2017).

Wilson, Claire (2014), 'How the Art of "Debate" Is Firing Up Public Discourse in Jordan', *Muftah*, <http://muftah.org/debates-firing-discussions-streets-jordan/#. V6ulNWNlmt8> (last accessed 5 January 2017).

World Bank (1996), *Tunisia: Poverty Alleviation: Preserving Progress while Preparing for the Future*, <http://web.worldbank.org/WBSITE/EXTERNAL/TOPICS/ EXTPOVERTY/EXTPA/0,,contentMDK:20208640~menuPK:435735~p agePK:148956~piPK:216618~theSitePK:430367,00.html> (last accessed 5 January 2017).

Yom, Sean L., and Wael al-Khatib (2012), 'Jordan's New Politics of Tribal Dissent', *Foreign Policy: The Middle East Channel*, 7 August, <http://mideast.foreign

policy.com/posts/2012/08/07/jordans_new_politics_of_tribal_dissent> (last accessed 5 January 2017).

Younes, Ali (2016), 'Jordan Violent Protests in Dhiban over Unemployment', Al Jazeera, 23 June, <http://www.aljazeera.com/news/2016/06/jordan-violent--protests-dhiban-unemployment-160623100230190.html> (last accessed 5 January 2017).

Yousef, Tarik M. (2004), 'Development, Growth and Policy Reform in the Middle East and North Africa since 1950', *Journal of Economic Perspectives*, 18.3 (Summer), pp. 91–116.

Zemlianski, Pavel (2008), *Methods of Discovery: A Guide to Research Writing*, <https://www.glowm.com/pdf/JM-research_Chapter%2010.pdf> (last accessed 19 January 2017).

INDEX